CW01647055

AUM SHINRIKYŌ AND RELIGIOUS TERRORISM IN JAPANESE COLLECTIVE MEMORY

A British Academy Monograph

The British Academy has a scheme for the selective publication of monographs arising from its British Academy Postdoctoral Fellowships, British Academy Newton International Fellowships and British Academy / Wolfson Fellowships. Its purpose is to assist individual scholars by providing a prestigious publishing opportunity to showcase works of excellence.

Rin Ushiyama is Lecturer in Sociology at Queen's University Belfast, a post he has held since 2021. He holds a Ph.D. in Sociology (2017) from Trinity Hall, University of Cambridge. Previously, he was a British Academy Postdoctoral Fellow at the Department of Sociology, Cambridge, and a Research Fellow at Murray Edwards College, Cambridge. He is currently a co-editor of *Cultural Sociology* (British Sociological Association/SAGE). He is a cultural and political sociologist interested in contested memories of violence, including war, terrorism, and colonialism with a regional focus on East Asia. His latest research investigates historical denial in the context of contemporary Japan and East Asia.

AUM SHINRIKYŌ AND RELIGIOUS TERRORISM IN JAPANESE COLLECTIVE MEMORY

Rin Ushiyama

Published for THE BRITISH ACADEMY
by OXFORD UNIVERSITY PRESS

Oxford University Press, Great Clarendon Street, Oxford OX2 6DP

© Author 2023
Some rights reserved.

This is an open access publication distributed under the terms of the Creative Commons Attribution Non Commercial No Derivatives 4.0 International licence (CC BY-NC-ND 4.0), a copy of which is available at http://creativecommons.org/licenses/by-nc-nd/4.0/.
For any use not expressly allowed in the CC BY-NC-ND licence terms, please contact the publisher.
You must not circulate this book in any other form and you must impose this same condition on any acquirer

British Library Cataloguing in Publication Data
Data available

Library of Congress Cataloguing in Publication Data
Data available

Typeset by Newgen Publishing
Printed in Great Britain by TJ Books Ltd, Padstow, Cornwall

ISBN 978-0-19-726737-0 (hardback)

For Jane

Contents

List of Figures and Tables

Figures

Tables

Notes on the Text

Parts of Chapter 3 appeared in the *International Journal of Politics, Culture and Society* (2019) as 'Latency through uncertainty: The 1994 Matsumoto Sarin Incident as a delayed cultural trauma' as a condensed version of the chapter, and parts of Chapter 6 originally appeared as 'Cultural trauma, counter-narratives, and dialogical intellectuals: the works of Murakami Haruki and Mori Tatsuya in the context of the Aum affair' as an article co-authored with Patrick Baert in *Theory and Society* (2016). Both articles were originally published under a Creative Commons Attribution 4.0 International License (https://creativecommons.org/licenses/by/4.0/).

Remarks on notation

Following academic and cultural convention, all Japanese names appear surname first.

Elongated vowels are notated with macrons (ō, ā).

Translations of Japanese texts and interview extracts are provided by the author, unless otherwise specified.

Acknowledgements

This project started with a simple question that arose over 10 years ago: why do Japanese people seem to react so negatively to the word 'religion' (*shūkyō*)? Little did I know then that tackling such a question would result in my writing a book about collective memory. Although this monograph cannot hope to give a complete picture of the deeply contested relationship between religion and culture in Japan, I have attempted to provide a partial solution to this question through the lens of memory and commemoration.

Writing this book would not have been possible without the support of so many people who generously offered their time and gave me words of encouragement. First and foremost, I express my sincere gratitude to my interviewees who were most candid about their experiences, corrected and challenged my assumptions about Aum, and continued to engage with my questions post-interview by email. Neither my Ph.D. dissertation nor this book would have been possible without their full cooperation. My fieldwork was also aided by the rich archival material at the Religious Information Research Center in Tokyo, which I'd like to thank for giving me access to Aum's out-of-print publications.

Patrick Baert, with whom I co-authored a journal article that forms the basis of Chapter 6, has been a consistent source of support and advice throughout my research career, starting with my Master's dissertation and continuing throughout the Ph.D. and a postdoctoral fellowship. His encyclopaedic knowledge, theoretical rigour, steadfast confidence in me, and above all, his warm personality, have made this book project possible. I could not have asked for a better mentor, colleague, and friend.

Over the course of preparing this manuscript, I have benefited from the critical feedback, input, and words of encouragement from numerous senior colleagues in Sociology, Japanese Studies, and Religious Studies. Although there are too many to name them all, I would like to thank in particular Eileen Barker, Lucia Dolce, Linda Flores, Inagaki Hiroshi, Kamata Tōji, Kohama Fumiko, David Lehmann, Marcus Morgan, Susan Palmer, Jim Richardson, and John Thompson. Erica Baffelli and Richard Gardner have been steadfast supporters of this project since its earliest iterations, and there are sections of this book I could not have written without their feedback and input over many years. As PhD examiners, David Inglis and Ian Reader gave me invaluable suggestions for improving both the theoretical framework and the empirical discussions, which I hope to have successfully incorporated into this book.

Much of the redrafting of the manuscript took place during my tenure as a British Academy Postdoctoral Fellow at the Department of Sociology, University of Cambridge, and as an Early Career Research Fellow at Murray Edwards College, University of Cambridge. The British Academy's generous funding offered me the time to concentrate on my research, and both the Sociology department and Murray Edwards were equally important for developing my career and pushing my research forward in new directions. Of course, institutions are only as good as the people inside them. Completing the manuscript would not have been possible without the help and encouragement of my friends and colleagues with whom I could openly share my anxieties and frustrations as an early career researcher. Thanks to Zeina Al-Azmeh, Jeff Barda, Federico Brandmayr, Masato Kato, Naim Bro Khomasi, Tiago Carvalho, Teije Donker, Peter Gardner, Dev Maitra, Helena Pérez Niño, Hillary Taylor, and Linzhi Zhang for their kindness and generosity over the years.

My present colleagues at the School of Social Science, Education and Social Work at Queen's University Belfast could not have been more supportive of this book project, for which I am deeply grateful. Jonathan Heaney, John Nagle, and Lisa Smyth have been outstanding mentors and colleagues, helping me learn the ropes of a university lectureship during the final stages of finishing the book.

I would like to thank Portia Taylor and the Publications Committee at the British Academy for their continued support as well as the anonymous reviewers for their constructive feedback which has significantly improved the manuscript. Two people deserve special mention for their part in helping me to finish the book manuscript. Ever since he served as a PhD examiner, Ian Reader has read multiple iterations of this book in part and in whole; each time, his constructive criticism has been indispensable. Eileen Barker, whom I've had the pleasure and privilege to work with for the past several years, has been no less generous with her time. With her unmatched knowledge of minority religions and precise editorial skill, she has suggested various ways for improving the manuscript to push it over the finish line. Needless to say, all remaining errors are my own.

Finally, I would like to thank my family for everything they have done for me. My parents went to great lengths for my education and have been cheerleaders for my career from the start. My wife Jane has supported me throughout this journey, from the earliest days of writing my PhD research proposal to applying for academic jobs and copy-editing the manuscript multiple times. I dedicate this book to her.

1

Introduction

More than a quarter-century has passed since the millenarian new religion Aum Shinrikyō released sarin, a deadly nerve agent, on the Tokyo subway system on 20 March 1995. The attack, known in Japan as the Subway Sarin Incident (*chikatetsu sarin jiken*), killed a total of 13 people and injured 6,000 more in the worst terrorist attack in post-war Japanese history. Yet, if one were to visit any of the dozens of metro stations affected by the attack today, one would be hard pressed to find any evidence that such an attack had taken place. There is no Tokyo equivalent to New York's 9/11 Memorial and Museum, or the 7 July Memorial at Hyde Park, London. The only memorial dedicated to the sarin attack is a small plaque at Kasumigaseki Metro Station, a key stop that serves the bureaucratic nerve centre of Tokyo. At Kasumigaseki, just past the Chiyoda Line ticket barriers, there is a black, metal plaque affixed to the wall. The plaque, perhaps no larger than a briefcase, is engraved with a short description of the attack and a tribute to the two employees who lost their lives. With the exception of the anniversary of the attack, when politicians and public figures give annual media interviews in front of the memorial, the plate recedes into the backdrop of normal life, unnoticed by tens of thousands of commuters that pass through the station every day.

The significance of the plaque goes beyond its inscription: it also encapsulates how socially powerful actors have defined the moral meanings of the subway attack and the string of violent crimes committed by Aum Shinrikyō, which have come to be known collectively as the 'Aum Affair' (*Oumu Jiken*). As the complex historical context of the attack is summarised as a brief description on a small plaque, the experiences of the victims are reduced to the number of casualties, and the dead are remembered only when it is convenient for the living. Every year on the anniversary of the attack, mass media reporters gather at Kasumigaseki Station, mantras of 'never forget' and 'remember the lessons of the Aum Affair' are recited by rote: exactly what must not be forgotten, or what the lessons are, are usually left to the audience's imagination. In their commemorative coverage, the Japanese mass media, much like mainstream media outlets around the world, have tended to uncritically reproduce cultural narratives that reduce the causes of Aum's extreme violence to dangerous 'cults' that 'brainwash' and 'mind control' vulnerable people.

It is only when we cast our eyes beyond the plaque and the mass media clichés that we can appreciate the full impacts of the Aum Affair on contemporary Japanese culture, politics, and religion. In the mid-1990s, the Tokyo attack and the subsequent uncovering of Aum's litany of crimes, including kidnapping, murders, and an earlier terrorist attack in 1994, sparked a sense that Japanese society was in crisis (Mullins 2016). Occurring just two months after the devastation of the Great Hanshin-Awaji (Kōbe) Earthquake that had killed more than 5,000 people, and taking placing during a period of sustained economic stagnation known as the 'lost two decades', the Aum Affair became a touchstone of Japanese culture that both exemplified and exposed fundamental flaws and tensions in society. The national meta-narrative that Japan would become ever more economically prosperous – and therefore happier – had come under question, perhaps more than ever before. The Aum Affair became a prism through which an array of commentators discussed various social problems, from youths' apathy and the breakdown of the traditional family structure to the emotional vacuity of consumer culture and the loss of alternative political ideologies following the collapse of the Soviet Union. Taken together, Kōbe, Aum, and the economic 'disasters' painted a very different picture to the utopian visions promised by post-war politicians, business leaders, and policymakers. Like many other parts of the world that experienced a 'memory boom' in this period, the year 1995 marked 50 years since the end of the Second World War and prompted many commentators to reflect on the half-century of post-war recovery and development.

In many ways, the Aum Affair was a 'watershed moment' that marked the end of an era marked by post-war recovery and growth and the beginning of a more uncertain and anxious – one might even say 'postmodern' – era (Mullins and Nakano 2016: 3). It is no understatement to say that the Aum Affair was an era-defining moment in Japan's cultural history. A tally of national television coverage between 1990 and 1999 found that the Aum Affair generated a total of 1,474 hours of news broadcasting, not including other television programming such as daytime talk shows (*waido shō*), debating programmes, and documentaries. The Affair constituted by far the greatest media topic of the decade. By comparison, news about the Imperial family ranked second at 673 hours of news coverage in the same period (Inoue N. 2011: 420).

Beyond these social commentaries and meta-commentaries, the Aum Affair also produced in its wake myriad cultural narratives, discourses, practices, and products that have transformed how people both inside and outside Japan conceptualise and interact with minority religions, millennialism, religious violence, and religious terrorism. One of the most transformative changes occurred in the

Japanese religious field. In the wake of the Tokyo attack, religious organisations were left reeling as they confronted a sea change in public attitudes towards religions, from one of apathy and indifference to open distrust and sometimes active animosity. Although extreme violence by new religions around the world is a relatively rare phenomenon, the Aum Affair drastically and permanently altered the terms of debate by introducing a new vocabulary for discussing religions as potentially dangerous to public safety and civil society (Ishii 2013; Winter 2018). Domestically, largely thanks to the success of 'anti-cult' activists and the mass media, the post-Aum public discourse introduced terms like 'destructive cults', 'brainwashing', and 'mind control' to the public. This new discursive landscape introduced a symbolic demarcation between legitimate 'religions' and illegitimate 'cults', the former category consisting of traditional institutions that serve local communities and offer 'correct' answers to deep fundamental questions, and the latter category encompassing an array of religious and spiritual groups that were depicted – often unfairly – as preying on the vulnerable to line the pockets of narcissistic and sociopathic leaders. As a result, many other religions, especially newer and foreign movements, have since had to navigate this precarious landscape in which any deviations from secular cultural norms risk accusations of being a 'cult' (see, e.g., Lewis 2016; Bromley, and Darnell 2008 for cult labels and discourses outside Japan).

Those directly affected by Aum's violent crimes faced altogether different problems in the wake of the terror attacks. Survivors continued to experience the physical and psychological after-effects of sarin poisoning for decades; some survivors of the attack found that the lack of awareness about post-traumatic stress disorder (PTSD) by friends, family, and colleagues made their recovery even harder. Widowed spouses and bereaved families expressed disappointment and anger that, despite the government's rhetoric of support and solidarity, material support from the authorities was not forthcoming. In response, some victims launched a campaign lasting 13 years calling for state-funded support, culminating in a law that provided financial relief to survivors and bereaved families.

Public discourses around the Aum Affair in the following decades have been further complicated by the fact that 'perpetrators' were some of the most outspoken participants in these debates. Commentators and victims were not the only ones to intervene in public discourses about Aum. The Aum Affair is fairly unique among cases of religious terrorism for its relative abundance of first-hand accounts by offenders, including individuals who committed these violent attacks.[1] Once we leave behind sensationalist media caricatures of Aum as a brainwashing

[1] In this sense, the Aum Affair is comparable to the deadly 1993 Waco, Texas siege by the Branch Davidians, which also produced a plethora of survivor accounts by former members (Wessinger 2009).

cult and its leader Asahara Shōkō as a cartoonish arch-villain, we can readily find rich autobiographical accounts and confessions by numerous ex-members who have renounced their faith following the Tokyo attack. Reflecting on their motivations for joining – and more importantly, staying – in the secretive organisation, many ex-members have warned others of the seductive appeal of believing themselves to be the self-appointed agents of truth and justice. Moreover, whilst media reports about the continued presence of Aum's successor organisations – Aleph and Hikari no Wa – have stirred public anxieties in local communities over the decades, a small number of actors have sought to ease tensions by exploring avenues for reconciliation through mutual dialogue and de-escalation.

The purpose of this book is to trace and reconstruct these multiple cultural discourses and practices surrounding the Aum Affair by examining how various actors – ranging from the Japanese government, policing authorities, and the mass media to victims, former Aum members, and lay social activists – have sought to define and shape public understandings about the origins and consequences of Aum's extreme violence. While the Aum Affair has been the subject of many academic and popular discussions, this volume explores the social, cultural, and political consequences of the Aum Affair through the lens of commemoration and collective memory. In contrast to everyday uses of 'memory' as a psychological and cognitive recollection of information and past events, 'collective memory' refers to social processes through which actors interpret and represent the past in relation to their collective and cultural identities. The term 'collective memory' has been used to describe and study a spectrum of political and cultural practices such as commemorative ceremonies, official statements, memorials and monuments, museums, history education, historical fiction, non-fiction, art, family history, and oral history. Studying this wide spectrum of social activities that reproduce certain interpretations of the past, this book defines collective memory as a short-hand term to describe a range of commemorative *processes* that take place dynamically in competitive 'struggles over meaning' (Olick 2016: 43–4). When powerful actors, such as the state and mass media conglomerates, endorse certain interpretations of the past, collective memory can appear to take on an objective quality, as these selective interpretations dominate various aspects of social and cultural life through commemorative ceremonies, memorials, statues, and artwork. In other words, certain representations of the past become 'hegemonic', socially accepted understandings of the past. However, this is not to say that such dominant representations are invulnerable to challenge. Commemoration is an ever-competitive process in which minority voices are present, if not always conspicuous. As such, this book endorses a multi-layered understanding of commemoration as occurring at various levels of social power, in which powerful elites, relatively powerless lay actors, and many people in between, possess varying levels of social resources (such as money, political power, cultural capital, social capital, and labour) to shape generalised and public interpretations of the past.

Pushing this principle further, it advocates perhaps a more controversial position. In order to gain a fuller understanding of how different actors interpret the past, we must pay attention not just to the traditionally 'subaltern' voices – the victimised, the traumatised, and the silenced – but also to those of offenders and 'perpetrators': those who exist beyond the boundaries of the moral community and who are seen as external threats to the body politic as a result of their past actions. Remembering the past is not just a simple process of recalling facts about the past. Public, shared forms of remembering are always political and moral acts inseparable from questions of identity and difference, inclusion and exclusion, and temporal continuity and discontinuity. As such, in studying the commemoration of violent events, studying the relative presence, location, and visibility of perpetrators' narratives sheds light on how communities impacted by violence address questions regarding the possibility of moral redemption, social reconciliation, and forgiveness. Some of the chapters here therefore devote a significant proportion of the discussions to the experiences and views of individuals presently or formerly affiliated with Aum and its successor organisations, whether through membership or through family relations. Needless to say, paying attention to perpetrators' narratives is not the same as treating them as *facts* at face value or sympathising with their views, let alone condoning their actions. As with any historical source or informant, we must exercise due diligence and beware of any omissions, inconsistencies, understatements, and exaggerations that such narratives may include. Nevertheless, understanding these minority voices – however disagreeable or repugnant they may be – and their effects on public discourse is essential to gaining a fuller appreciation of how private, personal recollections intersect with public, collective representations of the past.

The scope of this book

This book contributes to three areas of study. Firstly, it is centrally concerned with the long-term consequences of Aum's religious terrorism, focusing on how various actors including state authorities, civil institutions, experts, and laypeople responded to Aum's organised violent crimes and terrorist attacks over the past two-and-a-half decades.

In sociology of religion, the Aum Affair has invited comparisons with other cases of terrorism and violence by new religious movements (Lewis 2011) and millenarian movements (Wessinger 2011), and the history of Aum's path to violence has been an important area of research. In the English language, for example,

Ian Reader's (2000a) authoritative history of Aum Shinrikyō mobilises numerous interviews with current and former Aum members to uncover the complex doctrines centred on absolute devotion towards Asahara Shōkō (1955–2018), the group's founder and leader, as 'the omniscient guru'. The book meticulously recounts the process through which Aum gradually became a pessimistic and militarist organisation driven by a collective delusion that the world was on the brink of a world-ending nuclear war. Others have looked to individuals' personality traits for explaining Aum's turn to violence. Whereas Reader explains gradual changes in Aum's group dynamics over time with reference to different religious ideas and practices, psychiatrist Robert Lifton (1999) focuses on the role of Asahara as the ultimate source of Aum's destructive tendencies. Devoting a substantial portion of the book to Asahara's biography, Lifton argues that Asahara was a typical example of a person suffering from megalomania and that Asahara's obsession towards actualising his own prophetic visions of the apocalypse was the primary driving force behind Aum's violent tendencies. Other notable works in this area have focused on issues such as specific aspects of Aum's beliefs and practices (Baffelli 2018; Shimazono 1995; 1997; Watanabe 1998) as well as individual experiences of current and former Aum members (Baffelli 2012; Komiya 2011; Watanabe 2005), all of which have been illuminating for uncovering the complexities of life inside Aum at various levels of the organisation.

As insightful and informative as these preceding works have been, these analyses have tended to focus on the *history* of Aum Shinrikyō leading up to the Tokyo attack, and the *internal* dynamics of the group. By contrast, this book highlights the *consequences* of Aum's violence as instances of religious terrorism and investigates complex social networks of actors and institutions *external* to Aum Shinrikyō that sought to define the meanings of the Aum Affair. While there are numerous works that discuss the social consequences of the Aum Affair on a variety of topics including mass media (Gardner 1999; 2002a; Hardacre 2007), impact on other religious organisations (Baffelli and Reader 2011; 2012; Klein 2012; McLaughlin 2012; Ushiyama 2019a), and victim activism (Pendleton 2009; 2011, 2015), this volume attempts to paint a more comprehensive picture of how various actors in multiple fields have interacted with each other to compete over multiple and clashing interpretations of the Aum Affair.

To do this, this book pays particular attention to the Aum Affair as *symbolic representations* – how the event has been narrated, depicted, and discussed in news media, art, public discourse, political and legal debates, and social activism. Fundamentally, it argues that the 'consequences' of an act of terrorism cannot be solely judged by metrics such as the number of casualties and the amount of economic damaged caused. The social and cultural imprint that a terrorist attack leaves on a society must also be understood with reference to the 'importance' (whether this is framed in moral, political, economic, social, or cultural terms) that various stakeholders attribute to the event *post facto*.

Cultural sociology provides a useful vantage point for exploring these discursive processes of the attribution of meaning following large-scale violence. Sociologists such as Ron Eyerman, Jeffrey Alexander, Neil Smelser among others have coined the concept of 'cultural trauma' to describe violent events that become foundational to collective identities and come to hold profound moral and emotional weight for affected groups, even when they have no first-hand experience of the original events (Alexander 2004b; Eyerman, 2015; 2019; Smelser 2004b). In the past two decades, religious terrorist attacks such as 9/11, the 2005 London bombings, and the massacre at the Bataclan Theatre in Paris have left indelible marks on the national memories of the United States, the UK, and France respectively.

Although Aum's religious terrorism cannot be compared in a straightforward manner with these more recent cases of radical Islamic terrorism, it nevertheless offers an important case study for both scholars of religious violence and cultural sociologists alike. Just as the 9/11 US attacks and the 7/7 London bombings irreversibly altered American and British societies, not only did the Aum Affair leave a permanent mark on Japanese national identity and memory, it also initiated wide-ranging societal impacts relating to the state regulation of religion, changes to public transport safety, and enhancement of powers accorded to security agencies, and public attitudes towards minority religions. One of the central aims of this book is to bring the Aum case into conversation with other instances of religious terrorism and cases of religious violence by elucidating the ways in which various stakeholders have made competing claims about the Aum Affair as a monumental event in Japanese history.

This book also contributes to discussions about Japanese culture and memory. Currently, there exists a rich body of literature on memory in Japanese culture which has primarily centred around the legacy of Japanese imperialism and the Second World War. Indeed, divergent interpretations of war memory have been an important topic of research, producing a plethora of innovative work in memory studies (Buruma 2009; Dower 1999, Hashimoto 2015; Kim and Schwartz 2010; Saaler 2005; Saito 2017; Seaton 2007; Seraphim 2006; Yoneyama 1999). Building on these debates, the book offers to broaden the scope of debates on collective memory discourses in Japan through a detailed treatment of a major historical event, which, although not on the same scale as the Second World War, nevertheless had a momentous and irreversible impact on Japanese culture.

This is not to suggest, of course, that memories of the Second World War were entirely separate or insignificant to memory discourses about Aum. Indeed, memories of Japanese fascism and the war provided a consistent backdrop to how Aum's violence should be understood. Japan's violent repression of minority religions during the state sponsorship of Shinto between 1868 and 1945 formed an essential backdrop to heated political debates about whether freedom of religion could be extended to religious terrorist organisations and to what extent legislation required reform to allow greater state oversight of religions.

Just as memories about the Second World War proved to be important reference points for responding to Aum's violence, the Aum Affair has itself become a marker in cultural discourses about religious violence, heterodox religions, and 'cults'. The Aum Affair has served as an inspiration for numerous fictional works, including the 2009 novel *1Q84* by Murakami Haruki and the manga *20th Century Boys* by Urasawa Naoki (Thomas 2012; Yamada 2014), both of which feature charismatic leaders of religious cults turned terrorist organisations as antagonists. Whilst Japan's cultural landscape was never particularly welcoming towards new religious movements even before the Aum Affair, it set a precedent and a standard by which all other religions, especially newer organisations, were valued and judged in the public eye. The pervasive suspicion towards newer religious organisations have continued to influence political and social debates of large 'minority religions' such as the lay-Buddhist organisation Sōka Gakkai, the charismatic new religion Kōfuku no Kagaku (known in English as 'Happy Science') and most recently, the Unification Church (now the Family Federation for World Peace and Unification), following the assassination of former Prime Minister Abe Shinzo.

The third area of debate that this book hopes to contribute to relates to questions of collective mourning, remembrance, and post-violence reconciliation. The collective remembrance and mourning of a sudden loss of life is often a spontaneous act, in which disparate individuals come together to share and express grief, as frequently seen in vigils in public spaces following murders, accidents, and terrorist attacks. However, sustained commemoration over many years requires coordination by socially dominant actors. With the passage of time, fewer people typically become involved in the orchestration of regular commemorative actions, and remembrance of the past often comes to take on predictable, routine forms. This inevitable process towards smaller and more predictable expressions of memory also results in the *ossification* of memory, quite literally, as certain interpretations of history are fixed in stone as memorials, statues, and museums, and on memorial plaques such as the one found at Kasumigaseki Station.

Curiously, the Aum Affair did not produce many physical memorials, the reasons for which are investigated in this monograph. Put simply, there has been a persistent hesitancy, if not outright hostility, to the idea that *any* physical object that reminds people of Aum should be preserved for future generations. Furthermore, the remembrance of the Aum Affair over the past quarter-century has become routinised and standardised in different ways, especially in mass media discourse. In these popular representations, Aum has been conventionally labelled as a social evil and a quintessential marker as a cultural 'Other' to be ostracised and quarantined from mainstream society.[2] Consequently, these representations indirectly led to lasting tensions between remaining Aum members – who were

[2] It bears mention, however, that Aum (and later Aleph) also regarded mainstream society to be too polluted and segregated themselves from it.

themselves not involved in the criminal schemes orchestrated by senior members – and local residents who voiced concerns about their continuing presence in their neighbourhoods. From the late 1990s to early 2000s, these concerns led to some authorities breaking the law, citing public concern as a justification for unlawful and discriminatory practices. For instance, district school boards in several municipal councils moved to prevent Asahara's children – the youngest of whom were infants and toddlers at the time of the Tokyo attack – from attending compulsory education after nearby residents expressed opposition to the idea that their children would attend the same school as Asahara's children. These decisions were only reversed after the children's legal representatives began legal action against the school boards. Similarly, Asahara's third daughter, Matsumoto Rika, was refused entry to three private universities despite initially passing the admissions tests. Separately, some municipal authorities acted unlawfully by refusing to process resident records submitted by Aum members living in their municipalities. Aum successfully litigated against these municipal governments in many of the cases.[3] In the backdrop of this hostile environment, many former members who sought to readjust to a secular lifestyle also found themselves living in fear of being 'outed' as an 'ex-Aum' (*moto Oumu*) by security agencies, a prospect that could (and often did) lead to loss of employment. In condemning acts of evil committed by Aum, many public institutions acted against the constitutional values of equality, liberty, justice that they claimed to defend and uphold. As the symbolic antagonism of Japan as victim and Aum as perpetrator has become fixed in dominant cultural narratives, this binary division has also foreclosed potential opportunities for reconciliation and forgiveness. As of writing, the social rifts between civil society and Aum's successor organisations, Aleph and Hikari no Wa, have continued, with little possibility for resolution. The aftermath of the Aum Affair is demonstrative of one of the biggest and most common ironies of commemoration: what is originally intended as an act of civil repair and moral cohesion for a victimised community becomes the source of enduring social division for future generations.

Organisation of the book

In what follows, Chapter 2 begins by developing a theoretical discussion of key concepts relating to collective memory and how concepts from the field of memory studies facilitate an understanding of the social consequences of the Aum Affair. Through a detailed discussion of cultural trauma theory, this chapter highlights the role of commemoration as a key social mechanism through which violent and

[3] For media reports on court verdicts regarding municipal councils' rejection of Aum believers' resident records, see Chapter 5.

destructive events acquire crucial importance at the level of collective memory and identity. Conceptualising commemoration as a stratified, contested, and unending process, the chapter proposes a multi-layered model of public commemoration in which the uneven distribution of social resources define both the scale and content of commemorative speech acts, ranging from state ceremonies and official statements to self-publishing booklets, and staging demonstrations. This is followed by an introduction of three concepts by the literary theorist Mikhail Bakhtin's as pertinent and useful tools for understanding memorial practices. Firstly, Bakhtinian 'dialogue' describes an inherent and necessary property of competing commemorative speech acts grounded in difference of perspectives. Secondly, 'polyphony' describes the resultant co-presence of multiple, mutually irreconcilable perspectives that occurs through dialogue. Thirdly, 'heteroglossia' captures the hierarchical nature of discourse between disparate social actors and their speech acts, in which more powerful actors can impose dominant interpretations of social reality with greater ease than others. However, there is never total control over discourse – less powerful actors can challenge and disrupt taken-for-granted interpretations of the social world they inhabit. The resulting effect is that both polyphony and heteroglossia are ubiquitous features of competitions over representations of the past.

Chapter 3 begins with a brief history of Aum Shinrikyō, tracing its development from its foundation to the group's first indiscriminate terrorist sarin attack on the city of Matsumoto in June 1994. Outlining the doctrinal and organisation evolution of the group from a small provincial yoga class to a much larger national organisation with multiple communes across Japan, this chapter shows how Asahara developed religious justifications for violence and militarisation in a claim to have rediscovered an ancient form of Buddhism. Central to Aum's organised violence was the concept of '*poa*', a type of mercy killing. According to this concept – which was originally drawn from Tibetan Buddhism but gained a completely different meaning in Aum's terminology – Asahara, an omniscient being, could predict whether someone would commit evil deeds in the future; killing them before they committed those acts prevented them from accruing negative karma, thereby guaranteeing a better life in their next incarnation. Putting this principle into practice, Aum committed a series of violent crimes that included lynching of dissident believers, kidnapping of members' relatives for 'donations', and assassination attempts of rival religious leaders and critics. In June 1994, attempting a mass *poa* of the national population, Aum gassed the residential streets of Matsumoto City, central Japan, in an attack which killed eight and poisoned over 600 residents.

Reconstructing the immediate societal responses to the Matsumoto attack, this chapter shows that the attack failed to materialise as a traumatic moment in the national imaginary due to a combination of factors, including the scarcity of material evidence as well as missteps in initial police investigation that led to a false accusation against an innocent victim. This uncertainty over why the attack happened prevented investigators and commentators from presenting an authoritative understanding of why and how the attack had taken place. As a result, the event gradually became a 'mystery', which had devastated a local community but did not become a cultural trauma as such. It was only when the true perpetrators were discovered during the investigation of the Tokyo attack that Matsumoto regained a new meaning as part of the cultural trauma of the 'Aum Affair'. Subsequently, Matsumoto also become infamous not just for its scale and impact as Aum's first indiscriminate attack, but also for the ways in which the police and mass media pursued an innocent victim as a suspect.

Chapter 4 explains how advances made by the police in investigating Aum's controversies led Aum's leadership to instigate a hastily planned assault on Tokyo. The Tokyo attack immediately resulted in an outpouring of discourses about how the nation should respond to this hitherto unknown threat. The chapter discusses mainstream media reactions as found in newspapers and other print media, as well as responses by 'experts' and commentators who traced back Aum's violence to a variety of contextual factors ranging from macro-social conditions to toxic intra-group dynamics within Aum. Following the attack, government officials, security agencies, and mass media universally identified Aum as a malevolent enemy to be crushed with the full force of the law, situating Asahara as a power-mad leader who brainwashed his adherents in a plot to take over Japan by force. The cultural discourses surrounding Aum popularised new vocabularies to discuss the Aum Affair, including 'destructive cults' and 'mind control', contributing to negative cultural stereotypes about new religions in general as being socially deviant. As the investigation progressed, commentators also shifted moral responsibility away from ordinary members to a core circle of Asahara and his aides, identifying Asahara as the ultimate cause of Aum's turn to terrorism. In doing so, he was portrayed as a demonic figure who represented values antithetical to Japan's, as well as a profane individual devoid of any true religious charisma or redeeming personal qualities. These cultural discourses established the 'dominant narrative', in which members of Aum represented a 'foreign enemy' to be defeated and excluded, with little possibility for moral redemption or reconciliation.

Cultural discourses surrounding the Aum Affair soon turned into questions about how to commemorate the terror attacks, as well as how to implement institutional changes in response to the social problems that the Affair brought to light. Chapter 5 explores the reactions by state and civil actors including the government, the police, the mass media, and local residents living near buildings owned by Aum. The government was relatively quick to respond to reform laws such as strengthening the state's authority over religion and enacting new laws to place Aum's successor organisations under surveillance, but systematic governmental support for survivors and bereaved families was much slower. The national media, through commemorative reports, documentaries, and dramatisations, have continued to reproduce narratives of Aum as a destructive cult which manipulated believers into committing violent crimes using brainwashing and mind control. Some victims' experiences, such as that of Kōno Yoshiyuki – a survivor and initial suspect in the Matsumoto attack – have also been recreated in television dramas and on film. In contrast to the abundance of media narratives about Aum, however, there have been very limited efforts to preserve physical relics or build memorials.

The Aum Affair had a profound and transformative effect not only on the religious field but also on the intellectual field more generally, as scholars across the humanities and social sciences confronted a violent religious group that they were hardly aware of prior to the Tokyo attack. Assessing the impact of the event on academia and in public debate, Chapter 6 addresses the controversies and conflicts between religious scholars, anti-cult activists, and public intellectuals over mind control theory, which purported that some new religions psychologically manipulated their followers to commit crimes. Some religious scholars were excoriated for their inaccurate and careless past assessments of Aum, while others, especially anti-cult activists, achieved prominence by warning the public about the dangers of 'brainwashing cults'. This chapter then explores the works of two public intellectuals who challenged this orthodox 'brainwashing' paradigm: novelist Murakami Haruki and documentary film-maker Mori Tatsuya. In the two-volume non-fiction work *Underground*, Murakami conducts interviews with victims of the Tokyo attack as well as Aum believers and ex-believers. Instead of providing an authoritative account of Aum's violence, Murakami relies on dialogue to produce polyphonic narratives as told by the interviewees themselves. By contrast, Mori Tatsuya engages in dialogue through the medium of film. In *A*, his debut film released in 1998, Mori gains access to Aum's facilities and holds candid conversations with Aum believers, showing them to be less 'brainwashed' than the media suggested. In the sequel *A2*, Mori follows the clashes between remaining Aum members and local protest movements calling for the eviction of Aum members from neighbourhoods, capturing the deep chasm between residents and believers, as well as some moments of détente and reconciliation.

Chapter 7 reconstructs the actions of individuals who became public advocates for 'victims' of Aum Shinrikyō. In the immediate aftermath of the Tokyo attack, much of the media coverage had centred on the profiles and backgrounds of individual Aum members as perpetrators, paying comparatively less attention to the diversity of victims' experiences. Countering this relative dearth of public interest, three individuals played an influential role in articulating contrasting interpretations through their own pursuit of 'justice'. First, Nagaoka Hiroyuki, father of an ex-believer and a survivor of a murder attempt by Aum using a potent nerve agent, negotiated the difficult symbolic space between 'victim' and 'perpetrator' as he renamed his organisation from 'Aum Shinrikyō Victims' Society' to 'Aum Shinrikyō Families' Society' shortly after the Tokyo attack. Until the executions of the culprits, he had campaigned for the death sentences of Asahara's aides to be commuted to life sentences. Second, Takahashi Shizue, who was widowed by the Subway Sarin Incident, became a prominent advocate for victims' rights. In her personal capacity, she has also defended capital punishment as a necessary mechanism for retributive justice. Her group has published edited collections of memoirs of victims to commemorate the subway attack. Third, Kōno Yoshiyuki, survivor of the 1994 Matsumoto Sarin Incident, has defended the constitutional right of Aum believers to practice their faith, has been opposed to the death penalty, and has criticised discriminatory practices by local authorities towards Aum believers. Kōno has also explored possibilities for reconciliation between members and local communities by acting as an external auditor for Aum's successor organisation. The chapter shows that 'victimhood' does not have a single meaning, but is a relatively open category that is realised through public claims to victimhood.

The Aum Affair stands out from many other cases of religious terrorism due to the preponderance of narratives by individuals who identify and are identified as 'perpetrators', from low-ranking members to those committing murders and terrorist attacks. Interrogating some of these autobiographical, confessional accounts, Chapter 8 examines the remarkable variations in how former members have addressed issues relating to guilt, responsibility, perpetrators' trauma, and financial redress. Even though some ex-members endorsed the idea that being subjected to mind control techniques had led to the loss of their autonomy and rational thought, others, including some of the most senior members, explicitly rejected mind control theory by admitting their heinous actions were the outcome of their own volition driven by misguided faith. In recent years, two of Asahara's children have publicly reflected on their own traumatic upbringing and have reached contradictory conclusions about the nature of Aum's crimes and Asahara's mental condition after his arrest. Prior to his execution, Asahara's third daughter Matsumoto Rika had contended that Asahara required medical treatment for his erratic behaviour during custody and had stated reservations about her father's level of involvement in the crimes. By contrast, Asahara's fourth daughter, appearing in public under the alias Matsumoto Satoka, had argued that Aum was a brainwashing cult and that Asahara was faking illness to avoid execution. The rift between the two has continued even after Asahara's execution in July 2018.

The book concludes with a consideration of the controversial circumstances surrounding the executions of Asahara and his 12 associates in two separate rounds of mass executions in July 2018. Although the executions brought a sense of closure for some, it also sparked intense debates about the legitimacy and the necessity of the death penalty in the Japanese justice system. While the executions brought a conclusion to the Aum Affair in a legal sense, the executions failed to resolve many of the social problems that the Aum Affair created and exposed, from the ambivalent position of religion in Japanese politics and civil society to the cultural reliance on social ostracism as the main mechanism for addressing the cultural 'Other'. Ultimately, the post-Aum social landscape illustrates how entrenched patterns of commemoration ensure that cultural distinctions between 'victims' and 'perpetrators' remain permanent and irresolvable, thereby sustaining social divisions between different communities of meaning.

2

Towards a Multi-layered Account of Collective Memory

There can be no such thing as an isolated utterance. It always presupposes utterances that precede and follow it. No one utterance can be either the first or the last. Each is only a link in the chain, and none can be studied outside this chain.

M.M. Bakhtin (1986, p. 136)

Memory is a vast and broad concept that has received much attention across the humanities, social sciences, and natural sciences. It is perhaps because of this wide breadth that it is difficult to pin down precisely what we mean by memory, and why the concept has resisted domestication by any singular discipline. In ordinary speech, words like 'memory', 'remember,' and 'forget' have relatively straightforward meanings. One has a 'memory' of something if they can successfully recall a personal experience, such as an early childhood experience of their birthday party, or if they can summon information that they have 'memorised', such as a phone number, an address, or the multiplication table. 'Forgetting' is usually seen as a failure of memory, referring to an inability to recall experiences and information, or an attempt to erase the memory of particular events: one can 'forget' to lock the front door as they leave the house in a hurry, or one can try to 'forget' an unpleasant encounter with a colleague by taking an extended vacation. A systemic inability to recall information is usually considered a medical condition (such as amnesia and dementia).

In addition to these cognitive, neurological, and psychological properties, memory also plays a critical function for social life, such as family histories and generational identities, as well as identities of culture, ethnicity/race, religion, and nation. What we 'remember' is not purely personal; we remember, share, and re-narrate experiences and anecdotes as we are told them by our parents, grandparents, friends, partners and colleagues. Through various media, we consume and share stories of important historical events in the societies in which we live. Scholars have coined terms such as 'national memory' to describe a body of knowledge that a 'nation' collectively shares with reference to 'monumental' events, such as wars, political events, elections, demonstrations, and celebrations. Starting in the early 1990s, many parts of the world, especially Europe, North America, and East Asia, experienced a 'memory boom' – an upsurge of academic and popular discourses surrounding these 'national memories' that roughly coincided with the fiftieth anniversary since the end of the Second World War. Spanning across the humanities and social sciences in disciplines including history, literary criticism, sociology, anthropology, archaeology, and cultural studies, terms such as 'collective memory', 'cultural memory', and 'social memory' have captured these socially shared and reproduced aspects of memory and memorial practices (Erll 2011; Olick 1999; Olick, Vinitzky-Seroussi, and Levy 2011; Misztal 2003).

In the past several decades, the field of memory studies has decisively shifted from classical notions of collective memory as an enduring, objective structure that constrains individuals belonging to a society, to instead treat memories as contingent and contentious objects of political struggle within and between societies. As a result, the field of memory studies has produced a dizzying array of concepts and theories to highlight different types of commemoration, from official ceremonies and national holidays to media narratives, art, and street protests, which, through their performance, enact and realise partial (in both senses of the word) interpretations of the past; this book refers to these as 'commemorative speech acts'. The act of commemoration is a type of 'performative utterance', or a 'declarative' statement, in which the speaker creates, rather than describes, social reality through speech acts (Austin 1962; Searle 1995).

Building on these approaches that stress the contingency of commemorative processes, this chapter seeks to develop a sociologically driven account of collective memory that places the uneven differentials of power and resources as key factors that influence both the form (what kind of commemorative medium and method is used) and the content (what kinds of messages are disseminated through commemorative speech acts). As such, this chapter develops a theoretical approach informed by cultural trauma theory, as well as concepts by the literary theorist Mikhail Bakhtin. Specifically, it argues that Bakhtin's conceptual vocabulary of 'dialogue', 'polyphony', and 'heteroglossia' is eminently suited to a sociological analysis of contending cultural trauma narratives.

The goal of this chapter is neither to advocate for the creation of yet new categorisations of memory nor to proclaim the superiority of Bakhtinian theory above existing ones. Instead, the chapter proposes an approach that puts the agency of social actors at the heart of struggles over memory narratives within a socially stratified and historically dependent arena of discourse. It argues that this model is useful not only for understanding the long-term impact of the Aum Affair, but for understanding how the Japanese government actors, mass media outlets, civic institutions, and individuals responded to the perceived social crisis in disparate ways.

Collective memory as uneven commemorative processes

There are many ways to define 'collective memory', but at its core, the term stresses the fact that memory is not solely an individual's capacity to remember, but a type of common property shared by members of a group and passed down generations. The French sociologist Maurice Halbwachs was arguably the first to systematically theorise collective memory in this way. Halbwachs was heavily influenced by Durkheim's methodological holism, which argues that a society shares a singular 'collective consciousness' (Durkheim 2008). Following Durkheim's central argument – that the collective consciousness is more than the mere sum of its constituent parts but an objective social fact – Halbwachs held that society, as an external structural force, was integral to an individual's capacity to interpret the world: 'it is in society that people normally acquire their memories. It is also in society that they recall, recognize, and localize their memories' (Halbwachs 1992: 38). Nevertheless, Halbwachs was also careful to point out that collective memory was not coterminous with Durkheim's 'collective consciousness'. Whereas Durkheim highlighted the powerful normative and moral drive of a single collective consciousness shared by all members of a society, for Halbwachs, collective memory existed at the level of concrete social groups, such as occupational groups, religions, and family units that reproduced narratives about themselves across multiple generations.

Much of memory studies debates has emerged as a response to Halbwachs's influential formulation of collective memory as a supra-individual structure and an objective 'social fact'. On the one hand, Halbwachs's formulation is appealing because some aspects of social life are inextricably linked to experiences to which no single individual has a claim. Modern nation-states routinely create, reinforce, and reproduce national identities through commemorative events, museums, statues, street and place names, and national holidays (Billig 1995; Connerton 1989; Nora 1989; Winter 2010; 2014; Zerubavel 2003). Such an approach usefully highlights that collective memory, just like other social phenomena that precede and outlast any single individual such as language and religion, are objective *social facts*, rather than an aggregate of individual reflections of the past (Olick 1999).

On the other hand, the Halbwachsian approach has an implicit bias towards historical continuity and cultural conservatism: individuals can only receive and reproduce memories of their predecessors, but with little flexibility to change or challenge them. To overcome this stability bias, numerous scholars have highlighted how social actors actively shape how the past should be remembered with reference to concepts such as 'moral entrepreneurs' (Wagner-Pacifici and Schwartz 1991), 'agents of memory' (Vinitzky-Seroussi 2002), or 'memory choreographers' (Conway 2010a).

Others have stressed that 'national memories' or 'collective memories' are never unitary, but divided across structural inequalities and often imposed from above. For instance, the Popular Memory Group at the Birmingham Centre for Contemporary Cultural Studies (CCCS) highlighted the importance of vernacular articulations of memory beyond historical sources as told by and for elites. Reflecting the Birmingham School's wider interests in 'mass' culture, the Group called for an expansion of sources of 'memory' to include popular culture such as commercial works of biographies and autobiographies, fiction, television, radio, and film, as well as practices such as oral history and community publishing (CCCS Popular Memory Group 1982; Seaton 2007). In a similar vein, Schwartz and Schuman (2005) have noted that there are patent discrepancies between how elites portray historical events and figures, and how the masses remember them through individual recollections, suggesting that official institutions of memory such as commemorative ceremonies, national holidays, museums, monuments, and history textbooks are not necessarily reflective of *civic*, *public*, and *popular* memories more generally. It is not surprising that memory scholars have become increasingly alert to the need to study 'bottom-up' forms of commemoration and remembrance in addition to 'top-down' models which have tended to dominate influential studies of the past (Winter 2010: 317).

Indeed, a recognition that collective memory is reproduced along uneven distributions of economic, political, military, cultural, and social resources is critical for understanding why some forms of commemoration are possible but not others (Conway 2010a). For instance, public remembrances of historical atrocities may be banned by the state, as is the case for the remembrance of the 1989 Tiananmen Square massacre in China. Conversely, mass protests and collective civic action can overturn (quite literally) pre-existing symbols of the past through dramatic actions. Following the police murder of George Floyd in Minneapolis, Minnesota, in 2020, the Black Lives Matter protests led to the toppling of the statue of slave trader Edward Colston in Bristol, UK, and the removal of statues of Confederate leaders across the United States.

While the conflict between elite ('top-down') memories and mass ('bottom-up') becomes most visible at flashpoints such as these mass demonstrations against public 'sites of memory', it is important to note that elite and mass memories are not always contradictory forces. As this book argues, how 'elite' and 'mass' memories concur or clash with one another is an empirical, rather than a theoretical question. Ordinary people's willingness to challenge dominant representations of the past, whether at an individual or collective level, is dependent on specific contexts and variables including the size and power of counter-hegemonic groups and movements, the salience and the relevance of historical events and social issues at a specific given time, as well as 'political opportunity structures' such as the level of state repression, the level of pluralism among politicians, and ties between elite and ordinary actors.

Collective memory is not always conflictual, and indeed, as Durkheim originally argued with reference to religious rituals as a site for celebrating social unity, commemorative actions can often result in a strong sense of moral cohesion. This is especially true in the aftermath of terrorist attacks, when there is often a strong congruence between state, media, and civic reactions to the violence. These actors often employ frames of good and evil to celebrate their own values, while calling on external threats to be exterminated (Simko 2012; Smelser 2004a; Wagner-Pacifici 1986). In the wake of Islamic extremist terrorist attacks across Europe and America, buttressed by enduring public support for the 'war on terror', states have successfully strengthened their hold on individuals' behaviour, through greater investigative powers, enhanced security checks, greater surveillance in public spaces and online, and increased budget spending for security authorities.

This book does not seek to fully explain how and when ordinary people's perceptions of the past concur or diverge with those of elite actors. Instead, it proceeds with a basic presumption that collective memory is not always consensual, nor is it always agonic: cultural 'hegemony' – the agreement between elite and mass perceptions of social reality – is a contingent, rather than a necessary phenomenon that is to be explained through the empirical study of specific case studies. As this chapter proposes below, a sociological model of collective memory must be attuned to questions of social differentiation (in terms of the division of labour), as well as social stratification (in terms of the uneven distribution of social resources that make commemoration possible). Moreover, the model must be attuned to the direction of commemorative speech acts and discourses, in terms of whether such discourses agree or disagree with representations of social reality that elite actors seek to impose.

There are two distinct bodies of research on memory and social discourse that are conducive to developing such a theoretical outlook: cultural trauma theory, on the one hand, and Bakhtin's literary theory on the other.

Cultural trauma: Negative events as cornerstones of collective identity

Emerging concurrently, and in conversation with, wider debates on the relationship between collective memory and collective identity, cultural trauma has emerged as an influential and prolific research programme for studying the long-term, intergenerational trajectories of intensely negative events such as wars, genocides, terrorism, and other acts of violence. Cultural trauma is defined as an instance in which a collectivity experiences an 'acute discomfort entering into the core of the collectivity's sense of its own identity' (Alexander 2004b: 10). Cultural trauma developed as an explicit critique of 'naturalistic' theories of trauma which hold that entire collective groups such as ethnic groups or nations are automatically traumatised by horrific events. Instead, cultural trauma arises as a result of concerted efforts to attribute moral meanings to past events through narratives: 'cultural traumas are for the most part historically made, not born' (Smelser 2004b: 37).

The cultural sociologist Jeffrey Alexander identifies a four-step 'trauma process' by which stakeholders socially construct cultural trauma (Alexander 2004b: 12–15). Firstly, the nature of the pain and hurt must be identified; secondly, the victims must be named; thirdly, the relationship of the victims to wider collectivities must be established, and fourthly, responsibility and blame are attributed to perpetrators. Cultural trauma emphasises the fundamental role of symbolic representations, and the presence of supra-individual, cultural schemata (Alexander 2004a: 200): the events need to be 'coded', 'weighted', and 'narrated' according to binary oppositions such as victims and perpetrators, good and evil, purity and impurity, sacred and profane (ibid.: 202–4). Various 'carrier groups' of trauma such as public intellectuals, the state, the mass media, and survivors of violence play instrumental roles in relating the moral significance of an event to indirectly implicated audiences with no first-hand experience of it. When carrier groups are successful in the 'symbolic extension' from those directly affected by the event to wider audiences, cultural traumas can become important markers of cultural identity. As carrier groups and institutions successfully routinise these trauma narratives through commemorative processes, cultural traumas come to occupy an integral position in collective memory and collective identity. Cultural trauma has produced numerous and wide-ranging works on the importance of horrendous events in shaping collective identities, from slavery in African American identity (Eyerman 2001) and Holocaust memory (Alexander 2004a), to Japanese war memory (Hashimoto 2015; Saito 2006) and natural disasters (Eyerman 2015; Geilhorn and Iwata-Weickgennant 2017).

As a theory that emphasises the constructivist and contingent nature of commemoration, cultural trauma has been particularly successful in demonstrating how historical events result in suppressed or delayed articulations of trauma. For instance, Bartmanski and Eyerman (2011) show that the mass murder of Polish soldiers and civilians in the Katyn Massacre by Soviet forces during the Second World War failed to emerge as a national trauma in Poland until after the fall of the socialist regime in 1989, due to political repression and the weak political status accorded to victims. In drawing attention to cases of delayed or failed commemoration, cultural trauma provides a useful alternative approach to existing studies which have tended to privilege successful cases of commemoration (Conway 2010b: 448).

Despite its utility, cultural trauma suffers from two shortcomings which arise from the insistence that narratives, rather than broader processes of commemoration, should be the primary object of sociological analysis. The first problem relates to the analytical separation of 'values' from 'interests'. For cultural trauma theorists, the struggle over symbolic 'values' takes place on a different plane to that of the struggle over material 'interests'. As such, cultural trauma theorists insist that symbols and narratives need to be analysed on their own terms, rather than as reflections or instruments of economic and political interests. While the analytical separation of (symbolic) 'values' from (material) 'interests' is certainly a useful one, it is less useful when applied to investigating what certain forms of narratives and commemorative speech acts accomplish socially and politically. As discussed above, commemoration can never be entirely separated from questions about power and stratification: every commemorative speech act must eventually answer the mundane but inevitable question: 'who pays for what?' Jay Winter (2014) emphasises that commemoration entails a distribution of resources, such as construction materials, money, specialist knowledge, labour, and time. Who buys the land on which a memorial is built? Who pays for the architects, builders, landscapers, cleaners, and (if required) security guards? Who will clean, maintain, and repair the site of memory? Who organises and attends regular commemorative ceremonies? Winter notes through a discussion of First World War memorials that,

> [h]owever sacred the task of commemoration, it still touched all the chords of local loyalties, petty intrigues, favouritism, apathy, and indifference. It also was about contracts, payments, and profit...The business of commemoration was always that: a business, shaped by the character of the community that undertook it. (Winter 2014: 90)

If one acknowledges that all forms of commemoration are products of social resources and present interests of various stakeholders in one way or another, it follows that one must study these flows of material interests, political agendas, and commercial incentives in conjunction with, rather than separate from, the competition over symbolic representations.

The second problem arises from the first, in that the caesura between the 'material' and 'symbolic' worlds forecloses an analysis of the potential 'meanings' of the various commemorative media at the physical, material, and spatial level. To date, many cultural trauma theorists have been primarily interested in the 'meanings' and 'narratives' expressed through different media. However, this has meant that a consideration of the unique properties of different modes of commemoration which act as vessels of these narratives is often lacking in these analyses. To return to Marshall McLuhan's (1964) adage that the 'medium is the message', it is not simply the content of commemoration that requires analysis, but also the material medium that is itself meaningful for the reproduction of a particular memory narrative. As such, it is imperative to consider the material possibilities and 'agency' of different mnemonic tools and practices by considering how these vary in cost, duration, and affect.

For example, commemorative ceremonies on anniversary dates can invoke powerful emotions through vivid language and iconography. However, the duration of such heightened emotions through ceremonies is short-lived. As such, routinisation and professionalisation of commemorative ceremonies is necessary for them to have a more enduring effect on collective identity (Olick 2016: 57). By contrast, physical commemorative objects such as memorials and monuments are often costly in terms of time, money, and space. The spatiality and design of the site of memory may itself be meaningful; Wagner-Pacifici and Schwartz (1991) have highlighted how certain memorials such as the Vietnam Veterans Memorial act as sites of 'dissensual' memory politics, in which the physical design of the memorial site enables individual visitors from different political orientations to derive different meanings from them.

In short, materiality matters. Every commemorative speech act, from holding a minute of silence to constructing a monument in a public area, imposes a particular vision of the 'social organisation of time' (Zerubavel 2003). Questions such as whether the commemorative medium is a human being or a material object, or what is the colour, size, design, and material of the object are pertinent for exploring the 'meanings' of sites of memory which are not reducible to the content of 'narratives' as such. Cultural trauma theory's focus on abstract '(meta)narratives' and 'cultural codes' unfortunately neglects how materiality itself is a meaningful object of analysis in the circulation and reproduction of social memory.

Bakhtin's literary vocabulary: Dialogue, polyphony, and heteroglossia

If an analysis of commemorative 'narratives' in isolation is insufficient, how can one be more sensitive to these interaction between 'values' and 'interests' as well as to the meaningfulness of different commemorative media? Mikhail Bakhtin's three concepts of 'dialogue,' 'polyphony,' and 'heteroglossia' provide insights for capturing the conflictual and dynamic nature of commemorative speech acts. To be sure, this is not the first attempt to develop Bakhtinian concepts in memory studies. Notably, Jeffrey Olick (2007; 2016) has articulated a sophisticated theoretical model inspired by Bakhtin, Bourdieu, and Elias, arguing that commemoration is 'always fundamentally dialogical' (Olick 2007: 82). Olick's (2016) study of official German commemorations of the Second World War illustrates how actors address political issues surrounding the question of commemoration in a path-dependent manner, as political leaders respond to preceding events, official statements, and evolving political priorities. Highlighting a different aspect of Bakhtin's work, the anthropologist Andrea Smith has developed Bakhtin's concept of 'heteroglossia' – the co-presence of official and lay discourse – to explore how differentials in class, status, and ethnicity shape how contradictory official and lay discourses are co-present in how people narrate their autobiographies (Smith 2004). Contrasting French official discourses of 'race blindness' with French settlers' actual experiences of racism, Smith highlights how different social contexts shaped whether interviewees would refer to official or lay discourse: 'official voice was most widely used in large gatherings of relative strangers, whereas the contrasting voice was especially apparent in more intimate settings with only a few present, and never in mixed French – non-French company' (Smith 2004: 261). Smith argues how inequalities in race, ethnicity, class, and status can shape internally contradictory – but by no means incoherent – memories of the past.

While these studies have been helpful for highlighting different aspects of commemoration and collective memory, this chapter proposes that the concepts of 'dialogue', 'polyphony', and 'heteroglossia' cannot be applied to collective memory in isolation, but that they must be considered in tandem. The concepts of 'dialogue' and 'polyphony' are perhaps the most well-known of Bakhtin's theoretical formulations. Drawing on dialogue as an everyday practice, Bakhtin drew attention to how some literary genres emphasise the interaction of multiple voices expressing differing opinions.

For Bakhtin, whereas the epic poem represents the protagonist's point of view through an authoritative narrative voice, the novel – as exemplified by the works of Dostoevsky – represents a new literary genre in which multiple characters express contrasting, but equally legitimate, viewpoints (Bakhtin 1981; 1984a). Dialogue differs decisively from the concept of Hegelian dialectics or Habermas' concept of communicative action. Unlike dialectics and communicative action, in which two opposing perspectives are resolved to a superior argument, dialogue does not presuppose an end point (Sennett 2012). Instead, dialogue treats difference as a given; it continues indefinitely as a response to what has been said before, in anticipation of what will be said in the future. As a result, dialogue exposes a state in which different consciousnesses mutually illuminate one another, leading to a greater understanding between participants that does not result in agreement or a Hegelian synthesis (Bakhtin 1984a: 97). Although dialogue does not necessarily result in a resolution, it does anticipate social change. Since dialogue does not have a logical conclusion, any attempts to fix meanings are always open to challenge, rebuttal, and reinterpretation. Bakhtin stresses that no single participant gets the 'last word' (Bakhtin 1986: 170).

In Bakhtinian discourse, since multiple viewpoints are not fully resolved, dialogue always results in polyphony, a situation which he defines as a 'world of a multitude of objectively existing and interacting psychologies' (Bakhtin 1984a: 37). Although intimately connected, there is a subtle difference between dialogue and polyphony that makes them conceptually distinct: dialogue highlights the sequential nature of an interaction between different points of view; in contrast, polyphony highlights the co-presence of multiple opinions at a given time. Thus, dialogue can be understood as the *process* which gives rise to polyphony as a *product*.

In contrast to Bakhtin's better-known concepts of dialogue and polyphony, the concept of 'heteroglossia' has arguably received less attention in memory studies. Heteroglossia refers to the many 'accents', or 'speech genres', that exist according to existing social hierarchies. Within a linguistic system, there are many speech genres, that range from official state discourse, professional jargon and urban speech to regional dialects, polemic, and everyday language (Bakhtin 1981: 263). Like the Marxist philosopher Antonio Gramsci, who was similarly sensitive to the relationship between class and language, Bakhtin emphasised that inequalities were constitutive of social discourse. Different forms of speech genres are distributed according to differences in social characteristics, such as between official and non-official discourse, professional and lay language, and city and country.

This perspective is more pronounced in works by V.N. Voloshinov – one of Bakhtin's collaborators – who maintained that '[c]ommunication and the forms of communication may not be divorced from the material basis' (Voloshinov 1986: 21).[1] For Voloshinov/Bakhtin, as different social groups, each with their own 'accent' (speaking with multiple 'accents') speak to one another, language itself becomes 'an arena of the class struggle' (ibid.: 23). Bakhtin highlighted that each stratum of language has a certain 'direction'. On the one hand, official, 'sacred', 'high' discourse is characterised by a 'centripetal force': an attempt to bring ideological unity and to represent social reality in the interests of the ruling class. As with Gramsci's concept of hegemony, in which the existing social order is accepted by the masses as natural and inevitable, Voloshinov/Bakhtin argued that '[t]he ruling class strives to impart a supraclass, eternal character to the ideological sign, to extinguish or drive inward the struggle between social value judgments which occurs in it, to make the sign uniaccentual' (Voloshinov 1986: 23). For example, elite discourses such as legal documents, professional documents and academic papers seek to make generalisable and all-encompassing statements about entire populations across time. In commemorative speech acts, one can often find centripetal narratives during wars and following events such as natural disasters, terrorist attacks, and pandemics, when state leaders and figures of political and cultural authority call for unity amidst a 'national emergency' and potentially overpower dissenting voices through coercive state institutions.

[1] The 'true' authorship of the literary critics V.N. Voloshinov and P.N. Medvedev has been contested by scholars. Both figures were contemporaries of Bakhtin, although some have suggested Bakhtin wrote using their names to appease Soviet authorities to produce more distinctly Marxist literary theories. See also the Editor's Introduction in Bakhtin et al. (1994) and the Translators' Preface in Voloshinov (1986). This book follows Pam Morris's (Bakhtin et al. 1994) and Michael Holquist's (Bakhtin 1981: xxvi) suggestions in treating Voloshinov's *Philosophy and the Philosophy of Marxism* as co-authored works by Voloshinov and Bakhtin.

On the other hand, multiple speech genres or 'accents' that exist across society as 'low', 'mass', 'profane' discourse resist attempts by elite strata through a 'centrifugal force', leading to a dispersion of meaning through resistance, satire, and parody. Unlike Gramsci, for whom the masses' perception of the world was obscured by hegemony and 'common sense', Voloshinov/Bakhtin held that the opposition of speech genres across social divides provides linguistic signs with 'vitality and dynamism and the capacity for further development' (Voloshinov 1986: 23).

Although heteroglossia highlights the interaction of linguistic discourses between multiple strata as a relatively normal condition in society, Bakhtin recognised that the social differentials can occasionally be subverted at a societal level. In what can be considered a case of 'centrifugal' discourse that destabilises centres of social power, in *Rabelais and His World* (Bakhtin 1984b), Bakhtin draws attention to the 'carnivalesque' as a temporary state of the suspension of social hierarchies and norms, a type of 'anti-structure' (Turner 1982). The carnival, much like Durkheim's religious ritual which results in a moment of heightened emotions which he called 'collective effervescence' (Durkheim 2008), is an occasion in which the social differences that separate individuals temporarily break down, resulting in a moment of unity. During the carnival, social norms and expectations are subverted. 'Lowly' bodily functions of eating, excretion, and sex are on full display. Satire, parody, and blasphemy become permissible. The sacred becomes profaned, and the hidden becomes apparent. By upending existing cultural norms and social hierarchies, and as opinions are exchanged between people as equals, carnivals dissolve existing social structures, albeit temporarily.

Bakhtin's attention to the innate capacity of lay actors to engage in parody, satire, and other forms of resistance means that heteroglossia provides a more dynamic model than Gramsci's, in which ordinary speech is reduced to a reflection of elite interests and laypeople are assumed to be 'cultural dopes', unaware of their true class interests until prompted by 'organic intellectuals'. Heteroglossia stresses that, while lay actors are still subject to centripetal speech genres, they also have the innate capacity to challenge, parody, and attack these representations through centrifugal speech. Moreover, applied to the study of commemoration, an explicit consideration of heteroglossic aspects of commemoration overcomes a common tendency to equate commemoration to 'elite' and 'official' discourses by taking into consideration non-elite and subaltern actors in the creation of speech acts.

Conclusions: Three propositions for a multi-layered model of collective memory

Having considered these theoretical perspectives, this chapter concludes with three theoretical propositions that undergird the following chapters.

1. *Commemorative speech acts aim to reproduce collective memory with reference to collective identities in response to what has preceded them and in anticipation of what will follow*

Collective memory is not a rigid and stable social structure, nor is commemoration an unreflexive reproduction of knowledge about what has happened in the past. Nor can collective memory be reduced to an aggregate of individual psychological reflections about the past. As Halbwachs highlighted, cognition – or rather, recognition – of the past is always social, filtered through existing structural constraints, including language, social norms, kinship and friendship groups, and, as this book highlights, the mass media. Moreover, the style and content of specific commemorative media are dependent on cultural and historical factors that determine the discursive rules of what can and cannot be said.

Rather than treating collective memory as an unchanging social structure, collective memory is best understood as a shorthand to describe the collection of competing claims, symbolic representations, and social practices pertaining to shared understandings of the past. Some of these claims, when successfully shared across the population, have a structuring effect on individual perceptions of the past: they may even become taken for granted explanations about the origins and history of a society or a people. Thus, while this book has 'Japanese collective memory' as its focus, it does not mean that there is a permanent and objective social structure that all Japanese people are conditioned to accept. Rather, 'collective memory' refers to constellations of social practices that create and reproduce certain interpretations about what it means to be 'Japanese' across multiple generations. Collective memory is neither a purely 'objective' nor an impartial reflection of the past; as such, it is analytically distinct from 'history'.

Commemorative speech acts are concerted social efforts by individuals, groups, and institutions that create and reproduce partial interpretations of the past through a variety of mnemonics devices and practices across disparate social groups and across generations. Because there are always many ways to interpret the past, there is never a *single* 'collective memory'; even if certain narratives and symbolism become hegemonic, one can still expect to find multiple and mutually exclusive narratives and symbolism relating to the past.

Given that different social groups inevitably have different understandings of the past. especially regarding the factual, normative, and affective importance of historical events, commemoration is inherently dialogical – in the sense that each intervention responds to what precedes it – and polyphonic – in the sense that there are multiple perspectives coexisting in the same discursive space: this means that commemoration is always provisional and open to challenge (Olick 2016).

2. *Commemorative speech acts express moral meanings of the past through a range of symbolic and material mnemonic devices*

Commemorative speech acts, whether of positive or negative events, rely on symbolism to represent particular interpretations of the past with reference to fundamental values and norms. Symbolic expressions can range from physical sites of memory, such as monuments and museums, to mediated forms of communication, such as mass media, artwork, books, academic work and commemorative processes that rely on embodied practices such as oral history, commemorative ceremonies, demonstrations, music, and dance.

As cultural trauma theorists have argued, these representations of the past very often rely on a foregrounding of binary cultural codes consisting of positive and negative oppositions: good and evil, victims and perpetrators, sacred and profane, pure and impure. As such, sites of memory are replete with moral meanings and inseparable from appraisals of the past, making commemoration an intensely political struggle over who occupies the side of the 'good', 'sacred', and 'pure'. As commemoration relies on the reification and celebration of the 'in-group' as being on the side of the 'good', it can also intensify representations of certain groups as 'evil', 'profane', and 'impure', thereby justifying exclusionary or discriminatory behaviours and policies against those who are identified as 'perpetrators' and the cultural 'Other'. As Alexander and Breese (2011: xxxiii) note, cultural trauma construction does not necessarily result in civil repair; instead, it can lead to enduring social division, as cultural codes of good and evil, pure and impure, and victims and perpetrators become entrenched in civil discourse between opposing groups.

At the same time, cultural practices are meaningful beyond their expressions of abstract binary values through narratives. The materiality of commemorative media, such as the design, colour, and material of a memorial object, are themselves affective qualities even if they may not relate directly or explicitly to 'narratives' or 'values'. Similarly, the very presence of a memorial object demonstrates a willingness to remember, while its absence may suggest either an inability to remember or a desire to forget and exclude a certain event from public memory.

3. *Social resources required for the organisation of commemorative speech acts are unevenly distributed across society*

Many types of commemoration, from ceremonies and rituals to the construction of monuments and museums, are resource intensive. Commemoration requires a range of social resources such as time, capital, labour, physical space, access to media, political power, and social ties. These social resources are unevenly distributed across society, meaning that those with more social resources are likely to be able to engage in commemorative speech acts that are high-impact and far-reaching. For example, political elites hold the power to enact legislation, hold military parades, determine educational curricula, and set official holidays. Rich and powerful corporate actors such as mass media conglomerates can disseminate narratives and imagery that reach national or even global audiences. Economic elites may engage indirectly in commemorative speech acts through patronage and financing the creation of monuments, museums, and archives, or by funding research in a field of study related to distinct peoples or past events. These elite-controlled commemorative speech acts usually constitute the 'dominant' representations, or the 'master narratives' of collective memory that have structural effects on individuals' perceptions of the past.

As Bakhtin (among others) recognised, elites tend to use language in a 'centripetal' manner that neutralises and justifies the current social order. However, this is not always the case for all elites. Those in relative positions of privilege, but without direct access to political power – artists, novelists, academics, and journalists, to name a few – can challenge these dominant representations through counter-narration, by 'speaking truth to power'. These elites in intermediate positions can destabilise and challenge established meanings through 'centrifugal' discourse. Hence, social discourse cannot simply be reduced to an opposition between 'elite' and 'lay' discourse: discourse is multi-layered into numerous substrata, each of which can be oriented in 'centripetal' (towards the political and linguistic centre) or 'centrifugal' (towards the political and linguistic periphery) directions.

While social differentials of power have structuring effects on lay actors' perceptions of the past, they do not *determine* the outcomes of commemorative practices. It is indeed often the case that ordinary populations will be influenced by elite representations by the state and media, and history is replete with instances in which national populations are prone to propaganda about the mythical origins and the superiority of nations and ethnic groups. Yet, this is not to suggest that 'ordinary' people cannot challenge or question established narratives and frames. Even when lacking access to social resources, subordinate strata can still rely on different commemorative media with relatively lower barriers for entry, such as social media, public demonstrations, self-publishing, and commemorative ceremonies. The power of subaltern groups to engage in counter-memory means that 'elites' never truly have a monopoly over the meanings of the past. Whilst those at the centres of power enjoy a structural advantage in shaping collective memory within a society, given the centrifugal aspects of language among peripheral groups, 'there can be no consensus' of collective memory at any given time (Schwartz 2012: 529). Ordinary people are not under the influence of 'hegemony' or 'common sense' by default. Rather, elite 'master narratives' are always vulnerable to resistance, parody, and challenge. Every utterance, whether it comes from the elite or subaltern, anticipates a response; dialogue never ends.

The following chapters seek to demonstrate how each of these three principles is crucial for understanding the complex relationships between various actors involved in the narration and commemoration of the Aum Affair. The Aum Affair was a landmark moment for Japanese society, raising fundamental questions about the state of current society. However, perhaps more importantly, it was an event that exposed the fault-lines of who constituted the Japanese 'us' and the non-Japanese 'them'. These divisive categorisations, operating at the levels of civil society, religion, and ethnicity, have endured long after the immediate impact of Aum's violence has faded.

3

The Prelude to Destruction: The 1994 Matsumoto Sarin Attack[1]

Throughout scholarly as well as public discourse surrounding 'cult' violence and religious terrorism, Aum Shinrikyō is remembered first and foremost for its culpability in the horrific Tokyo sarin gassing. This is far from surprising, given the unprecedented nature and scale of the event: the Tokyo attack is often listed as one of the worst instances of 'cult violence' alongside other examples such as the mass murder-suicides of the Order of the Solar Temple in France, Switzerland, and Canada in 1994–1995, the 1993 deadly siege and fire by the Branch Davidians in Waco, Texas known as the 'Waco Tragedy', and the mass suicides of the Heaven's Gate group in California in 1997. However, due to the disproportionate public attention paid to the Tokyo attack, it is often overlooked that Aum's violence was not a one-off event: there was a period of about six years in which Aum became increasingly violent, not only towards outsiders but to its own members, especially against followers whose devotion to the guru was seen to be wavering. Regrettably, its various murders, murder attempts, and its first indiscriminate terrorist attack using sarin in June 1994 in Matsumoto – a mid-size regional city in Nagano Prefecture, central Japan – have tended to be sidelined in academic and media debates about Aum. The causes and consequences of the Matsumoto sarin attack merit special attention not only as a historical milestone in Aum's turn to mass violence as a means of achieving religious ends, but also because of its *lack* of national impact in the immediate aftermath of the attack. The Matsumoto attack killed eight and injured more than 600 residents in a residential neighbourhood, in what was then one of the largest terrorist attacks in living memory. Yet, surprisingly, despite the scale and the unprecedented nature

[1] Parts of this chapter appeared in the *International Journal of Politics, Culture and Society* (2019) as 'Latency Through Uncertainty: the 1994 Matsumoto Sarin Incident as a Delayed Cultural Trauma' as a condensed version of the chapter, originally published under a Creative Commons Attribution 4.0 International License (https://creativecommons.org/licenses/by/4.0/).

of the attack, in its immediate aftermath, the Matsumoto sarin attack did not become a 'national trauma'. Rather, the event became a 'mystery' that gradually faded into the backdrop of ordinary life for most Japanese people. It was only after Aum committed the second terrorist attack in Tokyo nine months later that the Matsumoto attack regained national significance in public discourse as part of the 'Aum Affair'.

Reconstructing Aum Shinrikyō's 10-year history, from its inception in 1984 to its first mass, indiscriminate terrorist attack in Matsumoto, this chapter elucidates how Aum evolved in a short span from its humble beginnings as a yoga class held in a condominium to a highly hierarchical organisation with militaristic visions justifying the deaths of ordinary civilians for realising their religious-political ambitions. In doing so, it highlights two related historical developments that were crucial in the lead-up and the aftermath of the Matsumoto sarin attack.

Firstly, Aum Shinrikyō underwent a gradual doctrinal transformation starting in 1988, when Asahara first used the '*poa*' ritual, which transfers souls to the next life, to cover up the accidental death of a follower. Just a few months later, Asahara had reformulated '*poa*' as a legitimate form of religious murder to kill a dissident follower. It is also around this time that the group's priorities also shifted from encouraging self-improvement and changing the world through conversion to preparing for an impending catastrophe through militarisation. From 1990, this principle broadened to permit the killing of ordinary citizens through indiscriminate terrorism, although Aum's earlier attempts at biological terrorism were unsuccessful. The Matsumoto sarin attack was the first successful enactment of '*poa*' on a mass scale.

Secondly, due to Aum's characteristics as a 'world-rejecting' (Wallis 1984), isolationist movement with much of the militarisation process taking place in Aum's communes in the remote countryside, state authorities, media, and academics were entirely ignorant of Asahara's eventual ambition to rule over Japan by force. Although Aum Shinrikyō had some media exposure in the period leading up to the terrorist attacks, including a general election campaign in 1990, the group's carefully choreographed self-presentation as a peaceful Buddhist movement concealed more sinister and violent aspects of their beliefs and practices. Partly due to this PR strategy, and the secretive nature of Aum's militarisation process, the knowledge of Aum's increasing militancy and pessimism was hidden from outsiders. Consequently, in the immediate aftermath of the Matsumoto attack, there was chaos and confusion over the actual circumstances of what had happened. The first media reports could only confirm that hundreds fell ill after breathing in a toxic gas. In the first weeks and months of investigation, the police and media wrongfully implicated a local resident as a potential suspect while Aum evaded scrutiny, until the police investigation progressed to identify them as the true culprits several months later. Aum was not publicly identified as the perpetrators until after the Tokyo sarin attack, after which point the Matsumoto attack belatedly became a significant moment for Japanese collective identity.

A close reading of the circumstances before and after the Matsumoto attack reveals how and why Aum was able to continue its militarisation programme to commit the Tokyo sarin attack nine months later. Moreover, the incident illustrates the pivotal role of certain professions such as the police, forensic scientists, medical workers, journalists, and other experts in establishing the 'facts' and in enabling other actors to create persuasive narratives and attribute moral meanings to violent events. This group of experts, whom this chapter calls 'fact-finders', struggled to correctly identify the causes, motives, *modus operandi*, and identity of the suspects in the initial months of investigation because of the unprecedented nature of the attack; as the first recorded case of chemical terrorism by a non-state actor, the incident did not fit with existing professional norms of police investigation and media reports. Throughout 1994, the Matsumoto sarin attack remained a 'mystery', which it was extraordinarily difficult, if not impossible, to comprehend and narrate the event as an assault at the level of national identity and memory, despite the psychological trauma and devastation experienced by local residents of Matsumoto. Generalising from this event more broadly, this chapter shows that public narrations of an event as a 'cultural trauma' can be delayed when 'fact-finders' struggle or fail to provide clarity over why the event occurred.

The making of 'Asahara Shōkō' the guru

Before he became 'Asahara Shōkō', the self-proclaimed omniscient guru and a messenger of Shiva, the man born as Matsumoto Chizuo was a young man who had repeatedly sought and failed to achieve the conventional markers of success, such as education, economic wealth, and cultural status. It is fair to say Matsumoto likely faced greater hardship as a child than most other children of his generation. He was born in 1955 to a family of poor *tatami* mat makers on the western coast of Kumamoto Prefecture, on the western island of Kyūshū. Biographical accounts suggest that Matsumoto's parents benefited little from Japan's post-war economic recovery during his early childhood, as they struggled to raise nine children of whom Matsumoto was the seventh.[2] Matsumoto was born with a congenital condition which caused blindness in one eye; although he still had functional vision in the other eye, he was sent to a state-funded boarding school for the blind from an early age. The decision was supposedly made to ease his parents' financial

[2] Takayama (2006). Some earlier biographical accounts stated he was the sixth child out of seven siblings, e.g., *AERA* (1995) 'Asahara kyōso no kyozō to jitsuzō: Oumu Shinrikyō o hiraita otoko Sarin to Oumu', 10 April, p. 13, but this appears to be incorrect. The discrepancy could possibly be due to deaths of Asahara's siblings in early childhood.

burdens. As a result, Matsumoto spent much of his childhood separated from his parents, relying on his older siblings for familial support (Fujiwara 2006; Takayama 2006). After completing compulsory education, Matsumoto initially planned to go to Kumamoto University to become a doctor, but did not formally apply as the university could not accommodate the visually impaired.[3] Despite this setback, he continued his studies in a bid to gain entry to the prestigious Tokyo University. While studying for his exams, he met and married his wife, Tomoko. In 1978, after multiple unsuccessful attempts to gain admission to Tokyo University, he used his vocational training to open an acupuncturist clinic in Funabashi, Chiba Prefecture.[4] He was forced to close this business in 1980 when he was fined for insurance fraud (Takayama 2006: 73). The following year, he opened another business selling Chinese medicine. Although the dispensary was commercially successful, it too was forced to close in 1982 when he was arrested and fined for selling unlicensed products. It was around that time that he began to develop a greater interest in religion. In 1981, he joined Agonshū, a new religion founded by a charismatic leader, Kiriyama Seiyū. Kiriyama claimed to have rediscovered the most ancient form of Buddhism by studying the *Āgama* texts of early Buddhism. Leaving Agonshū after three years, he began to call himself Asahara Shōkō and to organise regular yoga classes in a small condominium under the banner 'Aum Society' (*Oumu no Kai*). He was 29 at the time.

For the first few years, Aum Society was dedicated to self-improvement through an eclectic synthesis of teachings taken from yoga, esoteric Buddhism, and Chinese ascetic training known in Japan as *Sendō*. Training would include exercises such as yoga, meditation, and rituals known as *shaktīpat*, in which Asahara 'injected' spiritual energy into the participant to awaken different energy centres called *chakras* inside the body. The group's earliest activities did not have explicitly political aims. Instead, ascetic training was a means for developing supernatural powers, as evidenced by Asahara's first book *The Secret Method of Developing Supernatural Powers* (*Chōnōryoku Himitsu no Kaihatsuhō*) (Asahara 1991 [1986]), in which Asahara recounts the struggles of ascetic training, and claims to have attained the ability of flight among other superpowers.[5] The book's cover features a now-infamous photograph of Asahara, sitting cross-legged in the traditional meditative position, supposedly suspended in mid-air. Although less impressionable readers may notice from Asahara's ruffled hair that the photo was most probably captured while he was in the middle of a jumping motion, the photo

[3] *Asahi Shimbun* (2004) 'Kyōso 'kane to chikara' ani no yōni', 26 February, p. 39.

[4] Ibid.

[5] Specifically, Asahara claimed to help followers develop six *jinzūriki*, or godly powers, in Buddhist teachings: *jinsokutsū*, the power of free movement and flight; *ten'nitsū*, supernatural hearing; *tashintsū*, the ability to read minds; *shakumyōtsū*, the ability to discover one's past lives; *tengentsū*, the knowledge of past lives of others; and *rojintsū*, one's awareness of having reached nirvana (Asahara 1991 [1986]).

and the book's that yoga could help ordinary people gain supernatural powers were certainly eye-catching, even for the incredulous. Drawn by the book as well as Asahara's charismatic oratory skills, many young people joined the group, in no small part fuelled by a vibrant youth subculture interested in supernatural issues such as spirituality, superpowers, and the occult.

In 1986, the group changed its name to Aum Society of Sages (*Oumu Shinsen no Kai*). During this time, Asahara and his entourage made several trips to India to meet Tibetan Buddhist lamas, including the Dalai Lama; Asahara subsequently used photographs of him standing beside the Dalai Lama as a recruitment tool in publicity materials. Following these trips to the Himalayas, he announced that he had reached the final stage of enlightenment, and claimed himself to be the Final Enlightened One, a supreme being and the primary object of worship. The self-created title *sonshi* (sacred leader) emphasised Asahara's holiness, and Asahara promised to guide disciples towards enlightenment on the condition of absolute loyalty. Disobeying Asahara or objecting to his orders would demonstrate one's low level of spiritual attainment: the follower's ultimate goal was to become his 'clone' by replicating his virtuous qualities through absolute devotion. Following the group's transition from a yoga class to a fully fledged religion, adherents were encouraged to become full-time renunciant monks (also known as *shukkesha*, *samana*, or *shissha*) and set up communes throughout the country (Fujita 2011). In this period, Aum aimed to develop a religious utopia (*Shambhala*) of self-sufficient communes called 'lotus villages' scattered across Japan, in which Aum believers could live and practice their religion in perpetuity (Shimazono 1995).

The group changed its name again to Aum Shinrikyō in 1987, and continued to expand across the country, drawing from youths interested in yoga, spiritualism, and the occult. Most new members joined first as '*zaike*' members, or part-timers, attending classes and talks, and would then be strongly encouraged to become '*shukkesha*' (renunciants). In joining the movement full-time, '*shukkesha*' were expected to donate all their assets and belongings to Aum and to cut off all ties with their family members (the exception being if the family also joined).

Under this new system, Aum assiduously avoided contact with the outside world, fearing that contact with outsiders would result in exchanging ritually polluting influences – in their terms, 'bad data' – which would accrue negative karma and impede enlightenment. As such, followers were forbidden to consume outside media and entertainment. On a day-to-day level, '*shukkesha*' or '*samana*' were assigned tasks known as 'work' (*wāku*) and had to take part in daily devotional training, including meditation and 'prostration' (*gotai tōchi*) in which the trainee repeatedly places their limbs and head on the floor while reciting their devotion to the guru and Lord Shiva. Residing in shared dormitories with minimal personal belongings, they lived on a strict vegetarian diet of one meal a day. Corporal punishment for transgressions was common. In a ritual known as 'cleansing karma' (*karuma otoshi*), transgressors beat themselves or were beaten with bamboo swords. Sleep was generally discouraged as a sign of laziness. Celibacy was the norm, although married couples were permitted to live together, and marriage was also permitted with Asahara's blessing. While celibacy was strictly enforced for ordinary renunciants, Asahara was the exception: he had sexual relations with numerous female devotees known as *dākinī*, claiming that he was conducting Tantric initiation rituals.

In this new residential system, Aum developed an extremely hierarchical structure defined by individuals' level of spiritual attainment. In practice, however, those with higher educational qualifications tended to be placed in senior positions to work closely with Asahara. Once they reached a certain stage of spiritual attainment, they would be gifted with 'holy names' chosen by Asahara. Names were usually picked from deities, bodhisattvas, and historical figures in Buddhism: for instance, the spokesperson Jōyū Fumihiro was known as Maitrēya after the Boddhisatva, while Inoue Yoshihiro, a key participant in the Tokyo attack, was named Ānanda after one of Shakyamuni Buddha's 10 principal disciples. While this hierarchical system introduced a command chain in an increasingly complex organisation, Asahara always remained the ultimate source of religious authority and object of worship. Absolute obedience was the only successful path towards becoming the 'guru's clone', while harbouring doubts or asking too many questions were seen as evidence of insufficient devotion. *Mahāmudrā*, meaning a 'test of faith', was an important mechanism in this regard. Asahara – and later, other leadership figures – would give subordinates difficult or even unachievable tasks to test if they would carry out the orders dutifully and unquestioningly.

Young people comprised the majority of Aum's membership. Aum appealed to teenagers, university students, and graduates disaffected by the rigid hierarchies in schools and companies, and the consumerist excesses of Japan's 'bubble' economy. Typical of many new religions in Japan and elsewhere that grew in the 1970s and 1980s, domestic membership was generally young: in 1995, 47.5 per cent were in their twenties, and 75.4 per cent in their twenties or thirties (Shimazono 1995: 384). However, there were also some followers, including Hayashi Ikuo and Hayakawa Kiyohide (see Chapter 8), who were older than Asahara and had established careers before joining Aum full-time.[6] Some families joined as parents and children, which meant there were also older generations of followers in their fifties, sixties, and seventies, as well as infants and children. At its height, Aum had around 10,000 members domestically, between 1,100 and 1,200 of whom were full-time 'renunciants' living communally (Reader 2000a: 8; Shimazono 1995: 384).[7] In 1992, Aum expanded to Russia, where seniors members used the

[6] Like Asahara, both Hayashi and Hayakawa were transient members of Agonshū, although their membership was brief.

[7] Reader 2000a gives the estimate of 1,200 full-time *samana*, while Shimazono 1995 estimates there were around 1,100 *samana* at its height.

Moscow branch to establish political connections and procure military equipment (Inoue M, 2011). Over the next several years, the group also conducted international tours in India, Bhutan, Zaire (now the Democratic Republic of Congo), and Australia to raise its profile.[8]

Aum's doctrinal evolution

Although Aum claimed to have rediscovered an ancient form of Buddhism (*genshi bukkyō*), its beliefs and practices were unique to the group. Aum derided traditional Japanese Buddhism as corrupt, and even as departing from orthodox esoteric Buddhist texts and teachings. Aum produced its own texts to recite and study, and Asahara's sermons comprised the canon. In these sermons, Asahara drew on a wide range of sources from Tibetan Buddhism and yoga, but also from Christianity and New Age spiritualism and occultism (Ōta 2011). Influenced by Theosophy, Aum developed its own notions of 'astral' and 'causal' planes existing beyond the physical realm that only Asahara was able to freely access. Moreover, drawing from contemporary occult subcultures and conspiracy theories, Asahara developed antisemitic conspiracy theories that argued that key institutions such as the CIA, the US Armed Forces, and the Japanese Government were secretly controlled by Jews and Freemasons, and predicted that the world would end in 1999 in a massive nuclear war. These ideas were later reflected in Aum's increasing sense of urgency over the approaching apocalypse, as well as Asahara's identification of the Judaeo-Masonic conspiracy as both Aum's primary enemy and harbinger of doom. In this sense, Aum differs from other millenarian movements because its inspiration for a pessimistic eschatology came not just from existing religious scriptures, but also from secular conspiracy theories and Asahara's vivid imagination.

Although Aum did not begin as a militarist organisation, Aum's doctrines gradually developed to condone violence towards insiders as well as outsiders. Over time, Aum developed a tripartite structure of different 'paths' (or 'vehicles') to enlightenment. At the bottom was the lowest form of *Hinayāna* (*shōjō* or 'small vehicle'), which emphasised individual enlightenment. Above it was *Mahayāna* (*daijō* or 'large vehicle'), in which enlightened leaders sought to guide uninitiated masses to salvation through spreading the teaching. According to Ian Reader, *Mahayāna* was the dominant mode of thought in Aum's early period (Reader 2000a: 88). Indeed, Aum's regular periodical for its followers was titled *Mahayāna*.

[8] In Australia, Aum had searched (unsuccessfully) for a uranium mine on a sheep ranch with the eventual goal of developing nuclear weapons.

Finally, and most importantly, the *Tantra Vajrayāna* or *Tantrayāna* path (*kongōjō* or 'diamond vehicle') stated that the enlightened guru could introduce worldly changes to bring about a religiously virtuous end, including killing. Asahara situated his disciples as 'warriors of truth' (*shinri no senshi*), tasked with the salvation of the world. This became the predominant justification of Aum's activities from 1988 onwards (Jōyū 2012: 54).

Among the most important doctrines in *Tantra Vajrayāna* was the concept of *poa*. In accordance with fundamental Buddhist tenets, Aum officially forbade killing of any kind. However, Asahara made an exception to this rule by introducing a ritual of soul transference, derived from the Tibetan Buddhist ritual of *phōwa*. Originally, *phōwa* is a ritual of spiritual transference in which an enlightened guru guides the soul of another being at the point of death to the next life (Shimazono 1995; Watanabe 1998). Asahara first used the ritual in 1988 when Majima Teruyuki, a male adherent in his twenties, accidentally died during extreme ascetic training. Asahara conducted the *poa* ritual to transfer the believer's soul to the next life, and, eager to avoid a public scandal, ordered the body to be secretly disposed of in an industrial microwave oven. However, the word *poa*, at this time, did not have a fixed meaning. In a 1989 publication, Aum advertises a 'Poa Course', which offered a less strenuous training course to its adherents, consisting of a textbook, musical recordings, and regular recordings of Asahara's sermons, and a monthly 'poa gathering' (*poa no tsudoi*) (Asahara 1989a: 234–5).

Poa took on a new meaning in early 1989, when a disgruntled believer, Taguchi Shūji, who had witnessed Majima's death and had lost faith in Asahara, announced his intention of leaving and publicly exposing the death. Fearing that this would jeopardise Aum's ongoing bid to gain official charity status as a 'religious corporation', Asahara ordered Taguchi to be killed and the body destroyed (Fujita 2011). Since then, *poa* became a justification for killing individuals whom Asahara 'knew' would commit evil deeds in the future. By killing them before they committed evil acts, they would not accrue negative karma, and thereby would be guaranteed a better life in their reincarnation (Reader 2000a: 145–6). After Taguchi's murder, *poa* became a sinister euphemism for eradicating anyone whom Asahara considered unworthy of life.

The application of *poa* as a type of mercy killing would soon extend to individuals outside of the organisation. As with many other new religious movements that experience rapid growth among young members, tensions intensified between Aum and external stakeholders. Parents of young believers, many of whom were university students or even secondary schoolers, became concerned that they had abruptly cut off ties with their families to join what they viewed as a 'cult'. Parents and critics questioned Aum's aggressive recruitment strategies, as well as what they saw as exorbitant prices for various 'initiations'. Aum gave phials of Asahara's blood to adherents to drink in return for 'donations' above ¥1 million (approximately US$7000 at 1989 exchange rates).[9] Aum also sold bottles of bathwater that Asahara had bathed in (dubbed 'miracle pond'), to be drunk or used in cooking. Between October and November 1989, the weekly contemporary affairs magazine *Sunday Mainichi* ran a seven-part series criticising Aum's aggressive and expensive recruitment strategies as emblematic features of a cult. The series of articles led to parents coming together under the banner 'Aum Shinrikyō Victims' Society' led by Nagaoka Hiroyuki (see Chapter 7), father of a former university student who had suddenly become a devoted member of Aum and cut off ties with his parents. The new group was represented by the lawyer Sakamoto Tsutsumi, who had experience with dealing with alleged 'spiritual sales' (*reikan shōhō*), such as sales of expensive vases and other spiritual goods by new religions such as the Unification Church (the Holy Spirit Association for the Unification of World Christianity, now the Family Federation for World Peace and Unification).

Asahara ordered the murder of Sakamoto Tsutsumi soon after the formation of the Victims' Society. When Aum discovered that Sakamoto had recorded an interview with the national television broadcaster Fuji Terebi, three senior disciples, Aoyama Yoshinobu (who was also a qualified lawyer), Jōyū Fumihiro, and Hayakawa Kiyohide, harassed television executives into showing them the unaired interview, which was due to be aired at a later date (see Chapter 5). After the disciples reported back the contents of the interview to Asahara, he gave the order to kill Sakamoto by '*poa*'. At around 3 a.m. on 4 November 1989, six assailants broke into Sakamoto's house under the cover of darkness and strangled him along with his wife and one-year-old baby. The bodies were taken to remote mountains and buried separately across three different prefectures.

After Sakamoto's sudden disappearance, Nagaoka, along with Sakamoto's friends and family, campaigned for years to find the Sakamoto family through public appeals for information. There were clues at the crime scene that suggested Aum's involvement: for example, there was a badge given only to high-ranking members – known as a *purusha* – that had fallen off one of the assailants as they struggled. However, the Kanagawa Prefectural Police neglected to seriously consider Aum as a potential suspect, and instead suggested that Sakamoto had run away because of personal debt.[10]

[9] *Sunday Mainichi* (1989) 'Oumu Shinrikyō no Kyōki: Nisegusuri no kako to chi no gishiki', 22 October, pp. 30–35.

[10] Sakamoto's legal firm had ties with trade unions and the Japanese Communist Party, and historically had strained relations with the police. In the initial stages of the investigation, Kanagawa Prefectural Police had suggested to the media that Sakamoto had been caught up in leftist sectarian violence or had run away due to personal debt. These insinuations were entirely baseless (Egawa 1995: 51: see also ibid.: 41–93; Interview with Nagaoka Hiroyuki, March 2015, Tokyo).

In a strange twist, several months after the murders, Okasaki Kazuaki, who was involved in the murders of both the dissident believer Taguchi and the Sakamoto family, ran away from Aum with ¥300 million (approx. US$2 million) in cash.[11] He proceeded to blackmail Asahara that he would expose the murders unless his safety could be guaranteed. Asahara agreed to pay Okasaki off for a cash payment in exchange for his silence. Nevertheless, Okasaki sent an anonymous tip to the police with a detailed, illustrated map of where one of the bodies was buried. Unfortunately, the police made only a cursory investigation of the suggested location and were unable to find the body. Due to these errors in their investigation, the police did not formally investigate Aum for the family's disappearance despite persistent pleas from Nagaoka and Sakamoto's colleagues, and the case remained unsolved until after the Tokyo attack. Meanwhile, Asahara and his top disciples temporarily fled briefly to Germany, and in a press conference, vehemently denied any responsibility. To avoid their fingerprints being matched to those found at the crime scene, some assailants were ordered to burn off their fingerprints on hot frying pans – an order which they dutifully obeyed.

Besides conflicts with parents of believers, in Namino, Kumamoto Prefecture, Aum also faced stiff opposition from local residents who feared being overrun by an unknown group. As Aum established a large-scale commune in the remote mountainous village, the local municipal council refused to accept Aum believers' 'resident records' (*jūminhyō*), a legal proof of address – a decision that lacked a legal justification. In turn, Aum accused critics of religious persecution and sued the village for damages. The legal stand-off was resolved only in 1994 when the village agreed to purchase the land that Aum owned for a hefty sum, in exchange for the group moving out permanently. Despite these moments of friction which generated some publicity, these were mostly covered only in the local news, and Aum maintained a less sinister public profile in a bid to attract more followers.

Turn to militarism

Aum's promotion of the *Mahayāna* objective of converting the masses reached a turning point in early 1990, when Asahara and 24 other candidates stood in the general election and lost. Aum's bizarre campaign, in which adherents performed songs and dances wearing elephant-shaped hats depicting the Hindu God Lord Ganesha and *papier-mâché* models of Asahara's head, aroused public curiosity (Tsukada 2011). However, the candidates struggled to turn this curiosity into

[11] Although Okasaki's name is more commonly written as Okazaki in English, this is an error. Japanese media consistently write his name as Okasaki. See, e.g., *The Mainichi* (2018), 'Ex-AUM cult members pondered atonement before executions, supporters say', 27 July <https://mainichi.jp/english/articles/20180727/p2a/00m/0na/029000c> Accessed September 2021.

votes. Asahara himself won a mere 1,783 votes, or 0.3 per cent of the votes in the constituency, while others attracted votes in the scores and low hundreds (Tsukada 2011: 320–21). Dismayed at the election result and convinced that the election had been sabotaged by nefarious political forces, Asahara announced that Aum was now entering the *Vajrayāna* phase of activity, known as the 'Vajrayāna Plan' (*Vajrayāna keikaku*), focused on arming themselves in preparation for the apocalyptic war that would occur before the end of the millennium. Their focus of Aum's activities therefore shifted from preventing the apocalypse to surviving the apocalypse, in order to rule over humankind after Armageddon (*harumagedon*). Over the next several years, Asahara ordered the development of biological weapons such as botulism and anthrax, as well as chemical weapons including phosgene, VX, and sarin.

Using the rich financial and human resources at their disposal, Aum formed the Science and Technology team headed by Murai Hideo, one of Asahara's most trusted aides. Murai, with a master's degree in material science, became a central figure involved in virtually all of Aum's plots using chemical and biological weapons. Their largest commune in Kamikuishiki, Yamanashi Prefecture, became the laboratory for this secret programme. Located in the foothills of Mount Fuji, about 100 km west of Tokyo, the remote commune resembled not so much a place of worship and religious training as an industrial complex, marked by cuboid buildings made from white sheet metal and corrugated roofs – each one known as a *satyam* (*satian*) – scattered across the vast estate (see Figure 3.1). With few neighbours and far removed from the scrutiny of the media or the police, there was little risk that the secret programme would be exposed. The scientific team comprised many highly educated youths with postgraduate training in the natural sciences, including Endō Seiichi and Tsuchiya Masami, who manufactured the sarin used in the Matsumoto and Tokyo attacks. However, as amateur scientists who had given up careers in specialist fields, they struggled to make progress. In the first few years, the Science and Technology team failed to develop biological weapons, resulting in botched terrorist attempts in 1990 and 1993 using innocuous strains of botulism and anthrax respectively. They were eventually successful in developing chemical weapons, and they planned to mass-produce sarin in a purpose-built factory known as *Satyam* No. 7. The plant, however, was never completed due to difficulties in construction.

Even as this militarisation programme was taking place, Aum continued to maintain a façade as a peaceful organisation to attract new members. The *Mahayāna* route had not yet been entirely abandoned. In 1991, Asahara appeared on a late-night live talk show to debate with senior members of Kōfuku no Kagaku (Happy Science), a new religion led by the charismatic founder Ōkawa Ryūhō, and appeared on television shows and in magazine interviews to promote Aum's worldview. Moreover, the militarisation was designated 'secret work' by the Science

Figure 3.1 *Satyam* buildings in Kamikuishiki. Photograph by Yoshikawa Yūsuke, 1996. Reproduced under CC-BY-SA-4.0.

and Technology team, which was largely hidden from the purview of ordinary, low-ranking believers, let alone the media, police, or members of the public.[12]

Meanwhile, Aum set up a regional base in Russia, which, by some estimates, gained as many as 50,000 followers over several years (Inoue M 2011), although this number should probably be interpreted as the total number of attendees at events and concerts, rather than the actual number of devotees. In Russia, in addition to founding a classical orchestra and setting up an international radio station that it used for public broadcasting, Aum established personal connections with Russian elites, successfully procuring and smuggling military weapons and equipment including an AK-74 assault rifle, gas masks, gas detectors, and a Mi-24 helicopter. They had intended to mass produce the AK-74 themselves and the helicopter was supposed to be used in a plot to spray sarin over Tokyo, although they were unsuccessful in both plans.

[12] While the individual operations were hidden, other aspects of the 'secret work' were visible and were something of an open secret. For example, dozens of believers were involved in the construction of the sarin plant Satyam No. 7 at the Kamikuishiki headquarters. Few, however, seem to have seriously questioned the precise nature of what went on inside the building.

Aum's struggle to grow, and its lack of ability to attract the new followers Asahara had planned for, seems to have fed into his increasingly paranoid delusions that higher powers were working to destroy Aum. Asahara's conviction that there were spies sent in by the CIA led to the invention of a procedure known as 'Narco' (*naruko*) or 'spy check', in which believers were interrogated after being injected with sodium thiopental, a barbiturate which Aum considered to be a 'truth serum'. Later, the chief doctor Hayashi Ikuo (see Chapter 8), one of the assailants in the Tokyo attack, invented 'New Narco', in which suspected spies were repeatedly administered electric shocks to their heads to erase their memories.

Other modes of punishment for transgressions and perceived disobedience included solitary confinement in metal containers, being made to listen to Asahara's sermons for hours at high volumes, and being hanged upside down by a rope tied to their ankles (Takahashi 2012). One member, Ochi Naoki, died after he had been left hanging for hours (Reader 2000a: 16). Although Aum's ascetic training was always seen by its critics as extreme – inviting criticism that it was 'mind controlling' and 'brainwashing' members – newer practices ignored questions of consent altogether in order to demand absolute devotion towards Asahara. In 1994, the group introduced 'initiations' using hallucinogenic drugs to induce mystical experiences, and these initiations were combined with the practice of taking scalding hot baths (*onnetsu shugyō*) to sweat out the drugs from the body. These extreme training regimes led to multiple accidental deaths, which were again covered up through the secret disposal of bodies. In addition to ordering the detection and 're-education' of perceived defectors, Asahara also ordered two further known murders inside the organisation. In January 1994, Ochida Kōtarō, a former believer, was captured and strangled to death when he returned to the Kamikuishiki headquarters in Yamanashi Prefecture to rescue the mother of another Aum ex-believer. Several months later, Tomida Toshio, a *samana*, was killed when he was falsely accused of poisoning a well and acting for the Freemasons.

Between 1993 and 1994, Aum expanded the targets of *poa* to external stakeholders, and used chemical weapons to attack its 'enemies', including Ikeda Daisaku, the charismatic leader of Japan's largest Buddhist new religion, Sōka Gakkai. Some of these attacks were successful, resulting in the death of several individuals, but other assassination attempts, including attacks on the lawyer Takimoto Tarō and the journalist Egawa Shōko, were unsuccessful. Meanwhile, accelerating plans for Aum to become its own state, Aum restructured its internal hierarchy in June 1994, introducing a pseudo-governmental structure for its sections by creating various 'ministries'. The Science and Technology team, for example, became the Ministry of Science and Technology, with Murai acting as the Minister. Some 'ministries' were modelled on the Japanese government, such as the Ministry of Finance (*Ōkurashō*), and Ministry of Foreign Affairs (*Gaimushō*), while others were invented with new names, such as the Ministry for Treatment (*Chiryōshō*). Unsurprisingly, as a theocratic dictatorship, there was no need for elected politicians; by default, Asahara became the Holy Emperor (*Shinsei Hōkō*), the ultimate sovereign and source of all laws.

As Aum's chemical weapons programme developed, Asahara expanded *poa* to be applied to the public, possibly to test the effects of sarin over a wide area (Hayakawa and Kawamura 2005: 197). The attack had a practical aim of sabotaging a trial in which Aum was a defendant. Aum had purchased land in Matsumoto with the intention of building a residential facility, but without telling the previous landowner of this fact. Responding to local protests, the seller had sued Aum to nullify the transaction on the basis that Aum provided misinformation. The verdict was expected to be in the seller's favour (Reader 2000a: 209; Shimada 2012 (v. 1): 26). With the verdict due to be delivered on 28 June, Asahara ordered Murai Hideo to attack a residential complex for members of the judiciary, in order to kill or maim them.[13] On the night of 27 June 1994 at around 10.30 p.m., Aum's customised truck drove through the streets of Matsumoto spraying sarin. A gentle breeze carried the vapours throughout the neighbourhood, entering homes within minutes. Seven were killed in the attack, and an eighth victim died in 2008 from the physical after-effects of sarin poisoning. Scores were hospitalised overnight and hundreds more injured, as authorities struggled to comprehend what had happened in the quiet neighbourhood. Aum accomplished the two goals of testing a chemical weapon on a large population and delaying the outcome of the trial.

The immediate aftermath of the Matsumoto attack: The 'fact-finders' fail

The nation woke up to the news of the incident in sheer shock and confusion. Matsumoto was hardly an obvious target for terrorism. As a small city with a population of around 200,000 in the centre of Honshū – Japan's largest island – Matsumoto was not a typical target for domestic terrorists, who tended to focus on public institutions such as police stations, government buildings, and banks in major cities such as Tokyo or Osaka. Amidst the confusion, various emergency services and security agencies were tasked with piecing together exactly what had happened. As initial news reports suggest, evidence was sparse, and discerning what took place was a matter of pure speculation at this point in time. The morning after the attack, reporters only knew that many people had been killed or injured due to a nauseous gas, and that the symptoms were similar to pesticide poisoning;

[13] *Yomiuri Shimbun* (1995), 'Matsumoto sarin jiken saisho no hyōteki wa Nagano chisai shibu', 13 July (Evening Edition – henceforth Eve. Ed.), p. 19.

the headline of the evening edition of the *Asahi* newspaper on 28 June, the first printed reports of the attack, simply read '7 die due to mysterious poison gas'. The 'crimes scenes' were multiple and dispersed over a large area; as the culprits had sprayed sarin from a moving vehicle, they left behind very few pieces of physical evidence in their wake.[14]

This uncertainty, however, did not deter the police or the media from making accusations based on flimsy circumstantial evidence. The police immediately identified Kōno Yoshiyuki, a 44-year-old office worker and father of three who was the first to contact emergency services, as a key person of interest. By pure coincidence, his house was next to the car park where Aum had begun to spray sarin, and he and his family were the first to be poisoned. As Kōno recalled later in a memoir, on the night of the attack, he noticed a strange sound outside and found his dogs convulsing on the ground. As he came back into the house to alert his wife, he found her collapsed on the floor; as he called for an ambulance, he himself was also poisoned by the gas and was unable to move (Kōno 2001). His wife fell into a coma from which she never awoke, resulting in her eventual death in 2008, while Kōno and his eldest daughter were hospitalised.

Ignorant of the possibility that the event could have been a terrorist attack, both the Nagano Prefectural Police and the national press inferred that the toxic gas was the result of an amateur chemical experiment gone wrong. In this imagined scenario – which was not supported by scientific evidence – Kōno was trying to make a potent pesticide by mixing chemicals and called for help when it suddenly produced a toxic gas. On 30 June, the national newspaper *Asahi Shimbun* ran a story that relayed the Prefectural Police's position that 'the toxic gas was produced after some kind of mistake was made while combining chemicals.'[15] Following this line of enquiry, the media collated circumstantial evidence and eyewitness accounts that supported this hypothesis. Unsubstantiated reports claimed Kōno had admitted responsibility to his son and warned him to prepare for police investigation (Kōno 2001: 88). These implicit admissions of guilt were entirely fictitious; it is possible that the police had informally fed the information to the media, so that public reports of his culpability would pressure Kōno to confess (ibid.: 242).

Circumstantial evidence seemed to point towards Kōno's involvement – or, more accurately, the police and the media selectively pieced together evidence to imply his culpability. Initial forensic analysis indicated the presence of organophosphates, a compound commonly found in pesticides as well as nerve agents. In his garden, the supposed 'crime scene', the police found pesticides that he had kept in the garden shed as well as several buckets and dishes in the garden,

[14] *Asahi Shimbun* (1994), 'Nazo no yūdoku gasu de 7 nin shibō', 28 June (Eve. Ed.), p. 1; 'Gen'in wa? Naze jūtakuchi?', 28 June (Eve. Ed.), p. 14; 'Nemuri no machi o doku ga osotta', 28 June (Eve. Ed.), p. 15; *Yomiuri Shimbun* (1994), 'Nagano Matsumoto no chūshinbu jūtakugai de yūdoku gasu, 7 nin shinu', 28 June (Eve. Ed.), p. 1.

[15] *Asahi Shimbun* (1994), 'Matsumoto yūdoku gasu, chōgō misu de hassei', 30 June (Eve. Ed.), p.19.

which, in their flawed interpretation, had been used for mixing chemicals. Animals in the garden – including fish in the pond and his dogs – had died, while the grass had withered and browned, suggesting the use of pesticides. Furthermore, there were eyewitness accounts of a white 'mist' around Kōno's house, four hours before the initial emergency calls – possibly when Aum had begun to spray sarin from the truck.[16] One early newspaper report concluded that it was 'a situation in which it was impossible not to suppose that some kind of chemical had been spilled'.[17] Meanwhile, still receiving treatment in hospital, Kōno strongly denied any involvement and agreed to informal police interviews. He was effectively placed under constant police supervision as he recuperated in his hospital bed.[18]

In the first few days after the attack, the 'Matsumoto Toxic Gas Incident', as it was initially reported in the media, did not develop into a national trauma. Despite the tragedy experienced by the entire community, which was deeply affected and traumatised by the attack, powerful stakeholders such as the state and the mass media did not situate the event as one that affected fundamental values of the collectivity. Matsumoto's relative marginality as a small regional city arguably added to public perceptions of the event as a relatively distant phenomenon. Furthermore, although the attack caused panic locally overnight, there was no sense in national public discourse that there was a breakdown of social order. In all other parts of the country, life went on as normal, and there was little sense of systemic crisis, unlike the case in the Tokyo sarin attack nine months later.

For Asahara and his associates, the initial conclusions that the media drew from the incident – warning the public about mixing chemicals – was a source of great relief.[19] The *Asahi* wrote in its editorial on 29 June: '[w]hy did he try to make a pesticide by himself, what kind of pesticide did he try to make, why did it result in so many casualties? There are many unclear points, but it is a horrific event that should not have happened.' The editorial pontificated that 'this incident reiterates the fact that our lives are side-by-side with harmful chemicals'; it concluded, '[t]here are, in fact, many dangerous substances around us that, once we make a mistake of mishandling [them], could lead to irredeemable outcomes. This incident teaches us the eeriness of this fact.'[20] Although some scientists cast doubt on this 'accidental narrative' – given the scientific impossibility of creating such a toxic gas from pesticides and other chemicals found in Kōno's shed – both the police and media set up this narrative based on heavy speculation and scant evidence.[21]

16 *Yomiuri Shimbun* (1994), 'Matsumoto no yūdoku jiken shiroi kiri, 4 jikan mae kara', 1 July, p. 35.

17 *Yomiuri Shimbun* (1994), 'Matsumoto gasu jiko Jūtakugai no niwa de yakubutsu jikken!?', 29 June, p. 31.

18 *Asahi Shimbun* (1994), 'Matsumoto yūdoku gasu, chōgō misu de hassei', 30 June (Eve. Ed.), p. 19.

19 *Asahi Shimbun* (1994), 'Shirōto no chōgō ni ayausa san konnyū de gasu', 29 June (Eve. Ed.), p. 19; *Yomiuri Shimbun* 'Fukō de fukakai na yūdoku gasu jiko', 1 July 1994, p. 3.

20 *Asahi Shimbun* (1994), 'Yakubutsu to tonariau kurashi no kowasa', 29 June, p. 5.

21 *Asahi Shimbun* (1994), 'Shinkei gasu ni ruiji ka', 1 July (Osaka Edition), p. 31.

This 'accidental narrative' suddenly collapsed a week after the attack on 4 July, when forensic scientists formally identified the toxic gas as sarin.[22] The history of sarin as a chemical weapon developed by the Nazis – which 'even Hitler hesitated to use', as reported by one newspaper – introduced a new, sinister dimension to the incident.[23] Had investigators followed scientific advice, this discovery should have completely exonerated Kōno. In contrast to Aum's scientists, who produced the gas under strictly controlled conditions over several years of trial and error, Kōno did not possess the expertise, ingredients, or the apparatus for manufacturing and releasing the gas. Moreover, he had neither the motive nor the resources to be able to commit the large-scale attack single-handedly. However, instead of abandoning this line of enquiry, the police and media merely modified the accidental narrative to imply Kōno had produced the gas deliberately. This was partially due to the police's ignorance of sarin production methods (NHK Supesharu Shuzaihan 2013: 122), and partly due to the media's negligence in fact-checking and following alternative leads: some self-styled 'experts' erroneously suggested that sarin could be made by mixing chemicals in a bucket, implying Kōno's culpability (Kōno 2001: 138).[24]

The emergent frame of the attack as a deliberate act of indiscriminate terrorism created a sense of collective unease, raising the possibility of narrators situating the attack as a heinous attack on innocent civilians. However, public discourse about the Matsumoto attack did not materialise in this direction for multiple reasons. Firstly, the misidentification of the culprit meant that the attack was construed as the result of a local dispute, not as a politically motivated attack or an attack on legal institutions, which was Aum's original intention. To this effect, the media defamed Kōno to situate him as the culprit; this included an unsubstantiated rumour that a man (hinted to be Kōno) had boasted about a weapon that could kill dozens (Kōno 2001: 139; 171–4).[25] Secondly, the attack diverged from historical patterns of domestic organised violence in a cultural context in which religious terrorism was hardly considered possible. Far-right terrorists usually targeted prominent politicians and public figures, and usually did not target civilians while armed Marxist guerrillas preferred to use firearms and explosives. They tended to target public institutions, such as government buildings, public transport, and banks, not the residential streets of a regional city. When terrorist groups had attacked civilians in hostage situations in the past, such as the leftist hijacking of a commercial airplane in 1970 or the attempted coup by the novelist

[22] *Asahi Shimbun* (1994),Shinkei gasu "sarin" kenshutsu', 4 July, p. 1; *Yomiuri Shimbun* (1994), 'Matsumoto no shūdan higai Nachi kaihatsu no dokugasu "sarin"', 4 July, p. 31.

[23] *Yomiuri Shimbun* (1994), 'Sarin kakuheiki nami sasshōryoku', 8 July, p. 15.

[24] *Asahi Shimbun* (1994), 'Shinkei gasu "sarin" kenshutsu', 4 July, p. 1; 'Sarin seisei no kanōsei bunseki', 4 July, p. 15; *Yomiuri Shimbun* (1994), 'Matsumoto no chūdoku jiken shinkei gasu "sarin" kenshutsu', 4 July, p. 1.

[25] *Asahi Shimbun* (1994), 'Sarin izen nazo, nazo', 19 August, p. 3.

and ultranationalist activist Mishima Yukio, also in 1970, the culprits had claimed responsibility and made their political demands clear. Moreover, by the 1990s, a bloody history of sectarian violence among militant leftist groups had led to their decline, both in size and influence (Igarashi 2007). When these 'usual suspects' failed to claim responsibility for the attack, there were no clear targets for investigation beyond Kōno. It is likely that this motivated the police to continue to treat Kōno as the prime suspect. Thirdly, few other pieces of evidence emerged, prompting the police to obstinately rely on the tried and tested method of pressuring suspects to confess.

Expert analyses in early July concluded that Kōno could not have produced sarin with the ingredients and apparatus at his house.[26] However, the police continued to press Kōno for information as a key person of interest. He was never arrested or charged. When Kōno was discharged from hospital on 30 July, he held a press conference to challenge the vilification of his character and agreed to police interviews.[27] Kōno spent two days being questioned intensively, at which point his health deteriorated again. In my interview with him, held in 2015, he recalled that the police held him for up to eight hours per day, ignoring the doctor's note stating he should not be interviewed for more than two hours.[28] After this point, Kōno refused to be further interviewed, as he recognised that the police were trying to force him to confess.

After his release from hospital, Kōno began to actively contest predominant representations of him as a suspect by meeting with reporters and experts. They universally concurred that it was impossible for Kōno to have made sarin (Kōno 2001: 117–22). According to him, after cooperating with media interviews, by August, some newspapers had shifted their tone to suggest that Kōno was not culpable.[29] Although he was not fully exonerated, the plurality of media representations of Kōno, together with the absence of evidence, meant that the narrative of Kōno as a lone killer gradually lost its persuasiveness. Nevertheless, media outlets do not appear to have seriously explored alternative scenarios that exonerated Kōno; until he personally intervened by inviting reporters to conduct interviews with him, news gathering seems to have been almost solely dependent on the police, relaying their official position in radio, television, newspapers, and magazines.

Meanwhile, investigators struggled to identify the true culprits. Aum, likely having built confidence after confirming the potency of chemical weapons, kept

[26] *Asahi Shimbun* (1994), 'Ōshū shita yakuhin 24 shurui de sarin no gōsei fukanō', 11 July, p. 19; *Yomiuri Shimbun* (1994), 'Shūdan gasu chūdoku jiken fusso kagōbutsu, hakken sarezu', 6 July, p. 14.

[27] *Asahi Shimbun* (1994), '"Sarin no namae, hajimete shitta" Matsumoto gasu chūdoku daiippō tsūhōsha kaiken', 30 July (Eve. Ed.), p. 21; 'Aratamete kanyo o hitei Tsuhō shita kaishain ga taiinshi kaiken', 30 July (Eve. Ed), p. 21; *Yomiuri Shimbun* (1994), 'Matsumoto no dokugasu yūdoku jiken kaishain taiin', 30 July (Eve. Ed.), p. 11.

[28] Interview with Kōno Yoshiyuki, 10 April 2015, Kagoshima Prefecture.

[29] Ibid.

a low public profile while continuing to carry out assassination attempts against individuals using sarin and VX. Yet investigators failed to link these individual cases to Matsumoto. Over the next several months, the police gained evidence that one of Aum's proxy companies had purchased massive quantities of sarin ingredients, and that there were local reports of strange smells near Aum's headquarters in July 1994. Following these tips, the police covertly obtained soil samples containing sarin residue near Aum's facilities in September (NHK Supesharu Shuzaihan 2013: 128–9). However, these findings were kept from the public eye, and did not lead to a full investigation. There was still insufficient evidence to investigate Aum for Matsumoto, and a legal loophole meant sarin production was not itself a criminal offence. In contrast to the eagerness with which they had identified Kōno as a person of interest, the police were reticent to publicly name Aum as a suspect, as they feared being accused of religious persecution. The Nagano Prefectural Police therefore remained on standby, hesitant to launch a large-scale operation. As new information failed to publicly emerge and the investigation hit an impasse, by autumn 1994, media outlets largely fell silent and eventually stopped reporting on Matsumoto, stopping short of vindicating Kōno, or offering public apologies. Victims and bereaved families of the attack expressed sorrow and suffering at the individual level, but not in relation to collective identity or to cultural values.[30]

As such, for much of 1994, the Matsumoto Sarin Incident was a 'mystery' and an 'enigma', but certainly not a national trauma with moral implications for national identity.[31] Though commentators recognised the event as an 'eerie' (*bukimi*) and 'frustrating' (*modokashii*) case, it was not perceived as a traumatic assault on cultural values: throughout 1994, not once was the Matsumoto sarin attack identified as a 'terrorist attack' by national newspapers *Asahi Shimbun* or *Yomiuri Shimbun*.[32]

Perhaps illustrative of the relatively low media attention given to the event, a newspaper poll asked readers to vote for what they considered to be the most important events of 1994 (see Table 3.1).[33] The Matsumoto Sarin Incident barely made the top ten list, coming behind other events such as the summer heatwave and drought (No. 1), the Tokyo Yomiuri Giants – Japan's answer to the New York Yankees – winning the national baseball championship (No. 4),[34] rice shortages

[30] *Yomiuri Shimbun* (1994), 'Matsumoto no "sarin jiken" kara 2 kagetsu', 22 August, p. 30.

[31] *Asahi Shimbun* (1994), 'Sarin jiken no modokashisa', 3 December, p. 4; *Yomiuri Shimbun* (1994), 'Matsumoto sarin jiken kara 3 kagetsu', 27 September, p. 13.

[32] *Asahi Shimbun* (1994), 'Sarin jiken no modokashisa', 3 December, p. 4; 'Nippon, tadaima gogo 3ji' 30 December, p. 5; *Yomiuri Shimbun* (1994), 'Kyōsei no nakami ga towareta 94 sesou', 29 December, p. 3.

[33] *Yomiuri Shimbun* (1994), '1-i wa kirokuteki mōsho; dokusha ga eranda Nippon 10-dai nyūsu', 25 December, p. 14.

[34] This, of course, may have been influenced by the fact that, as the name implies, the Yomiuri media conglomerate owns both the newspaper and the baseball team.

1.	Record heatwave leads to serious water shortages.
2.	Astronaut Mukai Chiaki goes into space.
3.	Ōe Kenzaburō wins the Nobel Prize for Literature.
4.	Baseball team Tokyo Yomiuri Giants win the Japanese League.
5.	Airbus airplane crash lands at Nagoya airport, killing 264.
6.	Political instability after three Prime Ministers take office in one year.
7.	Bullying leads to a series of suicides.
8.	Rice shortages lead to price hikes.
9.	Sumo wrestler Takanohana is promoted to the rank of Yokozuna (the highest title).
10.	Seven die as a result of toxic gas 'sarin' (Matsumoto).

Table 3.1 Top ten news items of 1994 according to a *Yomiuri Shimbun* readers' poll.
Source: *Yomiuri Shimbun* (1994).

as a result of the drought that led to price hikes (No. 8), and the Sumo wrestler Takanohana's promotion to the highest rank of Yokozuna (No. 9). This stands in contrast to the Tokyo Subway Sarin Incident and the 'Aum Affair', which, in the same poll a year later, was voted as the second most important news event after the Great Hanshin (Kōbe) Earthquake.[35] In short, in 1994, despite the initial shock and media attention it generated, the Matsumoto Sarin Incident was overshadowed by other national events, and risked falling into oblivion in the absence of new 'facts' that could help construct new interpretations of the event. Meanwhile, unbeknownst to the outside world, Asahara and his scientists continued to press ahead with their militarisation programme; as Asahara's paranoia grew by the day, Asahara insisted that he was under attack from the US military, and justified *Tantra Vajrayāna* as the only way forward.

Conclusions

The fact that Aum transformed itself from a small suburban yoga class into a secretive armed movement in the remote mountains within the span of 10 years is both remarkable and disturbing. In constructing a deeply Manichaean worldview that dismissed the secular world as beyond saving, Aum's development as a group is unsettling not only for its justification of extreme violence, but also for the speed with which these practices became embedded in and normalised as a core practice by the leadership. In developing and implementing the idea of *poa* as a type

[35] *Yomiuri Shimbun* (1995), '95 dokusha ga erabu kokunai 10 dai nyūsu', 24 December, p. 14.

of mercy killing, Aum justified physical violence not just against dissidents and its own members but indiscriminately against the general population. Leaving behind Aum's original dreams of setting up peaceful, self-sufficient communes, Asahara's paranoid delusions, which were never seriously challenged or questioned by his subordinates, became the foundation for Aum's violence and criminality. As the imaginary struggle between Aum and the Judaeo-Masonic conspiracy escalated in Asahara's mind, *poa* became the main method by which Aum dispensed its macabre version of 'justice' by acting as judge, jury, and executioner of the entire Japanese population.

Nevertheless, it is also important to bear in mind that Aum's transformation from a yoga class to a violent armed group was neither inevitable nor typical of new religions. Aum's growth and the success of the militarisation programme hinged upon a number of contingent factors. For instance, it was an accidental death of an adherent in 1988 that engendered and institutionalised *poa* as a central component of Aum's illegal activities. Moreover, there were several opportunities to stop Aum's escalation of violence. These opportunities were squandered when the police mishandled the investigations after the disappearance of the Sakamoto family and after the Matsumoto sarin attack. It is entirely possible that Aum's militarisation could have been stopped earlier in its tracks had there been a more concerted scrutiny of the organisation beyond the small but vocal groups of believers' parents, anti-cult activists, and a handful of journalists.

While the Matsumoto sarin attack was an important turning point for Aum in embracing indiscriminate terrorism using chemical weapons, the event initially had a limited impact at the level of national discourse and national identity. As the true identity of the culprits, motive, and objective remained obscured, 'fact-finders' tasked with establishing the 'facts' of the event, such as the police, forensic scientists, and journalists, could not present a coherent picture of the event. Consequently, conventional 'carrier groups' of trauma narratives such as public intellectuals, journalists, novelists, and writers did not recognise the event as a 'traumatic' moment for the Japanese society at large.

The Matsumoto case, however, would gain a new significance in 1995, as Aum's secret plans were gradually brought to public attention. On 1 January, the *Yomiuri Shimbun*, Japan's largest national newspaper, ran an exclusive story reporting that sarin residues had been detected in the mountains of Yamanashi Prefecture, days after the Matsumoto attack.[36] Although the *Yomiuri* story did not mention Aum by name, other media outlets soon followed suit by publishing similar stories, some of which reported that the chemicals were detected near Aum's facilities. As Aum came under ever greater scrutiny and pressures for a police investigation grew,

[36] *Yomiuri Shimbun* (1995), 'Yamanashi no sanroku de sarin zanryūbutsu o kenshutsu "Matsumoto Jiken" chokugo, kanren kaimei isogu', 1 January, p. 1.

Aum was running out of options: it is not difficult to imagine Asahara growing ever desperate.

Indeed, pessimism pervades Asahara's 1995 book – which was released just three weeks before the Tokyo sarin attack – ominously titled *Disaster Nears the Land of the Rising Sun* (*Hi izuru kuni, wazawai chikaku*) (Asahara 1995b). The book – an edited collection of his previous sermons, talks, and publications – contains extended discussions about the inevitable and imminent end of the world brought about by a 'final war' (*saishū sensō*), including debates between Asahara and the resident scientists about how to survive nuclear bombs, electromagnetic waves, and chemical weapons. One sentence in particular stands out, in Asahara's brief prediction of what was to come in the year ahead: 'If the Japanese people now are accruing good deeds [*zengō*], '95 will be a fantastic year, and if they are accruing bad deeds [*akugō*], they will receive what they deserve' (Asahara 1995b: 128).

4

Shock and Anger: Societal Responses to the Tokyo Subway Attack

The *Yomiuri Shimbun*'s exclusive story in 1995 about the discovery of chemical residues of sarin near Aum's facilities put them under intense public scrutiny. Aum's plan to take over the government by force was now in jeopardy. Responding to the allegations of sarin production, Murai Hideo, Aum's chief scientist, immediately ordered the disposal of existing stockpiles of sarin and other nerve agents. Nevertheless, whether by accident or design, Aum continued to keep hold of a key ingredient required for manufacturing sarin.

Aum responded to media reports connecting them to sarin through zealous litigiousness, threatening and filing lawsuits against media outlets as well as other organisations for defamation. This included a libel lawsuit against Aum's rival organisation Kōfuku no Kagaku, which had explicitly named Aum as being behind sarin production. At the same time, perhaps a sign of Aum's increasing desperation, their violent crimes became even more brazen. On 4 January, a team of assassins approached Nagaoka Hiroyuki, the leader of the Aum Shinrikyō Victims' Society (see Chapter 7), spraying VX solution onto his neck as they passed him on a street. VX is a potent nerve agent which was used in the 2017 assassination of North Korea's deposed heir-apparent Kim Jong-Nam in Malaysia. The nerve agent affected Nagaoka almost immediately as he collapsed at home and was then hospitalised. Nagaoka survived but with severe physical impairments affecting his breathing and motor functions.

In a fortuitous turn of events, the Great Hanshin (Kōbe) Earthquake on 17 January diverted public attention away from Aum to another national tragedy that killed over 6,000 people, destroyed thousands of buildings, and left tens of thousands homeless. In response, Aum mobilised volunteers in Kōbe and distributed aid to participate in the rescue and recovery process as a publicity stunt. At the same time, it did not forget to boast that Asahara had correctly predicted the death and destruction of the Kōbe Earthquake less than two weeks earlier, and that worse was yet to come (see also Asahara 1995b; Takahashi 2012: 226–8).[1]

In late February, as part of Aum's aggressive fundraising scheme, a team of assailants kidnapped the 68-year-old public notary Kariya Kiyoshi in broad daylight, shoving him into a van as he screamed for help. In the preceding weeks and months, Aum had been pressuring Kariya's sister – a part-time member – to donate her assets, and Kariya had helped her to go into hiding. Anticipating conflict and fearing for his own safety, Kariya had left a note that if anything happened to him, Aum was likely to blame.[2] His worst fears came true as he was taken to the Kamikuishiki headquarters, where he was injected with sodium thiopental – commonly used by Aum as a 'truth serum' to interrogate suspected spies. He died hours later after having an adverse reaction to the drug.

As public calls for further investigation grew and, as the police gradually built up a case against Aum in relation to the Kariya case, Aum obtained information that a police raid was approaching. In the early hours of 18 March, Asahara reportedly gathered his closest aides inside a Mercedes Benz limousine as they travelled from a gathering in Tokyo back to their base in Kamikuishiki to plan the next course of action. There, it was agreed that a sarin attack on the Tokyo subway was necessary to divert attention and to delay the police raid. Using the leftover sarin ingredients, Endō Seiichi, a former veterinarian, and Nakagawa Tomomasa, formerly a trainee doctor, hastily concocted impure but still lethal quantities of sarin solution to be used in the attack. The sarin solution was placed in transparent plastic bags used for intravenous drips. As Aum was preparing for the attack, on 19 March, the Osaka Prefectural Police searched Aum's Osaka branch and arrested three members for abduction and imprisonment of a university student.[3] A large-scale police raid now seemed imminent.

At around 8 a.m. on 20 March, five men boarded trains on three different lines. On the Hibiya Line and Marunouchi Line, the assailants boarded trains travelling towards the city centre from opposite ends of the line. On the Chiyoda Line, only the westbound-travelling train was targeted. As they disembarked at the designated stop, they placed bags of sarin solution wrapped in newspaper on the floor and punctured them with sharpened umbrellas. Each assailant was then picked up by a getaway driver. The vaporised sarin gas quickly spread through the carriages. At Kodenmachō Station on the Hibiya Line, passengers kicked the bags onto the platform in a panic, inadvertently spreading the gas over a wide area. There was initially panic and

[1] One of Aum's claims was that the Great Hanshin Earthquake was a manmade attack using 'earthquake weapons' (*jishin heiki*).

[2] *Asahi Shimbun* (1995), '"Nanika attara keisatsu ni" no memo', 9 March, p. 35; *Yomiuri Shimbun* (1995), 'Shinagawa no kōdhō yakuba jimuchō rachi', 4 March (Eve. Ed.), p. 11.

[3] *Yomiuri Shimbun* (1995), 'Oumu Shinrikyō Osaka shibu o sōsaku', 20 March, p. 31.

confusion over the details of the attack, as emergency services initially reported that there had been a gas explosion near Tsukiji Station. This theory was quickly dispelled as it immediately became apparent that there was no damage to physical structures and that injuries were dispersed over a wide area across the metropolis. The damage was exacerbated when operators continued to run some of the train services, even as passengers were reporting strange smells and difficulties breathing.

While many commuters, unaware of the seriousness of what they had encountered, continued their journey to their workplace, hundreds more collapsed on the platform and in the station concourse, unable to move or breathe. As ambulances struggled to transport victims to the Emergency Rooms of nearby hospitals, taxi drivers and passers-by carried survivors to nearby hospitals to assist with the emergency response. Public transport came to a gridlock as commuters struggled to get to and from work. As TV camera crews flew overhead to capture the chaotic scenes on the ground, live television footage showed emergency vehicles lining the roads as survivors sat on blue tarpaulin sheets out in the cold, awaiting treatment. Hours later, the Ground Self-Defence Forces were called in to decontaminate the trains and the platforms. Photographs of soldiers in full-body protective suits against the ordinary backdrop of metro trains and platforms became iconic representations of the sudden collapse of everyday life.[4]

The attack killed a total of 13 and injured over 6,000 commuters. Unlike Matsumoto, the aftermath of which was marred by confusion over the methods and motives for the attack, the political message of the Tokyo attack was obvious. The three subway lines that the culprits targeted all passed through the bureaucratic nerve centre of Kasumigaseki – an area which houses various ministries, as well as the Tokyo District Court, High Court, and Supreme Court. The metro lines also served the central business district of Ōtemachi, and the popular retail districts of Shinjuku and Ginza, some of the busiest areas in the capital.

Media responses to the Tokyo sarin attack

Even as the nation struggled to grasp the true scale of the attack, there was no mistaking that this was a deliberate act of mass murder. Initial media reports of the gassing were unequivocal in condemning the attack as an 'unforgivable challenge to society' and called for a full investigation. Even before the media had named the perpetrators, commentators endorsed a morally dualistic framework of a battle between good and evil, suggesting that the attack was committed by a 'dark, twisted shadow lurking somewhere in this peaceful and prosperous society'.[5]

[4] See, e.g., the photographic report in *Sunday Mainichi* (1995), 9 April, v. 74(19), pp. 3–19.
[5] *Yomiuri Shimbun* (1995), 'Yurushigatai chikatetsu sarin jiken', 21 March, p. 1.

Some reports strongly hinted at Aum's involvement, suggesting that the attack was the work of 'multiple fanatics'.[6] Even if Aum was not explicitly named, journalists framed articles on the attack alongside articles and timelines discussing Aum's alleged involvement in sarin manufacture.[7] 'It is no exaggeration to say that the subway sarin incident is a horrific violence against all humans – no, against all life', wrote the weekly contemporary affairs magazine *Sunday Mainichi*.[8] Some outlets explicitly adopted the metaphor of a war: the conservative newspaper *Sankei Shimbun* hypothesised in its editorial on 23 March that 'we can suppose that the group [responsible] had not a shred of humanity', and that they had 'launched a unilateral "war" against good citizens'. The same piece argued that 'the situation demands that citizens bring together all the power to confront the criminal group.'[9]

Prime Minister Murayama Tomiichi immediately condemned the attack as 'unforgivable' and vowed to bring the perpetrators to justice.[10] Contrary to Aum's expectation that the attack would delay the impending police raid, the police conducted a search of the Kamikuishiki commune and headquarters on the morning of 22 March. The search warrant was related not to the Tokyo attack but to Kariya's disappearance.

The raid was a massive media event with few precedents. As media crowds thronged the roads leading up to Aum's commune, approximately 2,500 police officers – more than twice the number of full-time renunciants at the time – entered the premises wearing protective armour, gas masks, and camouflage uniforms (eye-catching but hardly useful for entering buildings).[11] Officers equipped with gas masks carried caged canaries to detect poison gases – surely more of a media stunt for the cameras than an actual safety precaution; as the officers entered the premises, the media competed to get the best photographs and films of the spectacle.[12] As the footage of the raid aired over tense orchestral background music, the spectacle resembled not so much a police search as a military operation capturing a fortress. Resistance from believers was scattered and futile, as protestors were promptly restrained and arrested, while others were taken to hospital in ambulances, apparently incapacitated and unconscious. This initial search and subsequent raids exposed the full extent of Aum's militarisation plan, as the

[6] *Yomiuri Shimbun* (1995), '(Shasetsu) Kyōshinteki na hankō o danjite yurusuna', 21 March, p. 3.

[7] *Yomiuri Shimbun* (1995), 'Chikatetsu dokugasu taisakushitsu o secchi', 20 March (Eve. Ed.), p. 3.

[8] *Sunday Mainichi* (1995), 'Sarin no senritsu: Gajōni fumikonda sōsa no kakushin', 9 April, v. 74(19), p. 20.

[9] *Sankei Shimbun* (1995), '"Senso" o shikaketa sarinma', 23 March, Editorial. General, International Affairs section.

[10] *Asahi Shimbun* (1995), 'Shūkan hōkoku', 27 March, p. 5; *Yomiuri Shimbun* (1995), 'Jūsōbi, bōdoku masuku de totsunyū. 'Oumu Shinrikyō' sōsaku 3.22 dokyumento', 22 March (Eve. Ed.), p. 2.

[11] *Yomiuri Shimbun* (1995), 'Oumu Shinrikyō o kyōsei sōsa', 22 March (Eve. Ed), p. 1.

[12] *Sunday Mainichi* (1995), 'Sarin no senritsu: Gajōni fumikonda sōsa no kakushin', 9 April, v. 74(19), p. 21; *Mainichi Shimbun* (1995), Oumu Shinrikyō kyōsei sōsa', 22 March (Extra), pp. 1–2.

police confiscated massive quantities of sarin ingredients, scientific apparatus, and a cache of military-grade equipment.

Over the next several weeks, as the media gradually unearthed Aum's past controversies, conflicts, and crimes, the collective label of the 'Aum Affair' (*Oumu Jiken*) emerged as a shorthand reference to a variety of crimes, including the Matsumoto attack, murders, assassination attempts, kidnapping, and extortion. In the sampled publications, the first use of the label 'Aum Affair' by national newspapers occurred in April 1995.[13] It is worth clarifying here that while the word 'affair' has connotations with political scandals in the English language – such as the Dreyfus Affair, Iran-Contra Affair, or the Profumo Affair – in Japanese, '*jiken*' ('affair' or 'incident') is used ubiquitously for any criminal cases including murders, kidnappings, fraud, and so on. For example, a case of murder would be referred to as a '*satsujin jiken*' ('murder incident'). As such, calling something an 'affair' or 'incident' by no means downplays the scale or significance of an event.

As the investigation progressed and Aum's culpability for the terrorist attacks became beyond question, the media adopted a dualistic narrative of a democratic, civilised nation locked in a 'war' against an irrational and hateful enemy. As this trauma narrative formed, the sarin attack on Tokyo undoubtedly created a 'moral panic', in which '[a] condition, episode, person or group of persons emerges to become defined as a threat to societal values and interests' (Cohen 1972: 28). In this narrative frame, Aum embodied the negative values of autocracy, theocracy, oppression, irrationality, and violence: the antithesis of Japan's civic values of democracy, secularism, liberalism, rationalism, and peace. The Tokyo sarin attack was an assault by a 'barbaric' criminal organisation plotting the destruction of the peaceful 'mature civilisation'.[14] Representative of the tone of many media outlets at the time, the *Asahi* situated the perpetrators as an existential threat to Japanese society in an editorial: 'These incidents are clearly a challenge to civil society. We must consider this to be not just a challenge to social security, but a challenge to the values of civil society. We must defend ourselves.'[15] Responding to the discoveries from the police investigation, Nonaka Hiromu, chairman of the National Public Safety Commission, echoed this sentiment, comparing the ongoing crisis to a 'war between nations' in which Japan faced an existential threat.[16]

The escalation of this narrative of a war-like conflict between Aum and Japanese society was no doubt exacerbated by Aum's delusional self-image as guardians of truth fighting against the rest of the world. While Asahara went into hiding, senior

[13] *Asahi Shimbun* (1995), 'Kamikuishiki de uyoku ga gaisen', 24 April, p. 18; *Yomiuri Shimbun* (1995), 'Oumu jiken ichiryōjitsuchū ni zenkoku issei kataku sōsaku e', 13 April, p. 31.

[14] Yamauchi, M. (1995) "Media jihyō: Oumu jiken no teguchi kaimeishi saihatsu bōshi o', *Yomiuri Shimbun*, 21 May, p. 16.

[15] *Asahi Shimbun* (1995), '"Nichjō" ga yugamerareta ikkagetsu (Shasetsu)', 21 April, p. 5.

[16] *Yomiuri Shimbun* (1995), '"Kuni to Kuni no tatakai no kan" oumu sousa de Nonaka Kokka Kōan Iinchō ga kyōchō', 25 April (Eve. Ed.), p. 2.

disciples appeared on mass media daily to feign innocence and to accuse the state of religious persecution. These figures included Hayakawa Kiyohide (see Chapter 8), a former landscaper and architect who played a major role in the procurement of military supplies from Russia; Aoyama Yoshinobu, a *samana* and Aum's resident lawyer; Murai Hideo, the chief of the Science and Technology team, and Jōyū Fumihiro (see Chapter 8), Aum's spokesman who hastily returned from his post in Russia to manage the organisation's PR strategy. Although few people watching their defences will have been convinced of their explanation that their massive supplies of sarin ingredients were for making pottery and pesticides – an explanation which belied their principle of no killing of animals and their endorsement of organic farming – the continuous media exposure of Aum's high disciples had the unexpected consequence of raising their profiles to the status of minor celebrities. In particular, Jōyū, a relatively young, photogenic figure who earned infamy for his mastery of sophistry, gained a following of young women who would wait outside Aum's Tokyo office and television studios in a bid to hand him bouquets.[17] Of course, these followers were small in number and transient. For the majority of the viewing public, the disciples' protestations that they were under attack by the American military, controlled by the Freemasons, would only have cemented the impression that Aum was a crazed and dangerous cult.

Public fears that Aum may commit another terrorist attack of a similar scale were justified and accurate, as Asahara continued to give instructions to carry out terrorist attacks. The *Vajrayāna* Plan to take over Japan was still in effect. In April and May, Aum attempted to spray hydrogen cyanide from a briefcase at Shinjuku, one of Tokyo's busiest stations. On the day of Asahara's arrest, 16 May, Aum sent a letter-bomb to the Tokyo Metropolitan Government, seriously injuring a government employee. These violent plots came to an end only after the most senior disciples were arrested.

Combating 'evil'

Given the intensity of the shock and anger that the assault on Tokyo generated, it is unsurprising that commentators immediately associated Aum with existing historical signifiers of evil and violence. Comparisons between Aum and Nazis were common in newspaper commentaries. Despite some fairly obvious differences in the size and scale of the two organisations, comparisons between Aum and Nazis were not entirely unfounded, from the apotheosis of the leader and the endorsement of a philosophy of a 'chosen people' to the open embrace

[17] *Yomiuri Shimbun* (1995), 'Oumu okkake shōjō tachi "Jōyū san ni hanataba" shūkyō niwa mukanshin demo dōjō', 11 May, p. 34; *Yomiuri Shimbun* (1995), 'Motto shizukani' 27 April, Osaka Edition, p. 12.

of antisemitic conspiracy theories, the gassing of innocent civilians in enclosed spaces – commentators likened the train carriages to 'gas chambers' – and the fact that Nazi scientists first developed sarin before the Second World War.[18]

Others drew comparisons between Aum and the United Red Army, an armed radical Marxist group that lynched its own members in bloody infighting and later took a hostage to a mountain lodge in 1972, ending in a deadly shoot-out. Although the United Red Army comprised several dozen members at most, compared with Aum's thousand-strong full-time members, commentators pointed out similarities between the two organisations, such as living in isolation from the wider society, self-identifying as vanguards of revolutionary change, justifying death and violence based on abstract principles, and killing insiders deemed to be insufficiently committed to their cause.[19] Unlike public intellectuals who saw similarities between Aum and Japanese society, as discussed in Chapter 6, these similes stressed the differences between the 'normal' values of civil society and 'abnormal', anti-social groups.

As Aum's position as an external evil to be purged and destroyed at all costs became consolidated, vigilance gave way to vigilantism in the form of retaliatory murder. On 23 April, Murai Hideo tried to enter Aum's Tokyo Office in Minami-Aoyama, as he struggled to push past a horde of media personnel. A man suddenly pushed past the media scrum and stabbed Murai in the arm and abdomen. Multiple cameras within an arm's distance from Murai captured the macabre scene as it happened, and news programmes immediately broadcast the scene on national television. The assailant, a marginal member of a *yakuza* (crime syndicate) group, later admitted that he was driven by anger towards Aum and a sense of vigilantism, and that he had intended to kill any of the high disciples that he recognised from television (Jōyū et al. 2013).

The vigilante killing of Aum's de facto second-in-command, who was a central figure in the militarisation programme and an accomplice in many of the murder cases meant that investigators and prosecutors lost a valuable source of information over the full extent of the militarisation programme. It also meant that when senior disciples were arrested, they would often deflect the blame onto Asahara and Murai whilst minimising the roles they had in Aum's criminal schemes.

As society remained on high alert for weeks, some criminal cases were attributed to Aum without sufficient evidence. A week after the Tokyo attack,

[18] *Asahi Shimbun* (1995), 'Tōkyō no chikatetsu sarin jiken', 21 March, p. 1; *Yomiuri Shimbun* (1995), "(Shasetsu) Kyōshinteki na hankō o danjite yurusuna," 21 March, p. 3. On gas chamber analogy, see *Shūkan Bunshun* (1995), 'Sonotoki, chikatestu no shanai wa jigoku to kashita', 30 March, v. 37(13), pp. 30–31; *Yomiuri Shimbun* (1995), 'Hibiyasen kenshō "hashiru gasu shitsu" sarin no kyōfu', 21 March, p. 35.

[19] *Asahi Shimbun* (1995), 'Jashūmon', 15 May (Eve. Ed.), p. 7.; *Asahi Shimbun* (1995), '"Kagami no tate" o Oumu ni', 3 July, Editorial, p. 5.

Chief of Police Kunimatsu Kōji was shot down outside his home by an unknown assailant. He was gravely injured but survived. Based on the timing and the shocking nature of the assassination attempt, the media strongly hinted at Aum's involvement.[20] Although several Aum members were arrested over the course of the investigation, they were never charged due to lack of convincing evidence. The statute of limitations expired in 2010, and the case remains unsolved.[21]

There were other instances where Aum was associated with criminality in general. In a separate case on 20 April, exactly a month after the Tokyo attack, a copycat criminal sprayed a pungent gas at Yokohama Station, causing panic. The assailant was initially suspected to be an Aum member, but it was soon revealed that he had no connections to Aum.[22] In June, shortly after Asahara's arrest, a man hijacked a domestic flight from Tokyo to Hokkaido and claimed that he was a member of Aum and demanded Asahara's release. After the hijacker was arrested, he confessed that he had no affiliation with Aum. Perhaps unsurprisingly in the aftermath of a terrorist attack, strange sights and sounds in public spaces frequently caused alarm and panic. In one instance, the police were called after two men in suits were spotted handling bags of white powder and containers of brown liquid near coin-operated lockers. Upon investigation, it emerged that the substances in question were nothing more than flour and fish stock.[23]

The prevalent sense that the nation was under attack and faced further threats of violence led the police to engage in legally questionable practices, such as arresting Aum members on minor criminal charges then interrogating them to gain information about more serious crimes (a practice known as *bizai taiho*, or *bekken taiho*). By the middle of May, over two hundred Aum members had been arrested for minor infractions including carrying a craft knife, having an out-of-date address on a driving licence, and using a false identity at a hotel, offences which might not ordinarily lead to arrest and prosecution.[24] Although some commentators expressed discomfort and concern that stringent police practices were damaging the rule of law and equality before the law, the government

[20] *Asahi Shimbun* (1995), 'Keisatsu toppu hyōtekini. Kunimatsu Keisatsuchō chōkan jūgeki jiken', 30 March (Eve. Ed.), p. 25; 'Kokumin ni mukerareta jūkōda (Shasetsu)', 31 March, p. 5; *Sunday Mainichi* (1995), 'Keisatsuchō chōkan sogeki de zōfuku sareta "tsugi" no kyōfu', 16 April, v. 74(20), pp. 28–33.

[21] In 2010, the Tokyo Metropolitan Police Department (Keishichō) held a press conference to mark the expiration of the statute of limitations for the shooting of the Chief of Police in March 1995. At the press conference, the head of the Public Security division named Aum as the culprit behind the attack without providing evidence. Aleph, Aum's successor group, promptly sued the Tokyo Metropolitan Government for defamation and won both the District Court and High Court judgments, receiving ¥1 million yen (around US$10,000) in compensation.

[22] *Asahi Shimbun* (1995), 'Doku gasu no akumu futatabi', 20 April, p. 31.

[23] *Yomiuri Shimbun* (1995), 'Kageki? Aitsugi fushinbutsu sawagi', 23 July, p. 31.

[24] *AERA* (1995), 'Keisatsu kokka ka kyōki tero shakai ka; bizai taiho ni sanpi ryōron', 22 May, p. 10; *Asahi Shimbun* (1995), '"Bizai Taiho" ni seifu fukuzatsu', 21 April, p. 2.

defended these actions as within the scope of existing laws and necessary for conducting a thorough investigation.[25]

The quest for ratings – uncovering Aum's inner workings

While the seismic impact of the Tokyo attack reverberated across the whole of society, it arguably had the most impact on mass media outlets. As the collective normative impulses to condemn acts of evil fused with capitalist interests of attracting audiences amidst a fierce competition for ratings, the 'centripetal' discourse of major mass media outlets was characterised by sensationalism, exaggerated claims, and unfounded or unverified allegations. The mass media competed with one another to expose the most shocking facts about Aum's beliefs and practices, from the everyday lives of ordinary renunciants such as their daily routines and diets, to more sordid and tabloid-friendly topics of 'forbidden romance' between believers and Asahara's relationship with the harem of lovers that he kept in his personal compound (*satyam*). Aum appeared not just in factual programmes and news reports. The Affair was a mainstay of 'wide shows' (*waido shō*) – daytime magazine programmes that have a broad focus on lighthearted, general interest topics like fashion trends, places to see, and celebrity gossip – which quickly found that Aum was able to attract more viewers than other topics.[26] In this sense, Aum became more than just an object of moral condemnation: it was the villainous antagonist of a social melodrama, an object of derision, humour, and parody (Gardner 2002b), and perhaps above all, a source of morbid entertainment (Hardacre 2007).

In unearthing the 'reality' of life inside Aum, the media particularly privileged the experiences of disillusioned ex-believers, who were able to provide intimate details of life as a *samana*, not just about their daily routines and training regimes but also about sinister practices such as the drugging of members in initiation rituals, sleep deprivation, corporal punishment, and solitary confinement. These testimonies seemed to corroborate the 'mind control' and 'brainwashing' thesis, reproduced uncritically in the mass media, that Aum was using such techniques to create an army of obedient 'robots' take part in a revolutionary war against the world.

[25] For critique of state power, see *AERA* (1995), 'Keisatsu kokka ka kyōki tero shakai ka; bizai taiho ni sanpi ryōron', 22 May, p. 10; *Asahi Shimbun* (1995), 'Bunmei ga towareru Oumu Saiban (Shasetsu)', 5 July, p. 5; 'Kyozetsu (miru, kiku, hanasu wa ima)', 18 October, p. 30; *Yomiuri Shimbun* (1995), '(Kiryū) bizai taiho tahatsu, ihō sōsa dewa', 27 May, p. 19. For a defence of the use of state powers, see *Yomiuri Shimbun* (1995), 'Oumu Sōsa wa tekisei; Maeda hōsō ga kyōchō', 22 April, p. 3.

[26] In my interview with film director Mori Tatsuya, who was a television director at the time, he noted that Aum Shinrikyo was the first event that broke down the barriers between news and entertainment, as news topics began to be discussed in day-time variety, magazine shows ('*waidoshō*'/'wide show'). Interview with Mori Tatsuya, 20 July 2016.

As the following chapters (Chapters 6 and 8) discuss, these media discourses around 'mind control' and 'brainwashing' demonstrated the evils of Aum as a dangerous and anti-social group and contributed to the mitigation of blame attributed to ordinary members. According to these interpretations, ordinary believers originally had good intentions of making the world a better place, but were deceived by the con-artist Asahara, who manipulated them into submission for his personal gain and vainglory. Some commentaries suggested that while Asahara's followers did not qualify as 'victims' in the ordinary sense, they were nonetheless deserving of sympathy and should be encouraged to reintegrate back into society.[27] Even the journalist Egawa Shōko (see Chapter 6), Aum's ardent critic, showed sympathy towards ordinary members by arguing that many of them had 'pure' personalities and were 'serious' but, unfortunately, were suggestible and naïve (Egawa 1995: 486). The self-help group for ex-members, the Canary Society (*Kanariya no Kai*) (see Chapter 8) has emphatically endorsed this narrative. By demarcating the moral responsibilities of rank-and-file *samana* from those of senior disciples higher up the chain of command, these discursive strategies removed low-ranking members from the circle of responsibility, while leaving open the possibility of rehabilitating them back into society through 'deprogramming' and other purported methods for 'reversing' the debilitating effects of mind control.

As more senior members were arrested over the course of the investigation, media attention turned to the question of when and how Asahara would be arrested. The former doctor Hayashi Ikuo (see Chapter 8), one of the culprits in the Tokyo attack who was arrested in early April, was the first senior disciple to confess to his role in the Tokyo attack. After his defection, Asahara's arrest seemed all but inevitable. On the morning of 16 May, replicating the spectacle of the first police raid in March, two hundred media personnel waited outside the Kamikuishiki facilities, eagerly awaiting the moment of Asahara's arrest.[28] As hundreds of police officers gradually made their way into the building complex, Asahara was found several hours later in a secret attic disguised by a false door.[29] The arrest was one of the biggest media events of the decade. On the day, 'the six network channels in Tokyo produced a total of more than one hundred hours of Aum coverage' (Hardacre 2007: 175), averaging a viewing figure of 55.7 per cent across the country.[30] With Asahara's arrest, mass media outlets gradually toned down the coverage as the perceived threat of another imminent terrorist attack declined and as the public gradually became bored with the over-saturation of information.

[27] *Asahi Shimbun* (1995), 'Ippan shinto to hanzai, musubitsukenaide', 1 May, p. 22; 'Kyōdan no fukai yami ni semare', 17 May, p. 5.
[28] *Asahi Shimbun* (1995), 'Mieta? Ame to kiri de hōdōjin katasukashi', 17 May, p. 29.
[29] Ibid.
[30] *AERA* (1995), '55.7 (Key Number)', 29 May p. 72.

While the mass media competed frantically for the viewers' attention through sensationalism, this is not to suggest that viewers were passive recipients, or that they uncritically supported the Manichaean frame of a war between Aum and the Japanese nation. Writing to newspapers and responding to surveys, some viewers complained about the excessive coverage, such as the repeated playback of Murai's gruesome murder, and suggested that the mass media were practicing a different kind of 'mind control' on its viewers.[31] Members of the public were divided over broadcasters' decisions to invite senior Aum members on air, which effectively provided an alleged terrorist organisation with a publicity platform. Others complained of the repetitive content and lamented that excessive information about Aum was pushing other social issues out of public discussion.[32] One example which arguably captures the mood of those who had grown weary of the media frenzy is a *senryū* – an aphoristic, satirical, or humorous poem written in *haiku* form – published in a newspaper (Gardner 2003: 22):

Konsento hazushi Oumu to en o kiri	I've cut my link to Aum by unplugging the television[33]

Matsumoto re-signified

While the media continued to cover the Tokyo attack as the main story, they also competed over new details surrounding other cases of Aum's organised crime and violence. One of the most significant developments in this regard was the return of the Matsumoto attack in public discourse. As the investigation progressed, it became increasingly evident that Aum had perpetrated the attack, and that the victim and survivor Kōno Yoshiyuki had been a victim of widespread character assassination. This development prompted the police and media to make public apologies to Kōno for their mistakes just months earlier. Alongside news reports on the latest developments surrounding the Tokyo sarin attack, a flurry of 'sincere apologies' appeared in newspapers, magazines, and on television. In June, nearly a year after the attack, the Nagano Prefectural Police issued a public 'expression of regret' (*ikan no i*) surrounding the circumstances of the investigation.[34] Representing the police system, Nonaka Hiromu, the chairman of the National Public Safety Commission, met Kōno in person to offer a public apology on

[31] *Asahi Shimbun* (1995), '"Mitai" "Fukai" Shichōsha no me (Terebi to Oumu hōdō)', 6 June, p. 9.

[32] *AERA* (1995), 'Hontō no koto ga shiritai, Pushhon Ankēto Oumu hōdō', 5 June, p. 60.

[33] Translation provided by Richard Gardner (2003).

[34] *Yomiuri Shimbun* (1995), 'Matsumoto sarin jiken Nagano Kenkei ga Kōno san taku otozure "ikan no i"', 12 June (Eve. Ed.), p. 19.

19 June.[35] Of course, the simultaneous flurry of apologies was not simply the outcome of the goodwill and sincerity of media outlets and the police. At the start of the year, Kōno had sought legal aid from the Japan Federation of Bar Associations for violation of human rights and had already begun legal action against many major media outlets. Eager to avoid potentially costly lawsuits and compensation, media companies swiftly made agreements with Kōno to publish public apologies in exchange for the lawsuits being dropped (Kōno 2001: 214–27).[36]

As commentators could finally narrate the symbolic significance of the Matsumoto attack with greater factual certainty, the event gained new and altered meanings in public discourse in three key respects. Firstly, as the media began to reattach new meanings to Matsumoto in relation to the wider cultural trauma of the Aum Affair, it gained a new meaning as a turning point in Aum's path to militarisation. However, because of this latency in the emergence of trauma narratives, Matsumoto never developed into a cultural trauma independent of Aum's other violent crimes.

Secondly, the public image of Kōno Yoshiyuki went through a complete reversal, as his image transformed from a suspect of a major terrorist attack to an innocent victim and survivor who was wrongfully maligned by the entire nation. In the retelling of the attack, the media recast Kōno as the quintessential victim-hero protagonist, who stoically stood his ground in the face of formidable adversity. In this new narrative, he was victimised three times over: he was personally injured and hospitalised; his wife fell into a coma from which she never regained full consciousness until her death in 2008, and his reputation was harmed by the accusations. Kōno was widely praised for facing an intensely difficult situation with dignity and aplomb. Though Kōno himself never personally spoke as a representative for Matsumoto's victims and bereaved families, his public interventions now gained more gravitas than any other individual victimised by the attack.

This new cultural status enabled Kōno to become a public figure, as he decried the process of investigation and forceful attempts to extract a confession, as well as the speculative and irresponsible media coverage.[37] Since then, Kōno has gone on to establish a career as a public speaker and an activist promoting the rights of victims of crime (see Chapter 7).

Thirdly, the commemoration of the Matsumoto attack has taken on a qualitatively different character to the commemoration of the Tokyo attack. The discovery of the true culprits of the attack has meant that the media had to confront their past mistakes, rather than simply condemning the perpetrators. Newspapers published

[35] *Yomiuri Shimbun* (1995), 'Matsumoto sarin "yōgisha atsukai ni danchō no omoi" Nonaka Kokka Kōan Iinchō, Kōnosan ni shazai', 20 June, p. 31.

[36] Interview with Kōno Yoshiyuki, 10 April 2015.

[37] *Asahi Shimbun* (1995), 'Matsumoto sarin jiken', 8 July, p. 37; 'Matsumoto sarin jiken no daiichi tsūhōsha, Kōno Yoshiyuki san no owaranu takakai', 17 July, p. 35; *Yomiuri Shimbun* (1995), 'Matsumoto jiken de Oumu no Asahara hikoku ra taiho', 17 July, p. 31.

special reports examining the flaws and missteps by both the media and the police, such as the media's reliance on the police for information, the police's method of extracting confessions through intensive interrogation instead of following scientific experts' advice that Kōno could not have made a potent nerve agent.[38] As a result, as the following chapter elaborates, the commemoration of Matsumoto has centred around remembering the event as a case of false accusation, not just as Aum's first terrorist attack using sarin. It is evident that many mass media outlets were embarrassed and humbled by Kōno's vindication. However, whether or not the media have since successfully incorporated the lessons learned from their initial coverage of Matsumoto – such as relying on the police for information and presuming the guilt of suspects before going to trial – is an entirely separate question that warrants a more systematic study beyond the Aum Affair alone.

Tracing the social causes of Aum

Compared with the initial cacophony and media frenzy in the first two months after the Tokyo attack, the second phase of public discourse, after Asahara's arrest, tended to be more measured, reflective, and in-depth. Media discussions generally shifted in emphasis from competing to report the latest facts about Aum to debating about the current state of society in relation to the Aum Affair as a moment of national crisis. For much of the Japanese public, everything about Aum appeared to them to be peculiar and 'foreign', from their dress, diet, and long, barely pronounceable 'holy names' given to senior members, to religious jargon consisting of *katakana* – a script used for loan-words and foreign names, as opposed to conventional Buddhist terminology written in *kanji* and *hiragana*.[39] Yet, Aum could not be written off as simply a foreign cult; it was undeniably a domestic movement whose rise in popularity required domestic explanations. Why had so many highly educated youths abandoned conventional success to commit extreme violence in the name of a guru? While public discourses about Aum encompassed multiple topics, there were several recurring themes that commentators generally converged towards.

Anomie

Consciously or not, many commentators invoked the spirit of the sociologist Émile Durkheim by diagnosing Aum as a symptom of an underlying social

[38] *Asahi Shimbun* (1995), 'Kōno san ni owabi suru', 14 June, p. 5; 'Matsumoto sarin jiken', 8 July, p. 37; *Yomiuri Shimbun* (1995), 'Kenshō "Matsumoto sarin" hōdō', 7 July, p. 19.

[39] Indeed, Aum made a conscious attempt to use terminology drawn from Pali and Sanskrit, rather than to draw on the equivalent terms in Japanese Buddhism.

illnesses that afflicted contemporary society. Among the most commonly identified malaises was a sense of stagnation and hopelessness (*heisokukan*), which might be compared with Durkheim's concept of *anomie*, a pervasive sense of lack of moral regulation. At a societal level, with the decline of student left-wing movements and the fall of socialism, there were few social and political causes that offered a viable alternative to consumer capitalism. Amidst a drought of alternative political ideologies, counter-cultural movements like Aum offered alternative religious ideologies that promised a life outside of the capitalist system.

In a theoretically flawed but nevertheless influential book, *Live the Endless Everyday* (*Owarinaki Nichijō o Ikiro*), the sociologist Miyadai Shinji proposed that young men and women responded differently to the general atmosphere of *anomie* that pervaded contemporary society (Miyadai 1995). According to Miyadai, whereas young women embraced the uncertainty by living everyday life hedonistically, young men – who sought a stabilising meta-narrative – sought the promise of absolute certainty as promised by movements like Aum. This, he argued, accounted for the over-representation of young, highly educated men in Aum's leadership. Miyadai's thesis, which rests on an essentialist view of gender and assumes highly gendered responses to social crises, is highly problematic to say the least, but it does illustrate the prevalence of a sense of directionless-ness that many commentators identified as the cause of (both secular and religious) millenarian culture, of which Aum was one of the most destructive examples.

Education

Searching for explanations for why so many highly educated people were 'lured' by Asahara's grandiose assertions and outlandish claims about the coming apocalypse, some commentators singled out the education system as a societal dysfunction. Japan's hyper-competitive education system, in which school and university entrance exams determined the trajectory of students from an early age, encouraged memorisation of facts over nurturing critical thinking faculties. In this interpretation, the school system produced talented individuals who excelled at scientific problem-solving, but who lacked the capacity for independent thinking and moral judgement. When youths became disillusioned with the material rewards that secondary school grades or a university degree could offer, they abandoned the secular life to seek relief in religion and spirituality.[40] One newspaper commentary warned that Aum was an indictment of the

[40] *Yomiuri Shimbun* (1995), '"Oumu" o unda jidai (ge)', 27 May, p. 30.

education system, arguing that 'we cannot ignore the fact that the knowledge learned at school held no meaning for young believers.'[41]

The rigid hierarchical structure of young people transitioning from school to higher education and into permanent employment also attracted criticism. From this perspective, Japanese organisations, whether in corporations or in academia, valued experience and age over individual merit. Commentators speculated this was a source of much frustration for talented scientists and professionals, who were eager to prove their abilities as soon as possible. In this respect, the religious path offered by Aum offered an attractive career for youths who looked for meritocracy. Unlike corporations where age took precedence (*nenkō joretsu*), young believers could be promoted quickly to manage money, people, and power inside Aum.[42] Through the Science and Technology team, Asahara promised young scientists what ordinary universities and companies could not: funding and facilities to conduct their own research 'for the future of humanity', even if that meant developing weapons of mass destruction.[43] Nevertheless, such an interpretation must be counter-balanced by the subjective narratives of the members themselves. Many renunciants who left their scientific backgrounds were disillusioned by the promises of medical and scientific advances in the first place and continuing with their research was hardly a priority for the vast majority of followers. Instead, they saw the life of an ascetic monk, training for enlightenment, to be a far more attractive 'career option'.

Popular culture

Although it was not linked to Aum as a direct cause, popular culture shared the blame in indirectly influencing the group's delusions about the apocalypse and its self-identified role as the chosen people fighting against evil. Commentators pointed out that Aum had developed its unique religious vocabulary through a syncretic blend of various religious traditions and popular culture, such as sci-fi anime and manga from the 1970s and 1980s. In many Japanese science-fiction works from this period, there were popular tropes of a band of heroes struggling against an evil enemy, often in post-apocalyptic settings, such as *Space Battleship Yamato* and *Mobile Suit Gundam*. According to commentators, Aum had supposedly used these narrative structures as templates, imagining themselves as heroes who would rebuild civilisation from the ashes of destruction.[44] Indeed,

[41] *Yomiuri Shimbun* (1995), 'Kyōiku mo yusaburu oumu "gakumon fushin" haikei ni taiō chūmoku sareru chūkyōshin', 7 June, p. 17.

[42] *Asahi Shimbun* (1995), 'Kyōdan no tokuisei', 5 June, p. 7.

[43] *Asahi Shimbun* (1995), 'Nerawareta "zunō" tachi sennō de "robotto" ni', 28 May, p. 29.

[44] For a detailed discussion, see Gardner (2008). On the one hand, Aum condemned popular culture and mass media as forms of mind control by the Judaeo-Masonic conspiracy; on the other hand, it heavily used manga and anime for promotional activities.

some of the ideas from sci-fi had entered Aum's vocabulary. During the militarisation period, Aum introduced air purifiers known as 'cosmo-cleaners', designed to protect Aum from poison gas attacks by the Freemasons; the name of the device was taken a device used in *Space Battleship Yamato*, which purifies nuclear radiation (Jōyū 2012: 135; Shimada 2012 (v. 1): 216). In a way, then, there were commentators who saw Aum as reflective of some of the destructive impulses and desires which were popularised in popular culture.[45]

Some commentaries suggested that Aum was an iteration of '*otaku*' subculture: communities (usually dominated by men) who obsess over certain hobbies and interests such as trains, manga, anime, and video games. In a newspaper column, the sociologist Inamasu Tatsuo drew comparisons between Aum and Miyazaki Tsutomu, a notorious paedophile and serial killer who was known as an '*otaku* murderer'. Like Miyazaki, who was reported as being a shut-in and an anime fanatic, Inamasu argued that Aum had shut itself off from the 'real world', preferring to live in a delusional fantasy and choosing to exact violence on the 'real world' that they despised.[46] While the connections between cultural works like *Space Battleship Yamato* and Aum's worldview are difficult to deny, the fact that critics singled out subcultures like manga and anime as pernicious influences on youth's 'healthy development' reflects a wider prejudice of its time against *otaku* subcultures. By drawing similarities between new religions and subcultures, these commentaries located both phenomena as deviating from the norms of a 'healthy' and functioning society.

Transnational influences

While these normative commentaries usually attributed the rise of Aum to domestic causes, some commentators broadened their focus to identify transnational and global transformations for Aum's success. Some commentaries argued that Aum had successfully exploited broader international geopolitical changes. Russia, in particular, had become a fertile ground for new religious movements in the social, economic, and political turmoil following the fall of the Soviet Union.[47] Critics pointed out that the growth in demand for religious movements within Russia had enabled Aum to establish and exploit political connections to aid their militarisation process.[48] Similarly, Asami Sadao, a Christian theologian, outspoken 'anti-cult' activist, and a staunch advocate of mind control theory (see Chapter 7),

[45] *Asahi Shimbun* (1995), 'Onaji byōri ga shakai nimo aru', 19 May, p. 5.

[46] Inamasu Tatsuo (1995), 'Koseika ga unda shin-kachikan', *Yomiuri Shimbun*, 8 June, p. 15.

[47] *Asahi Shimbun* (1995), 'Oumukyō Roshia de kyūbōchō. Soren hōkai, wakamononi seishinteki kūhaku ya shōrai eno fuan', 1 April (Eve. Ed.), p. 1.

[48] *Yomiuri Shimbun* (1995), Oumu Shinrikyō kaigai mo shinshoku Roshia seikai nimo jinmyaku hōfu na shikin de kyoten tsugi-tsugi', 16 May (Eve. Ed.), p. 3.

pointed to a global trend in the growth of new religious movements, which, in his account, had originated in the United States. In Asami's view, new religions are quintessentially modern phenomena found in developed countries, made possible through the constitutional freedom of belief. In his opinion, structural conditions such as the freedom to choose one's faith, uncertainties about the world, and the perception of social decline created the conditions for millenarian thought to flourish. Aum's rise was therefore not necessarily unique, but characteristic of many developed societies.[49]

Comparing Aum with other 'multinational religions' (*takokuseki shūkyō*) such as the Unification Church and the Peoples Temple, the social anthropologist Nakamaki Hirochika argued that these religions sought to create religious utopias that transcended national borders. Nakamaki suggested that Aum was an extreme development of this 'borderless' form of religion, except that Aum sought to establish its own religious polity through a violent revolution, instead of simply breaking down national borders.[50]

While some of these discussions are insightful for moving beyond the inward-looking analyses of Aum as a social pathology borne out of structural faults within Japan, these commentaries also tended to emphasise the foreign-ness of Aum as existing separately from indigenous (and therefore legitimate) religious culture and implied a mistrust of new religions or cults as foreign and potentially harmful intrusions into Japanese culture and identity.

Religion under attack

The Aum Affair had a tremendous impact not just on new religions – which suddenly found themselves tarred with the same brush as Aum – but also on more established, traditional religions whose very purpose in society was being questioned. Many of these commentaries treated the category of 'religion' with a great deal of scepticism and saw it as fundamentally external and possibly threatening to a healthy civil society. While religions – especially newer charismatic religions – have historically encountered negative media coverage and moral panics in Japan (Dorman 2012a), public confidence in religions hit a new low following the Tokyo attack.

There were generally two kinds of criticisms levelled against religions. Firstly, new religions, with much shorter histories than traditional religions, and often founded by charismatic leaders, were increasingly seen in a negative light as exploitative and predatory. Moreover, even if new religious movements did not

49 *Yomiuri Shimbun* (1995), 'Shinshūkyō o sasaeru "senshinkokubyō"', 18 May, p. 14.

50 *Yomiuri Shimbun* (1995), 'Fuan no jidai (4) "Shūkyō = Kokka" kōsō. Nakamaki Hirochika', 18 May (Osaka, Eve. Ed.), p. 5.

have political ambitions comparable to Aum's, their involvement in social and political affairs was usually met with suspicion and hostility. The Aum Affair only served to intensify the cultural 'otherness' of new religions within the religious field, as well as in wider civil society. Secondly, traditional religions, too, came under attack for their declining social relevance. It was often the case that people who joined Aum were utterly uninterested in what existing Buddhist sects in Japan had to offer, preferring to discover the 'original' form of Buddhism as taught by Asahara. For youths that joined Aum – and for many others as well – traditional Japanese Buddhism had become a mere custom for conducting funeral rites (*sōshiki bukkyō*), deprived of deeper meanings and unable to provide spiritually fulfilling answers to life's fundamental questions.

The Japanese public's categorical rejection of 'religion' as a positive influence on society, or even as a constitutive element in civil society, has been described by various scholars as an 'allergy to religion' (*shūkyō arerugī*) (Inoue 1999; Reader 2012; Shimazono 2001). This trend is most clearly evident in a newspaper poll conducted by the *Yomiuri* three months after the Tokyo attack.[51] While a clear majority of respondents (77 per cent) acknowledged that Aum was an exceptional case and not representative of religions in general, the proportion of people identifying as religious had declined to 20 per cent, compared with 26 the previous year. The poll also underlined the irrelevance of religion in everyday life: 70 per cent of respondents answered that religion was not important for a happy life, and 87 per cent of respondents answered that they had never thought about joining a religious organisation. Negative impressions about religious organisations were also prevalent: 33 per cent thought aggressive proselytisation strategies by religions were common, and 40 per cent agreed that religious organisations were greedy about money. In another survey conducted by the *Asahi* in September 1995, 34 per cent of the respondents stated that they had gained a negative impression of religion in general after the Aum Affair.[52] Although more recent polls have suggested a slight uptick in the percentage of people identifying as religious (Nishi 2009: 66–7), there is no doubt that the Aum Affair intensified negative stereotypes of religion in public opinion, a situation which has persisted to the present day (Reader 2012). Moreover, as the following chapters reveal, the Aum Affair inevitably became an obligatory reference point for subsequent public and policy debates about how much the state should regulate religions. This subsequently led to intense political struggles between Kōmeitō – the political party with deep ties to the lay Buddhist religion Sōka Gakkai – and its rivals, over the reform of the Religious Corporations Act.

[51] *Yomiuri Shimbun* (1995), 'Oumu jiken to shūkyōkan, "Shūkyō banare" ichidan to kasoku', 27 June, p. 13.

[52] *Asahi Shimbun* (1995), 'Kōreisō de "mushinkō" kyūzō. Shūkyō dantai e kibishii shisen', 23 September, p. 21.

Religious organisations responded to the widespread public distrust of 'religion' in various ways. Some new religions, who feared being accused of being a 'cult', modified their activities by reducing their public-facing activities, moderating their millenarian worldviews, and consolidating their existing membership base instead of attracting new members (Baffelli and Reader 2011; McLaughlin 2012). Some representatives from older, more established Buddhist sects also stressed their differences from Aum by arguing that Aum presented a false understanding of Buddhism by straying from its fundamental tenets of peace and non-violence.[53] However, many more organisations chose to stay out of public debates altogether, perhaps eager to avoid attracting negative publicity (Kisala 2001: 108–10). In other words, many religious organisations chose to avoid the limelight, instead preferring to remain a marginal presence in civil society.

One of the enduring effects of the Aum Affair that has affected all religions operating in Japan has been the concretisation of a binary between 'religions' and 'cults'. Although various terms such as '*inshi jakyō*' ('lewd and evil religion'), '*shinkō shūkyō*' ('newly established religion'), '*ese shūkyō*' ('fake religion'), and '*giji shūkyō*'('pseudo-religion') have existed for decades to denigrate new religions and to distinguish them from more established religions, the term '*karuto*' ('cult') entered the popular lexicon in the aftermath of the Tokyo attack to become a generic term for controversial religious movements and businesses seen as predatory and unscrupulous, including self-help seminars (*jiko keihatsu seminā*) and multilevel marketing (Sakurai 2014; Ushiyama 2019a).

The popularisation of this binary distinction between 'religions' and 'cults' in public discourse has been a double-edged sword for many religions operating in Japan. On the one hand, this coding has provided them with a strategy for positioning themselves as 'religions' in contrast to 'cults' such as Aum and other controversial religions. On the other hand, the entrenchment of this cultural binary in public discourse has meant that religions became vulnerable to accusations of being a 'cult' by, for example, disaffiliated ex-members and their families, who have often taken leading roles in mobilising against controversial movements. Like North American anti-cult movements, their Japanese anti-cult equivalents have often been led by close relatives of members of controversial religious movements to accuse leaders of engaging in 'brainwashing' and 'mind control'. However, unlike North America, where Christian anti-cult groups have tended to act separately from secular counterparts (Cowan 2002; Richardson and Introvigne 2007), Japanese anti-cult movements have attracted the support of religious practitioners, who have collaborated with activists to disseminate 'brainwashing' and 'mind control' theories and to engage in 'deprogramming' and 'exit counselling' to persuade (or in some cases, to coerce) members of new

[53] Kitabatake Kiyoyasu (1995), 'Dentō bukkyō yo, kikikan o idake', *Asahi Shimbun*, 21 June, p. 4.

religions to renounce their faith. Some religious practitioners, then, have chosen to treat the contentious distinction between 'religions' and 'cults' to be self-evident and to give support to individuals and groups that are categorically hostile to many controversial religions. Today, the Japan Society Cult Prevention and Recovery – originally founded as the Japan De-Cult Council in the wake of the Aum Affair – lists Buddhist priests and Christian pastors among its directors.[54]

The making of a villain: Asahara the antagonist

The prevalent image of Aum Shinrikyō as an exogenous enemy attacking the Japanese nation was inseparable from the public's fascination for Asahara Shōkō. As more information surrounding Aum's controversies and violent crimes emerged over the course of the investigation, public sentiment and interest inevitably turned towards Asahara's biography, personality, and motives. In this period, Asahara received intense and critical attention accorded only to the most notorious of social antagonists, comparable to Western villain archetypes comparable to Hitler, Stalin, Mao, Saddam Hussein, and Osama Bin Laden.

Consequently, various commentaries converged around the image of him as a symbol of ultimate evil, a 'demonic figure', in whom 'ambiguities of moral character are erased, so that the commemorated figure is seen as fully, intensely, and quintessentially evil' (Ducharme and Fine 1995: 1311). Through this symbolic transformation, Asahara achieved the status of 'nonpersonhood', in which 'all that remains from the public's perspective is the evil core' (ibid.: 1312). In short, Asahara – or rather, the signifier 'Asahara Shōkō' – became the vessel for a range of negative signifieds: dictatorship, irrationality, deviance, criminality, megalomania, paranoia, and a love of violence.

This process of demonisation, however, was more complicated than merely condemning him as the leader of a terrorist organisation. There was no single, stable image of Asahara; rather, representations of him as evil incarnate changed gradually as the investigation progressed and as more biographical details about him emerged. Asahara's public image underwent a twofold transformation, from an obscure leader of a relatively small religion to the primary antagonist with whom the entire nation was now in conflict. Firstly, in a process which this chapter calls the 'distillation of evil', the moral responsibilities for Aum's various crimes were eventually traced back to Asahara as a criminal mastermind, as disciples claimed that Asahara had coerced or manipulated them into committing crimes. As a result, the 'circle of responsibility' gradually narrowed to identify Asahara

[54] Japan Society for Cult Prevention and Recovery (n.d.), "What is The Japan Society for Cult Prevention and Recovery: JSCPR?" <www.jscpr.org/english> Accessed November 2021.

as the *sole* source of Aum's violence. Secondly, Asahara's status as a 'sacred evil' would not be complete without a wholesale denial of the legitimacy of Aum's belief system and the denigration of his religious charisma, and any other positive human qualities he may have possessed or displayed. In this second process of what this chapter terms 'profanation of character', commentators sought evidence – amply supplied by disaffected ex-members – that he was merely a conman, disguised as a holy man. In doing so, numerous commentators argued that Asahara had effectively 'duped' vulnerable people for personal profit, and that he lived a hypocritical life characterised by avarice, lust, and gluttony that contradicted his own ascetic principles. If the 'distillation of evil' made an ordinary human into a demonic being, the 'profanation' process demystified the godly status that Asahara had given himself, by painting him as an unremarkable, hypocritical, and even pathetic, ordinary man.

Distillation of evil

While the narrative that Aum members had been brainwashed or mind-controlled by the leadership had been circulating almost immediately after the Tokyo attack, the possibility that the senior leadership, too, could have been mind-controlled by Asahara was raised only after the arrests and defection of the culprits behind Aum's terrorist attacks. The defection of Hayashi Ikuo in early April was one of the earliest and most dramatic examples of an Aum member's public renunciation of faith, but many other disciples followed suit by publicly denouncing Asahara. Notably, Inoue Yoshihiro, who had directed the ground-level operations, relinquished his membership during the trials and published an open letter urging remaining believers to quit.[55] Hayakawa Kiyohide, a core member who was an accomplice in several murder cases (see Chapter 8), also denounced Asahara's refusal to take responsibilities for his orders.[56] By the beginning of October 1995, 36 out of 61 Aum defendants whose trial proceedings had begun had defected.[57]

Relying on these accounts by disillusioned ex-members, the media constructed an image of Asahara as the archetype of a tyrannical leader. Commentators identified him as a megalomaniac, which, when combined with his constant fear of betrayal and paranoid delusions about conspiratorial forces, drove Aum to indiscriminately murder on ordinary civilians on a massive scale. As an example of Asahara's cold-blooded ruthlessness, the murders of the Sakamoto family gained

[55] *Asahi Shimbun* (1995), 'Sonshi wa ego o jissen saseta dake. Oumu, Inoue hikoku, Shinto ni dakkai yobikake', 29 December, p. 22.

[56] *Yomiuri Shimbun* (1995), 'Sakamoto bengoshi jiken "Sonshi shiji nanoni kyōjutsu sezuni kitanai' Hayakawa hikoku, kibishiku hinan', 23 September, p. 35.

[57] *Yomiuri Shimbun* (1995), 'Oumu saiban "joban" no sōkatsu', 1 October, p. 8.

a new significance after their bodies were finally discovered in September 1995. The *Yomiuri Shimbun* denounced the attack as showing not 'a shred of humanity' for taking the life of a 14-month-old baby and identified the event as the 'origin' of Aum's organised crimes.[58]

Another common rhetorical strategy was to compare Asahara with other pre-existing archetypes of tyrannical leaders. An article published in *AERA*, a weekly contemporary affairs magazine, made direct comparisons between Aum and the Nazis, suggesting there were uncanny similarities between them: the absolutism and the unique charismatic personalities of the leader, an extremely hierarchical organisation, the use of scientific technology for violence, and the involvement of intellectual and ambitious youths.[59] Some directly compared Asahara's charisma and ambition to Hitler by stating that Asahara was a 'crazed dictator on a par with Hitler'. Reports highlighted that Asahara, as an admirer of Hitler and Mao, emulated the hierarchical structure to consolidate his dictatorship and to pursue his personal ambitions.[60] To underline this point, a newspaper article quoted a sermon in which Asahara had discussed Aum's 'mind control' programme with reference to Hitler and Mao. In this sermon, Asahara had stated that 'if Aum Shinrikyō has a great mind control system, that would be the greatest thing. You must continue to mind control and brainwash new members. Hitler was a political dictator. Mao Zedong was dictator of thought. And I am considering becoming a dictator of belief to guide you towards an ultimate form of enlightenment.'[61] Notwithstanding the absurdity of comparing dictators of global powers responsible for the deaths of tens of millions with a religious leader whose influence peaked at just above a thousand full-time followers, these analogies nevertheless concretised Asahara's public image as a totalitarian dictator fundamentally opposed to civic values of liberty and democracy.

Commentators also turned to Asahara's biography to trace his self-transformation into an omniscient guru. In brief biographical summaries of Aum members, Asahara was described as having a lust for power from an early age, with a dream to become a politician.[62] In this narrative, commentators speculated that Asahara's difficult upbringing contributed to his desire to be upwardly mobile, which turned into a feeling of being rejected from the world after his businesses failed. Born with congenital glaucoma with one eye and raised in a large family with constant economic hardship, Asahara was sent to a boarding school for the blind from an early age. As a result, he supposedly bore a grudge against his

[58] *Yomiuri Shimbun* (1995), 'Oumu no genten no itamashii ketsumatsu', 7 September, p. 3.

[59] *AERA* (1995), 'Nachisu to Oumu-kyō wa nisugite kowai', 1 May, p. 8.

[60] *Yomiuri Shimbun* (1995), 'Oumu Asahara dokusai taisei. Guntai to sokkuri. Shukkesha o 14 kaikyū. Hitorā sonkei', 26 May, p. 19.

[61] *Asahi Shimbun* (1995), 'Kyōfu aori busōka, "tero shūdan" e henyō', 6 June, p. 25.

[62] *Yomiuri Shimbun* (1995), 'Oumu Shinrikyō "Chikatetsu sarin" yōgisha 41 nin no yokogao', 15 May, p. 5.

parents for abandoning him.[63] His dominating personality developed further at school, as he used his remaining eyesight to dominate and bully his handicapped classmates.[64] Tracing continuities between his childhood and his adult career as a guru, some commentaries observed that Asahara had written in the elementary school leavers' essay that his dream was to build a 'robot kingdom'.[65] Although this may simply have been the innocent musings of a child growing up with the popular sci-fi series of the time, such as *Astroboy* and *Testujin 28-gō*, this sentence was interpreted as an ominous foreshadowing of Asahara's ambition to turn humans into obedient and mindless 'robots' for his personal kingdom. Even after leaving school, Asahara encountered difficulties as a young man. After working as an acupuncturist for several years, his Chinese medicine business collapsed when he was arrested and fined for falsely claiming the effectiveness of his products. His failure at conventional success encouraged him to pursue success through yoga and spirituality.

The commentary provided by the philosopher Umehara Takeshi is a typical example of this narrative, as he makes a link between Asahara's upbringing and his subsequent career as a religious guru before turning to indiscriminate terrorism: '[t]here can be no mistake that the Subway Sarin attack emerged from the darkness of Asahara Shōkō's soul', he stressed.[66] Unlike other religious leaders before him, who confined their sphere of influence to the religious realm, Asahara exercised no such restraint. According to Umehara,

> the *ressentiment* inside him – in other words, his hidden grudge – must have been far too strong. He was born and raised as a disabled child in Japan's poorest class, subjected to every kind of humiliation.[[67]] This humiliation created within him hatred of gigantic proportions; this hatred became an ambition to become a politician to rule Japan, but when this ambition faltered, he created a separate sacred realm different to this world, became the ruler of that sacred realm, and sought revenge upon the world itself.[68]

For Umehara, religion served exclusively as a means for Asahara to quench his endless thirst for power and ambition by manipulating vulnerable youths into becoming his 'slaves'. Through these biographical readings and other rhetorical devices, Asahara became the quintessential super-villain, driven by a thirst for revenge. These media discourses distilled the negative qualities of megalomania,

[63] *Yomiuri Shimbun* (1995), 'Zettaikachi fuzai no shakai gensō o ataeta Oumu', 7 June, p. 8.

[64] *Yomiuri Shimbun* (1995), '(Shōgen Shūmatsu no Kyōdan) Kanbu 10 nin no Sugao (1) Asahara Shōkō daihyō', 17 May, p. 14.

[65] *Asahi Shimbun* (1995), 'Kyōfu aori busōka, "tero shūdan" e henyō', 6 June, p. 25.

[66] *Asahi Shimbun* (1995), 'Chitekina yajū umidasu gendai no higeki', 2 June, p. 4.

[67] This is likely a veiled reference to rumours that Asahara hailed from a '*hisabetsu buraku*', or discriminated settlements, which have been historically discriminated against.

[68] *Asahi Shimbun* (1995), 'Chitekina yajū umidasu gendai no higeki', 2 June, p. 4.

hatred, and murderousness into Asahara's personality, identifying him as the singular and ultimate source of all Aum's evils.

It is crucial to note that, while many commentators were eager to diagnose Asahara with a catalogue of mental illnesses, such as narcissistic personality disorder and paranoid schizophrenia, they were eager to avoid assertions that he was *clinically* insane – arguing this would be tantamount to suggesting that he should not stand trial for reasons of insanity. Thus, although commentators portrayed him to be a 'crazed' character, they never questioned whether Asahara was fit to stand trial. Indeed, questioning Asahara's sanity itself became a social taboo. It was only Asahara's defence team, family members, and a minority of public figures and intellectuals such as Mori Tatsuya (see Chapter 6) who suggested that Asahara was not fit to stand trial and too ill to be executed. Whatever flawed traits and personality disorders he possessed, in legal and medical terms, Asahara was, and continued to be, in good physical and mental health until the very moment of his execution.

Profanation

While Asahara quickly gained a unique status as a demonic figure, this was only one side of his public status as a villain and 'Public Enemy No. 1'. Like many other villains in social dramas, Asahara was and continues to be, a frequent object of parody and ridicule in popular culture. Reports ranged from exposures of Asahara's hypocritical behaviour, ex-believers' 'tell all' stories about his lavish lifestyle and satirical cartoons in the tabloid print media gossip about his sex life that resembled a celebrity exposé. These media depictions repudiated Asahara's self-professed image as an enlightened guru, the messenger of Lord Shiva, and the second coming of Christ, representing him instead as a two-bit conman, a hypocrite, and an 'ordinary man'. Thus, if the distillation of evil elevated his status to a signifier of 'sacred evil', the process of profanation of character acted to publicly discount and discredit any amount of 'holiness' that Asahara claimed or that his followers ascribed to him.

In this discursive pattern, commentators described Asahara not as a religious leader, but as a poor impersonation of a true religious practitioner. This is a rhetorical strategy that is common in criticisms levelled against other charismatic leaders of controversial minority religions. Founders of religious movements have been frequently criticised for their lavish and ostentatious lifestyles. For example, Bhagwan Shree Rajneesh (who later went by the name Osho) of the Rajneesh movement was notorious for his fleet of Rolls Royces that he kept on the Rajneeshpuram ranch commune in Oregon. Asahara was no exception to this trope, and his material excesses were all the more pertinent due to Aum's asceticism and vegetarianism, which was strictly enforced on members. For many commentators, Asahara' s extravagant behaviour – not to mention his rotund figure – seemed to contradict his very own teachings which emphasised control over one's bodily desires. Using information provided by former aides and written instructions about his meals, the media described his daily habits, such as eating out at expensive restaurants, and what he would eat while travelling, which, contrary to his Buddhist principles, included meat and fish dishes.[69] In the news coverage of the trial of Asahara's former bodyguard, the bodyguard complained about Asahara's enormous appetite as he devoured multiple main courses in one sitting and took his entourage on a tour of 'family restaurants' (*famiresu*) for a month.[70] Rejecting Asahara's religious charisma, the ex-member dismissed Asahara, stating, 'he's nothing like a holy man, he's just like any old man you find on the street' (*tada no ossan*).[71]

If Asahara's was a hypocrite in many commentators' eyes, he was also depicted as a sly conman who was able to dupe thousands of people to feed his insatiable ego. In these representations, he was not a serious *yogi* with a deep religious conviction, but merely a conman interested only in money and power.

'I think he was a formidable conman', said the novelist Takamura Kaoru in a newspaper interview:

> The incident in which he made and sold fake drugs, which you could call his starting point, is also a scam … There is nothing religious about it. Even the 'ability to float' is advertised as a supernatural power, but in the light of scientific common sense, this is a lie. You lie that once you reach the stage of 'Final Enlightenment' you can fly, and attract believers. This is a scam. From beginning to end, it's all been a scam.[72]

Commentators like Takamura argued that Asahara's true motivation lay not in his religious interest, but a desire to 'get rich quick'. The expensive initiation rituals, sales of his bathwater, training courses and merchandise, as well as the recruitment strategy of forcing new members to donate all their material possessions and assets to the organisation were all evidence of Asahara's boundless greed.

Echoing Takamura's view, the non-fiction writer Inose Naoki concluded that Asahara should not be understood as a religious figure, but a con artist and a

[69] *Yomiuri Shimbun* (1995), 'Satian "hinpu no zōshoku" rōdōsha wa soshoku, hatarakizume, kanbu wa senyōsha, gaishoku', 18 April, p. 31; *Yomiuri Shimbun* (1995), 'Asahara daihyō ni komaka na settai tebiki', 9 May (Eve. Ed.), p. 1. In Aum's doctrines, Asahara, who had transcended the cycle of karmic rebirths, could not accrue negative karma himself by eating animals.

[70] *Asahi Shimbun* (1995), ' "Seija Asahara, asobuwa kuuwa" genmetsu shi hihan. Shinpen keigo tantō no hikoku', 6 September, p. 35. "Family restaurants" in Japan refer not to family-run restaurants, but to restaurants which cater to families, especially with young children, with a wide variety of food available to order on the menu, from traditional Japanese cuisine to "Western" (*yōshoku*) dishes.

[71] *Yomiuri Shimbun* (1995), 'Oumu saiban "joban" no sōkatsu', 1 October, p. 8.Here, '*ossan*', a phonetic corruption of '*ojisan*' (meaning uncle or middle-aged man), can carry derisive connotations, similar to calling someone an 'old man' in English.

[72] *Asahi Shimbun* (1995), 'Takamura Kaoru san (Oumu no Yami: Intabyū tokushū: 90)', 23 June, p. 2.

'psychopath' interested solely in his own success: 'the essence of how the founder Asahara ran the organisation lies in fraudulence.' Analysing Asahara's personality, Inose emphasised Asahara's arrest record for mis-selling drugs as the true 'origin' for his career. Arguing that Asahara was a typical psychopath who had a talent for lying, Inose concluded that:

> The misunderstanding began when we took Asahara to be a religious practitioner. He came into the world as a psychopathic leader, dressed up in the 'plush doll' [*nuigurumi*] of religion to raise money with remarkable brutality. As such, we can say that the vast majority of believers were defenceless victims worthy of our sympathy, who were preyed upon by a psychopathic leader because they sought spiritual salvation.[73]

Like the public discourses that supported the 'mind control' narrative, commentators like Takamura and Inose eschewed giving any recognition to Aum as a legitimate 'religion', or to Asahara as a legitimate 'religious practitioner' (*shūkyōsha*). By describing Asahara as a hypocrite and conman, media discourses denied that Aum's *raison d'être* could be religious in nature and presented Aum as a poor imitation of a 'real' religion. Moreover, just like the process of distillation of evil, profanation focused the moral responsibility for Aum's crimes to Asahara, locating him as the singular source of profanity, moral corruption, and symbolic pollution.

Discourses that profaned Asahara's personality, religious charisma, and motives also exposed Japan's dominant cultural biases about stigmatised groups considered to be 'profane' and 'outside' of the moral community. Although not circulated in quality newspapers or on television, less scrupulous media outlets circulated various conspiracy theories about Asahara's family background and Aum's organisation ties to underworld elements. For instance, there were unverified assertions that traced Asahara's family background to Zainichi Koreans – the ethnic Korean diaspora settled in Japan for generations – or claimed that he came from areas known as *hisabetsu buraku* (also known as *dōwa chiku)*, inhabited by a historically dominated and ostracised class of people (Lifton 1999: 15). These rumours circulated in tandem with related speculations about Asahara's underworld ties to North Korean agents and *yakuza* crime syndicates. These profanation strategies revealed more about enduring negative stereotypes of minority groups as 'profane' and 'symbolically polluting' in mainstream media and less about Asahara's 'true' character and personality.

To summarise, commentators extensively relied on both symbolic processes, distillation of evil, and profanation, to focus attention on Asahara as the ultimate villain in the trauma drama. In doing so, predominant discourses established an interpretive frame which situated Asahara as the source and embodiment of all

[73] Inose Naoki. (1995), 'Oumu jiken tsuranuku sagisei', *Yomiuri Shimbun*, 17 May, p. 5.

that is profane and dangerous to the body politic. As later chapters argue, this frame had a profound impact not only on the trial proceedings of the culprits and how former believers came to terms with issues of guilt and individual moral responsibility (see Chapter 8) and the discrimination against Asahara's immediate family (see Chapter 8), but also on wider policy discussions about the state regulation of religion (see Chapter 5) and public anxieties about cults as a source of social unrest (see Chapter 6).

Conclusions

As 1995 drew to a close, Aum-related coverage shifted from sensationalism to more measured reports about the trial proceedings. Although the trial hearings, especially Asahara's, continued to generate great public interest, a period of relative calm returned to news reporting. Nevertheless, by the end of the year, the Aum Affair had become a media event of a scale rarely seen before. On day-time variety shows (*waido shō*) alone, the Aum Affair had generated over 500 hours of footage by mid-June and over 1,200 hours by the end of November. Once news programmes were also included in this figure, the Aum Affair likely generated well over 2,000 hours of TV programming in 1995.[74]

Meanwhile, throughout 1995, Aum displayed few obvious signs of remorse or reform, even after the arrests of its leader and the defection of some of its most senior members. As Asahara issued instructions to his followers to continue training, ordinary members – if they hadn't already left already – maintained the status quo without explicitly addressing issues about collective guilt and responsibility. Some suspects, wanted for their alleged roles in Aum's terrorist attacks, continued to evade capture. Hayashi Yasuo, one of the five assailants in the Tokyo attack, was on the run until his arrest in December 1996. Hirata Makoto, a getaway driver in the kidnapping of Kariya Kiyoshi, turned himself in to the police on New Year's Eve 2011, and Takahashi Katsuya and Kikuchi Naoko were both arrested several months later in 2012 (see Chapter 8). The group's most senior remaining member, Jōyū Fumihiro, was arrested in October 1995 for perjury and falsifying documents relating to a land deal in Kumamoto Prefecture in 1990, and Aum was left without any leaders who possessed the know-how or charisma to steer the group forward. In a limbo, rank-and-file members chose to continue their secretive lifestyles and maintained as little contact with the outside world as possible. There is no doubt that Aum's refusal to formally admit responsibility or to issue a public apology contributed to the public perception that Aum was

[74] *Yomiuri Shimbun* (1995), 'Oumu to terebi kyōmi hon'i de rinri itsudatu, hōdō no geinōka', 22 December, p. 13. This figure includes non-news programmes as well.

indeed a 'destructive cult' that could not be reasoned with, and that it needed to be dismantled at whatever cost.

This dominant public discourse that emerged in the immediate aftermath of the Tokyo attack had a lasting and indelible impact on all sectors of society. Dominant actors and institutions employed symbolic oppositions such as good and evil, sacred and profane, democracy and autocracy, and rationality and irrationality to condemn and reject Aum's extreme violence and apocalyptic theodicy. Drawing comparisons with past examples with the Nazis and terrorist groups such as the United Red Army, various stakeholders universally identified Aum as an existential threat to the nation. Through this process, the dominant trauma narrative identified Aum as a dangerous brainwashing cult and Asahara as the embodiment of evil devoid of any redeeming features.

On the one hand, these representations were arguably both necessary and inevitable for civil repair: the narratives of a foreign threat attacking the nation helped the public to make sense of an unprecedented event that paralysed one of the world's biggest cities while the nation was still recovering from the trauma of the Great Hanshin Earthquake just two months previously. As the subway attack coalesced into a national trauma, the event marked a fundamental and irreversible point in Japanese collective memory. The Tokyo sarin attack became a national crisis that prompted an urgent re-examination of the various structural problems affecting contemporary society, such as youths' despair over excess consumerism and materialism, an education system which rewarded rote learning rather than critical thinking, and hierarchical organisational structures that rewarded only obedience to authority.

On the other hand, the media frenzy surrounding Aum as a brainwashing 'death cult', and metaphors of Aum as a social 'disease' to be eradicated 'by whatever means necessary' had deleterious effects on the rule of law.[75] The collective hostility towards Aum provided a normative justification for legally questionable practices of the police making arrests for minor offenses and indirectly contributing to the vigilante killing of a key witness and suspect, who died before facing justice. Furthermore, as news coverage of Aum transformed into its own genre of entertainment, a 'trial by media' of Aum's various alleged wrongdoings failed to reflect on the institutional failures that were exposed after the Matsumoto sarin attack, in which the mass media relayed information as told by the police at face value without independent fact-checking.

Importantly, these various narratives about the Tokyo subway attack revealed not so much about the 'true' nature of Aum and Asahara as they brought to the foreground Japan's latent cultural prejudices about social groups which civil society regarded as the cultural 'Other'. By drawing comparisons between Aum

[75] *Yomiuri Shimbun* (1995), 'Oumu no kiken na byōkon o issōseyo', 7 June, Editorial, p. 3.

and *otaku* subculture, for example, commentators highlighted that both phenomena lay outside what constituted 'real' or 'proper' Japanese culture. Moreover, speculative rumours about Asahara's family background exposed and reproduced Japan's deep-seated racialised stereotypes against ethnic Korean and *burakumin* communities.

While the perception of the Aum Affair as a national crisis subsided with the arrests of Asahara and senior members, the 'Aum Affair' was far from over. The subway attack left in its wake difficult political questions about whether to ban and dissolve the organisation, how religious organisations should be regulated in the future, and whether victims should receive compensation. Moreover, there remained a much more open-ended question for a myriad of stakeholders: how should the Aum Affair be remembered?

5

Commemorating Crisis: State, Media, and Civil Responses to the Aum Affair

The arrests of Asahara and his aides in mid-1995 reduced the possibility that there might be more terrorist plots, bringing a sense of momentary closure and relief. However, the arrests did not resolve all the problems that the Aum Affair had brought to the fore. Just as similar controversies surrounding 'cults' and cult violence around the world have prompted state interventions and the regulation of religions, the Japanese government faced a raft of problems and questions, such as whether Aum should be banned, how the financial damages caused by Aum should be repaid to various stakeholders, and whether existing laws governing religions were fit for purpose. In court, due to the sheer number and magnitude of the crimes committed, trials were slow, complex, and contentious. Public anxieties about the continuing presence of Aum members living in their neighbourhoods persisted for years, as there remained strong public demands for security agencies to continue to monitor Aum's activities.

In short, what started as the 'Aum Affair' (*Oumu jiken*) gradually become the 'Aum Problem' (*Oumu mondai*): how the state and civil society should interact with remaining Aum members in a 'post-Aum' society. The Aum Problem was also a problem of collective memory. There appeared to be a consensus of public opinion that the horrors of the Tokyo subway should not be forgotten. For many victims and bereaved families, forgetting Aum's crimes was hardly an option. They had no choice but to remember and relive the traumatic moments that they had suffered. Moreover, for many survivors and bereaved families, remembrance was a personal duty and ethical obligation to honour those who died. Yet, the victims' willingness to remember and commemorate the attacks stood in direct contradiction with another impulse shared by various segments of society to forget the trauma of the Aum Affair as much as possible. The psychological and social drive to erase – and to symbolically cleanse – marks of Aum was particularly acute for communities neighbouring Aum's shared accommodation.

For them, the complete eviction of Aum believers from their neighbourhood and the eradication of all physical remnants of Aum's facilities was non-negotiable for recovering their ordinary lives 'before Aum'.

This chapter examines this conflict between the will to remember – or more accurately, the will to *selectively* remember – and the will to forget by focusing on the interactions between actions by dominant institutions and responses by lay actors. While the following chapters will discuss actions by a variety of actors, it is important to focus first on elite institutions, as elite groups enjoy a disproportionate advantage in managing and controlling not just the collective memory of a given society, but also the social organisation of time itself (Zerubavel 2003).

Various levels of government have the means and the capital to stage officially sanctioned forms of commemoration that range from commemorative ceremonies and national holidays, to monuments and memorials, street names, and education curricula. The option of building memorials and statues, of course, is also open to elite non-state actors; hence powerful historical figures have sought to preserve an image of themselves as represented through statues, as recent protests against statues of European and American colonialists and slaveholders in recent years have demonstrated only too well. Whatever the commemorative process involved, they all require substantial investments of economic capital, political power, labour, and time, that less privileged actors may not have the means to provide. As a result, elite representations of the past often become the hegemonic frame through which national memory is reproduced. Dominant representations of the past provide cultural templates for interpreting not only actions of the past, but also for understanding present and future events: collective meta-narratives – such as ethno-national self-identities, histories of conflict, and categories of friends and enemies – provide ready-made answers for social issues in predictable, almost algorithmic, ways.

As Bakhtin (1981; 1986) highlighted, elite public discourse has a tendency to benefit the status quo. 'Elite' and 'official' speech genres, he argued, work for the benefit of the ruling class by concentrating meanings to the linguistic and political centre, which he called 'centripetal' discourse. Official languages of bureaucracy, law, and academia provide authoritative and unquestioned representations of the world that neutralises 'the way things are'. Elite discourse therefore stands above, and in opposition to, vernacular speech and provincial dialects, which challenge and disperse meanings through their 'centrifugal' characteristics away from the political centre.

In this heteroglossic – vertically stratified – structure of commemorative speech acts, socially dominant actors' responses in dealing with the aftermath of the Tokyo attack are essential for understanding the 'official' representations of Aum that have persisted in public discourse in the following decades. Although the state and the mass media had different interests at stake, they both converged on the framing of Aum Shinrikyō as a 'destructive cult' and a perennial threat to the body politic. This dominant narrative has been reproduced through criminal trials, legislation, mass media coverage, and municipal governmental policies. For state authorities such as the Public Security Intelligence Agency (PSIA), Japan's national intelligence agency, this narrative has enabled them to secure a legal mandate to carry out regular searches of premises belonging to Aum and its successor organisations – possibly in perpetuity – while municipal governments have defended policy decisions to unlawfully exclude Aum from receiving municipal services based on the perceived threat that Aum represents to public safety.

As with all forms of commemoration, elite commemoration is selective with what information it seeks to impart and reproduce. While dominant representations of Aum have relied on this representation of Aum as a 'destructive cult', elite responses to Aum's violence have also been marked by occasions of non-commemoration, where there are notable silences and omissions surrounding events when they apparently failed to follow the best course of action. For instance, until relatively recently, the police had rarely acknowledged missteps in investigating the first violent crimes committed by Aum. Similarly, the mass media have tended to avoid public discussions of the 'TBS Video Scandal', in which the TV broadcaster TBS was indirectly implicated in the murders of the anti-cult lawyer Sakamoto Tsutsumi and his family. By and large, with the notable exception of commemoration of the Matsumoto sarin attack, neither state authorities nor mass media outlets have systematically addressed their own shortcomings through their organisational responses to the Aum Affair.

State responses – Aum and the law

Cases of religious terrorism and religious violence often result in state responses which seek to identify and prevent similar instances from happening in the future. Although these may not fall under a formal definition of 'commemoration', studying state responses to terrorism through legislation nevertheless helps to elucidate the permanent and sweeping social effects of terrorist attacks on a society, as well as how states and state authorities form institutional memories about how to respond to current and future terror threats.

For instance, in the context of terrorist attacks by religious motives such as the 9/11 US attacks and the 7/7 London bombings, states have generally responded through an overhaul of governmental powers such as greater oversight of religious organisations, tightened security measures on public transport, and enhanced surveillance online as well as in public places. On the one hand, these measures are often accepted by the public as inevitable and necessary to reduce the risk of future attacks; for example, tighter airport security checks and the restriction of liquids on airplanes have become the global norm. On the other hand, terrorist attacks have frequently provided governments with a justification to enhance their legal powers at the expense of individual freedoms. Responding to the 9/11 attacks, the USA PATRIOT Act greatly strengthened state powers to search and collect personal data about its citizens, while in the UK, the Prevent strategy – initially introduced as part of the anti-terrorist CONTEST approach in 2003 as a response to 9/11 and significantly strengthened after the 7/7 London bombings – has made it mandatory for public institutions to report potential cases of radicalisation to the authorities (Qurashi 2018).

In other contexts, the perceived threats of newer religions to public safety and public order have resulted in legislation that specially targets minority religions. In France, responding to cases of violence by new religions including the murders and mass suicides by the Order of the Solar Temple and seeking to address a moral panic about cults, the government enacted the 2001 so-called 'About-Picard Law'. The Act legally demarcated the differences between authentic 'religions' and 'cultic movements' (*mouvements sectaires*) and created a new category of criminal misdemeanour called 'abuse of weakness' (*abus de faiblesse*) of vulnerable individuals. The law also enabled the state to dissolve religious groups whose executives have been found guilty of certain crimes. In 2004, Arnaud Mussy, a leader of a small millenarian group called Néo-Phare was convicted of the new crime of 'abuse of weakness' after one of his followers committed suicide (Altglas 2010; Palmer 2011). It is important to note that not all state responses have been grounded in cases of religious violence. In the past two decades, the Chinese government has adopted from Euro-American discourses and legal categorisations of officially sanctioned 'religions' and illegal 'cults' (*xie jiao*, translated as 'evil cult') to crack down on minority religions including the Falun Gong and the Church of Almighty God (Edelman and Richardson 2005; Irons 2018; Richardson 2011; Yang 2012).

Like many other national governments responding to terrorism, the Japanese government faced a range of legal and political obstacles in the wake of the Tokyo attack. Some legal hurdles were relatively simple to overcome, such as making sarin production a criminal offence.[1] Other, more sensitive, problems regarding the state regulation of religion touched upon fundamental constitutional values of freedom of religion and freedom of association. Put simply, can a religious group that has committed terrorism continue to exist?

There were four key legal developments in the state's handling of the 'Aum Problem': firstly, the government initially attempted to dissolve Aum through an application of the controversial Prevention of Destructive Activity Act (commonly known as *habōhō*, shortened from *hakaiteki katsudō bōshi hō* in Japanese, abbreviated here to PDAA); secondly, the reform of the Religious Corporations

[1] Sarin tō ni yoru jinshin higai no bōshi ni kansuru hōritsu 1995, 21 April. Act No.78.

Act altered the accreditation method for granting preferential tax exemption to religious organisations; thirdly, the enactment of a new set of 'Aum Laws' placed Aum's successor under state surveillance and held the group financially accountable for damages, and fourthly, the belated creation of a set of laws provided state-funded financial relief to victims of Aum's murders and terrorist attacks.

Prevention of Destructive Activity Act (PDAA)

Following the arrests of Aum's leadership, the focus of public debate shifted from bringing suspects to justice to discussing how the remaining organisation should be regulated and possibly disbanded. In October 1995, the Tokyo District Court revoked Aum's 'religious corporation' status, a charity status that gave Aum not only preferential tax treatment but also a mark of public respectability. The Tokyo government had granted the status to Aum in 1989, despite opposition from believers' parents. Following the revocation of the status, officials confiscated Aum's assets and Aum lost its formal status as a legal body, hereafter becoming an unincorporated organisation (*nin'i dantai*). Aum sued to void the decision but the revocation was well-grounded in law, and the decision was upheld by the Tokyo High Court in December 1995, as well as by the Supreme Court in January 1996.

Whilst the revocation of Aum's public status was relatively straightforward, the question of whether Aum should be disbanded completely was altogether separate and much more complex. With Aum's leaders in custody, remaining members – although fewer in number – continued to live in shared accommodation across the country much as before. The government's initial plan was to apply the Prevention of Destructive Activity Act (PDAA) to Aum to forcibly dissolve it. The PDAA is a repressive law established in 1952, originally intended to curtail leftist activism in the context of the Cold War and McCarthyism in the United States. Theoretically, the Act could be applied to individuals or groups and enabled the state to forcibly dissolve and outlaw anti-social, 'destructive' groups that threatened domestic security (Reader 2001: 228). Liberal and leftist parties, including the Social Democratic Party of Japan in the 1994–6 coalition government, had previously opposed the Act on the basis that it gave too much power to the state and that it potentially violated Article 21 of the Constitution, which guaranteed freedom of association. The debates were further complicated by the fact that, given the Act's historical context, it had not explicitly provisioned for *religious* terrorism or the disbandment of religious organisations. A forced dissolution of a religious organisation potentially contravened the constitutional freedom of religion as enshrined in Article 20 of the Constitution.

The application of the PDAA was widely supported by public opinion, with 79 per cent of the public stating in a straw poll that it should be applied to Aum.[2]

[2] *Yomiuri Shimbun* (1995), 'Shūkyō hōjin hō kaisei 83% ga sansei, tai Oumu habōhō tekiyō 79%', 23 November, p. 1.

Amongst politicians, however, opinion was more mixed. The ruling Social Democratic Party, which had vehemently opposed the Act's enactment in 1952, was initially reluctant to apply the PDAA, due to its sweeping powers and lack of precedence, with some party members considering the Act unconstitutional. In October 1995, Prime Minister Murayama Tomiichi made a special request to the Ministry of Justice demanding 'extra prudence' in making an application for the application of the PDAA. Members of the Liberal Democratic Party, nominally the junior coalition partner, were also split over whether the application was essential, given that the key culprits had already been arrested.[3]

Among the national newspapers, editorial opinions were divided along the political spectrum. The conservative paper *Yomiuri Shimbun* defended the move as necessary and urgent.[4] By contrast, the *Asahi Shimbun*, historically a flag-bearer of progressivism, opposed the application of the PDAA, arguing that it was unconstitutional and merely handed the Public Security Intelligence Agency (PSIA) more investigative powers and funding that it did not need.[5] The Japan PEN Club (the national branch of the free speech advocacy organisation PEN International) and the Japanese Federation of Bar Associations both opposed the application of the Act as unconstitutional and a breach of fundamental liberties.[6]

While it may first appear counter-intuitive that so many politicians were anxious about disbanding a group that had just committed the largest-ever terrorist attack at the heart of Japan's largest metropolis, these divisions amongst politicians, mass media, and other stakeholders can only be understood with reference to long-term institutional memories of political and religious repression under the pre-1945 militarist regime. Under the military-fascist state, which ended only with Japan's defeat in the Second World War, all forms of organisations, including political parties, professional organisations, trade unions, and religions, faced the stark choice between collaboration with the government or severe and violent repression. Religious persecution prior to Japan's defeat in 1945 was both widespread and violent. As Benjamin Dorman (2012a) argues, Shinto worship was enforced upon the national population between 1868 and 1945 as a civic duty comprising part of the 'national body' (*kokutai*) ideology, and authorities and mass media vilified new religions in particular as 'lewd and evil cults' (*inshi jakyō*). Perhaps most notably, the new religion Ōmoto, a movement founded in the late 19th century by Deguchi Nao, was persecuted and shut down by state authorities on two separate occasions in 1921 and 1935. The group was investigated on suspicion of

[3] *Yomiuri Shimbun* (1995), '"Habōhō" Murayama Shushō no taido itten; yotō nai no shinchōron han'ei', 4 November, p. 3.

[4] *Yomiuri Shimbun* (1995), 'Habōhō no tetsuzuki wa shukushuku to susumeyo', 15 December, p. 3.

[5] *Asahi Shimbun* (1995), 'Habōhō rongi wa uwasuberi da', 28 September, p. 5.

[6] *Asahi Shimbun* (1995), 'Iken no utagai koi 'pandora' no hō', 18 December (Eve. Ed.), p. 7; *Yomiuri Shimbun* (1995), 'Oumu Shinrikyō ni taisuru habōhō tekiyō hantai seimei', 6 October, p. 19.

lèse-majesté and for the violation of the Peace Preservation Act, a notorious law that initially targeted left activism but later expanded to curtail any form of religious and civil activism that the authorities saw as a threat to public order. On both occasions, its leader and Nao's son-in-law Deguchi Onisaburō was arrested and detained. In the second police raid, other members of the leadership were tortured, and the headquarters were razed to the ground. The leadership was eventually acquitted of all charges in 1942, but not before dozens of followers were killed under torture and the group suffered massive financial and reputational damage. The bloody history of violent religious persecution, combined with the PDAA's dubious legacy as explicitly anti-Communist legislation, prompted many stakeholders to oppose the Act being applied to Aum. For progressives and liberals, the freedom of association and freedom of religion were inalienable rights, even if this meant begrudgingly allowing Aum to exist, while conservative politicians that wanted to see Aum dissolved were fearful of being linked to the difficult legacies of the pre-1945 regime.

The Prime Minister eventually gave the go-ahead to the PSIA to dissolve Aum through the PDAA at the end of 1995.[7] However, the government's plan to forcibly dissolve Aum did not come to fruition. In 1997, the Public Security Examination Commission, a body under the Ministry of Justice that considers PDAA applications, rejected PSIA's claims, ruling that the application did not meet one of the necessary criteria for dissolving a group that the group in question presented an imminent security threat and that it could engage in repeated destructive activities in the future.[8] As authorities sought alternative solutions to disband or regulate Aum, the group continued to practice much as before, albeit under the close scrutiny of law enforcement.

Religious Corporations Act (RCA)

The second significant legal development that occurred in parallel with debates about PDAA was a proposed reform of the Religious Corporations Act (*shūkyō hōjin hō*, RCA). The original Religious Corporations Act, passed in 1951 by the Supreme Commander for the Allied Powers led by the US, formed a relatively laissez-faire framework in which regional governments oversaw the registration and monitoring of religious organisations by granting recognised religions the status of a legal person and offering them preferential tax rates. Under existing laws, Prefectural Governors granted religious corporation status to individual

[7] *Yomiuri Shimbun* (1995), 'Oumu ni habōhō tekiyō. Nennai nimo kaisan seikyū tetsuzuki', 14 December, p. 1; *Asahi Shimbun* (1995), '"Hō no ginen" kienu mama. Oumu Shinrikyō ni habōhō tekiyō e', 15 December, p. 2.

[8] *Yomiuri Shimbun* (1997), 'Oumu Shinrikyō e no Habōhō tekiyō no seikyū Kōanshin ga kikyaku kettei', 31 January (Eve. Ed.), p. 1.

organisations, with relatively little oversight from the central government. As the historical circumstances surrounding Aum's accreditation process became clearer, critics highlighted some flaws in the existing legislation: Aum had exploited the religious corporation status as a badge of public respectability to attract new members and had benefited from lower tax rates to run side-businesses, including a merchandise shop, a restaurant, and a computer hardware shop. More seriously, the decentralised administrative system meant that the Tokyo Metropolitan Government, with which Aum was registered, had no oversight whatsoever of Aum's illegal activities in its headquarters in Yamanashi Prefecture, 100 km to the west of Tokyo.

Like the application of PDAA, RCA reform had overwhelming public support, with 85 per cent agreeing that the law needed to be reformed, surely a reflection of the public distrust towards 'religions' as something that is outside and in tension with 'civil society'.[9] However, like the debate surrounding the PDAA, widespread public support did not translate into cross-party consensus, as the RCA quickly became the topic of intense party politics. The conservative LDP saw the RCA reform as an opportunity to undermine Kōmeitō, a party supported by members of the lay Buddhist movement, Sōka Gakkai. Although the LDP and Kōmeitō have had coalition agreements since 1999, the two parties had had a strained and often hostile relationship in the second half of the 20th century, as Sōka Gakkai's ambitious and forceful proselytisation tactics to transform Japan's religious landscape had come under repeated public criticism. Thus, the LDP wanted to use the RCA reform to weaken Kōmeito's influence on national politics. Unsurprisingly, the opposition party, New Frontier Party (NFP), which had arisen out of a short-lived merger between Kōmeitō and several other parties between 1994 and 1997, opposed sweeping RCA reforms.

New religions were also conflicted over proposed changes. The Federation of New Religious Organisations (*Shinshuren*) – which represents many Japanese new religions and has had a historic rivalry with Sōka Gakkai – supported the LDP but lobbied against the reforms, fearing that this would have the double effect of increasing political interference into religions and decreasing the ability of religions to intervene in political issues (Klein 2012). Eventually, the pro-reform faction won, and the reformed Religious Corporations Act was passed in December 1995, coming into effect in September 1996. The changes were relatively limited in scope, and less restrictive than many religious organisations had feared. The reformed Act brought the registration system under central administration by the Ministry of Culture (renamed in 2000 as MEXT: the Ministry of Education, Culture, Sports, Science and Technology) for religions operating

[9] *Yomiuri Shimbun* (1995), 'Oumu jiken to shūkyōkan, "Shūkyō banare" ichidan to kasoku', 27 June, p. 13.

across multiple prefectures.[10] It also expanded the state's authority to investigate religious organisations and required registered organisations to file annual financial records for greater transparency (Inoue N 2011: 410–12).

Security laws

The third wave of legal responses that institutionalised and routinised state responses to the Aum Affair in law was a new set of security-related laws pertaining to Aum's legal obligations and long-term surveillance of the group. These changes sought to hold Aum legally and financially accountable, even after it had lost its status as a religious corporation and had been declared bankrupt.

Following the PSIA's unsuccessful attempt to disband Aum through the PDAA, the state saw a need for new legislation that would enable authorities to continue to monitor Aum continuously. The 1999 Act Relating to the Regulation of Organisations Which Have Committed Indiscriminate Mass Murder (*Musabetsu tairyō satsujin kōi o okonatta dantai no kisei ni kansuru hōritsu*), abbreviated here as the Organisations Regulation Act (ORA, *Dantai Kisei hō*), effectively replaced the PDAA for keeping Aum under state surveillance. As the name suggests, the Act placed groups that have committed indiscriminate mass murder under state supervision for an initial period of three years, with the possibility for extending it indefinitely. Unlike the PDAA, which forcibly dissolved any organisation targeted by the security authorities, the ORA enabled organisations to continue to exist, subject to various conditions such as regular submissions of reports of financial and personnel details, as well as complying with unannounced searches by the police and PSIA.

The Act was a major victory for security agencies, especially the PSIA. Prior to the Aum Affair, in the face of a decline of right-wing and left-wing terrorism in the 1980s and 1990s, the PSIA had faced the possibility of severe budget cuts and possible closure. The enactment of the ORA came at an opportune time that secured the agency's future longevity. The legislature also passed a corollary Act which enabled the state to recover assets belonging to organisations monitored under the ORA.[11] The law ensured that Aum's successor organisations remained liable for the same financial liabilities and obligations, even if they set up new groups or changed their name. In the end, the effects of the ORA were relatively limited; after all, security authorities had been continuously monitoring Aum's activities even before the ORA was passed. Perhaps more disconcerting were the public's responses to the ORA being applied to Aum. Once the courts permitted ORA to be applied to Aum,

[10] Shūkyō hōjinhō no ichibu o kaisei suru hōritsu, 1995. Act No.134.

[11] Tokutei hasan hōjin no hasan zaidan ni zokusubeki zaisan no kaifuku ni kansuru tokubetsu sochihō, 1999. Act No. 148.

this re-ignited public anxieties towards Aum's remaining members, triggering local resident protests demanding Aum's expulsion from their neighbourhoods across the country. In response, municipal governments cited the ORA as a normative (if not legal) justification for implementing discriminatory policies against Aum members.

Compensation for victims

The fourth set of laws relating to financial assistance to victims developed much more slowly than security-related laws. From the initial response immediately after the Tokyo attack until 2008, the government held that victims should seek financial compensation from the perpetrators through the civil courts, and that the government was not party to these disputes. As a result, victims of Aum's crimes faced significant hurdles in recovering financial losses. The first obstacle pertained to the fact that Aum was unable to repay vast sums of compensation that the courts awarded to claimants including individual victims, the Tokyo Metro Company, the Tokyo Metropolitan Government, and the national government. As a result, Aum was formally declared bankrupt in 1996. Secondly, as bankruptcy law stated that official bodies and corporations were entitled to recover debt before individual claimants, these individuals would have received a much smaller share of the compensation than they were originally awarded in court. Following extensive lobbying by victims led by Takahashi Shizue (see Chapter 7), the government passed a special law in 1998 to prioritise individual claimants over official bodies. Although this was a small victory for victims' rights advocates, Aum's limited assets meant that only a small proportion of the compensation was recoverable.

As a result of extensive activism by victims' rights groups, in addition to gradual broader shifts in state responses to crime, the 2004 Basic Act Relating to Victims of Crime (*hanzai higaisha tō kihon hō*) fundamentally shifted the state's stance on victims' entitlement to state assistance.[12] The Basic Act spelled out responsibilities for national and municipal governments to proactively assist individual victims of crime. This paved the way for the enactment of the landmark 2008 law, The Act Relating to the Provision of Payments for the Relief of Victims of Aum Shinrikyō's Crimes (*Oumu Shinrikyō hanzai higaisha tō o kyūsai suru tameno kyūfukin no shikyū ni kansuru hōritsu*), abbreviated here as the Victims Relief Act (VRA). The law set up a system of one-off relief payments to victims and bereaved family members of Aum's crimes, including the 1989 murder of the Sakamoto family, the two terror attacks, and other murders and assassination attempts. Crucially, this excluded victims who were members or ex-members at the time.[13]

[12] Hanzai higaisha tō kihon hō, 2004, 8 December. Act No. 161.
[13] *Asahi Shimbun* (2008), 'Oumu kyūsai yōyaku', 12 June, p. 37.

Beyond the financial implications for the victims, the VRA was a symbolic statement of the state's denunciation of crimes committed by Aum. The first article of the Act situated the moral impact of Aum's violent crimes as a heinous assault on the nation's governing institutions. It declared that provision of assistance in the form of relief payments was significant for making clear the state's stance in their fight against terrorism.[14] The relief fund, which was funded by the state in conjunction with private donations and successor organisations, provided financial aid to 5,859 applicants to the sum of ¥2,806,400,000 (approximately US$280 million) until the programme concluded in 2010 (National Police Agency 2010). However, a minority of victims refused to accept compensation on the basis that they did not wish to be reminded of the attack.[15] Whatever the original intentions, the legislation was a fault-line which caused a clash between the will to acknowledge and remember, on the one hand, and the will to forget and move on, on the other.

Criminal trials of perpetrators

Besides legislative measures designed to prevent similar cases from occurring in the future, the Aum Affair resulted in hundreds of criminal trials involving scores of defendants on a raft of charges. Due to the sheer number of cases being considered, and the fact that many of the defendants stood accused of multiple serious charges, trials of the leadership took several years, with Hayashi Ikuo being one of the first culprits to receive a life sentence in 1998. Asahara's trial took considerably longer, with the first verdict passed down in 2004 and finalised in 2006.

Asahara's trial was complicated by the numerous charges that he faced, the amount of evidence, the number of witnesses called to testify, Asahara's behaviour, and the defence team's strained relationship with the court. Asahara's behaviour during the detention was a source of considerable controversy. During the first months that he was placed under custody, he sent messages to his adherents via his lawyer to continue their training.[16] In the trial proceedings, he initially pleaded not guilty. As the hearings progressed, however, his comments became increasingly erratic and incomprehensible, before eventually falling silent for the remainder of the trials. Whether this was voluntary or the result of deteriorating mental health has been fiercely contested.[17] During the appeals process, Asahara's

[14] Oumu Shinrikyō hanzai higaisha tō o kyūsai suru tameno kyūfukin no shikyū ni kansuru hōritsu, 2008 18 June. Act No. 80.

[15] *Yomiuri Shimbun* (2010), 'Chikatesu sarin "wasuretai" kyūfukin shinsei jitai mo', 19 March, p. 39.

[16] *Yomiuri Shimbun* (1995), 'Asahara hikoku ga gokuchū kara kyōdan ni soshiki gatame shiji Kōan chōsachō, habōhō tekiyō no konkyo ni', 2 October, p. 1.

[17] For contrasting responses to Asahara's silence during the trials, see Aonuma (2007) and Mori (2012). Aonuma is confident that Asahara's silence was a sign of his attempt to evade responsibility, while Mori asserts that he was visibly mentally ill during the final hearings (Chapter 6).

defence team released a whistle-blower account by a prison inmate, who described Asahara as being unable to communicate with the guards, barely able to stand, and incontinent (Asahara Kōsoshin Bengonin 2006). Although some – including Asahara's third daughter Rika, and the filmmaker Mori Tatsuya – had called for a stay of execution on medical grounds, some critics argued that Asahara was simply faking illness to avoid the death penalty.

The trials of other key culprits were also lengthy and complicated, partly due to Murai Hideo's untimely death. While some culprits such as Niimi Tomomitsu never renounced their faith in Asahara, many others did, and claimed that they were coerced or under the influence of mind control (see Chapter 8). However, claims of mind control were almost entirely rejected by the court, which ruled that all the individuals had acted out of their free will. As an exception, Inoue Yoshihiro, who led the ground-level operation in the Tokyo attack and orchestrated several terrorist attacks during the investigation, was initially sentenced to life, as the verdict acknowledged the effect of mind control. However, on appeal, the sentence was revised up to the death penalty, ruling that he had acted voluntarily. By the end of the 'Aum trials' (*Oumu saiban*), a total of 13 people had been sentenced to death by hanging. Many of them were members of Murai Hideo's Science and Technology team, having been personally involved in the manufacture of deadly chemicals as well as the terrorist attacks. Others, such as Hayakawa Kiyohide, Minister of Construction, and Inoue Yoshihiro, Minister of Intelligence, were accomplices in multiple cases of murder and assassination attempts. Of the five assailants that placed the sarin bags on the train carriages, only Hayashi Ikuo, who killed two in the attack, escaped the death penalty on the basis that he had shown evidence of genuine regret and remorse. By contrast, Yokoyama Masato, whose attack resulted in no fatalities, received the death penalty. Four of the getaway drivers for the Tokyo attack also received life sentences, while the fifth driver, Niimi Tomomitsu, was sentenced to death by hanging for his role in the Sakamoto murders and the Matsumoto and Tokyo attacks.

While the cases were ongoing in the criminal court, there were also numerous disputes in the civil court. Aum and its successor organisations have repeatedly appealed against the application of the ORA, which has been renewed to the present day. Notably, following the release of Jōyū Fumihiro from prison in late 1999, Aum announced that it would rename itself Aleph to signal a new beginning. This was seen as a strategy to avoid being subject to laws which specifically named Aum Shinrikyō: however, this move was ineffectual, as the ORA extended to any successor organisation deemed to have continuities with past groups. In 2007, following several years of animosity between Jōyū's faction, seen as a 'reformist' faction, and the 'loyalist' faction led by Asahara's wife Tomoko, Jōyū announced a split from Aleph, forming his own organisation, Hikari no

Wa. As of late 2021, both Aleph and Hikari no Wa continue to be monitored under the ORA.

State responses – commemoration by official bodies

The legal developments discussed above affected different areas of the law and varied in scope and effect. Nevertheless, the implications of responding to the Aum Affair through legislation were clear; the national government had recognised that Aum's crimes were significant for the nation-state and required a wholesale response. Yet, while acknowledging the national significance of the Aum Affair through legislation, the government has played an insignificant role in the coordination and choreography of commemorative processes beyond the legal arena. Large-scale events, such as commemorative ceremonies and symposia have been hosted almost entirely by private actors, with politicians and state officials playing a secondary role as participants and speakers.

In a notable exception to the state's apparent reluctance to commemorate, the Police Museum in Tokyo held a temporary exhibition in March 2015 to mark 20 years after the Tokyo attack. Held in the temporary exhibition hall, the exhibition consisted of numerous photographs, newspaper clippings, and informational panels that explained the historical background of Aum's violence and the police's responses to Aum since the Tokyo attack. Recordings of radio communications between emergency services played repeatedly in the background, recreating the tense atmosphere in the moments after the Tokyo attack. The exhibition also displayed replicas of protective suits worn by the Self-Defense Forces to avoid contamination, alongside other protective suits from security forces around the world. The exhibition justified the continued surveillance of Aum's successor organisations on information panels, reiterating the state's position that Asahara's teachings continue to compose a central component of activities by Aleph and Hikari no Wa, and that they could yet turn to terrorism. Perhaps unsurprisingly, the exhibition also displayed signs of selective amnesia: the exhibition made little mention of the police's flawed response to the disappearance of Sakamoto and his family in 1989, and glossed over their inadequacies in handling the investigation of the Matsumoto attack.

Elsewhere, the state has played a marginal role in commemorating the Aum Affair. Instead of hosting state-sponsored commemorative ceremonies, it has become customary for government representatives such as the Prime Minister and cabinet ministers to regularly visit Kasumigaseki Station on the anniversary of the Tokyo attack to offer flowers and to give media interviews. There are possible reasons for politicians' reluctance to take a leading role in commemorating the attack. For instance, the government may have been reluctant to choreograph official commemorative ceremonies at a time when its official position was that it would not provide state-funded financial assistance to victims, or state institutions may have wanted to avoid greater public scrutiny of uncomfortable facts in the years leading up to the Tokyo attack, such as the Tokyo Metropolitan Government's decision to grant religious corporation status to Aum, and the mishandling of police investigation in the years prior to the Tokyo attack.

Although there have been few official commemorative events, these official institutions have nevertheless engaged in the reproduction of memory narratives in different ways. In particular, the PSIA, Japan's equivalent to the UK's MI5 or the US's NSA, has been a steadfast advocate for the most stringent laws to be applied to Aum and has continuously reproduced narratives of Aum as a continuing security threat. The Aum Affair revitalised the PSIA at a time when its *raison d'être* as a bulwark against political radicalism had increasingly come under question following the end of the Cold War and the decline of far-left and far-right terrorism.[18] For the agency, the Aum Affair constituted an opportunity to redefine its purpose to identify security threats beyond political radicalism and to demonstrate its indispensability in its fight against 'cults' as a new security threat (Hughes 1998). One of the strategies the PSIA has employed has been to reiterate the continuing threat that Aum, Aleph, and Hikari no Wa pose to public safety. For instance, in a 2002 news article in *Japan Times*, a quality English-language newspaper on Japanese affairs, the PSIA spokesman emphasised that Aum 'is no less dangerous than it was seven years ago, in the sense that all of its members are under mind-control to worship Asahara', and that the membership 'is sufficient (for the cult) to engage in terrorism on a grand scale' (Matsubara 2002). These official statements have enabled journalists from inside and outside of Japan to sustain public anxieties about the scale and activity of Aum's successor organisations.

The PSIA has also pushed the official narrative of Aum as a perennial security threat through the dissemination of uncertain and unverified information through the mass media. In an illustrative case in 2000, two months after the ORA came into effect and several weeks before the fifth anniversary of the Tokyo attack, security agencies announced that Aum had been developing software for major contractors including government agencies and major telecommunications corporations (Sims 2000). This revelation raised fears that Aum had infiltrated government agencies, and that they could exploit the software for cyberterrorism or to steal confidential information.[19] Responding to the reports, the Japanese

[18] *Asahi Shimbun* (1995), 'Habōhō ni tsuyomaru kigu Oumu kyō eno dantai kisei hō tetsuzuki', 29 December, p. 4.

[19] *Yomiuri Shimbun* (2000), 'Oumu ga sennyū shita sofuto kaihatsu', 2 March, p. 3.

telecoms giant NTT announced it would review the software, while government officials and corporate executives expressed their intention to avoid doing business with Aum-related companies in the future (ibid.). To date, there has been no concrete evidence to suggest that Aum members had ever intended, or had the capacity, to commit cyber-terrorism or to steal sensitive government information. It also seems incredulous that Aum would risk jeopardising one of its core revenue streams by engaging in cyber-crime at a time the organisation was already under intense scrutiny by law enforcement. Nonetheless, official releases such as the potential 'risks' of Aum committing another high-level terrorist attack have been relayed by media with relatively little scrutiny, helping to sustain this narrative. To this extent, there is much credence to the claim by Asano Ken'ichi, a former journalist and professor of journalism studies, that the media have colluded with security agencies to portray a simplistic image of Aum as a murderous cult without independently examining the veracity of claims made by the authorities (Dorman 2001).

The PSIA's reiteration of Aum as a social menace have continued through successive applications to renew the three-year surveillance period, which have been approved by the Public Security Examination Commission. The PSIA's consistent portrayal of Aum and its successor organisations is demonstrative of the 'centripetal' nature of official discourses that attempt to fix meanings in ways that are advantageous for socially dominant groups and institutions. It also illustrates how symbolic representations of Aum as a mind-controlling cult and Japan's vulnerability to future terrorist attacks are directly tied to material and political interests of different state agencies. Despite its initial defeat in the debate over the PDAA, the PSIA's victory through the enactment of the ORA has given the organisation a powerful legal mandate to supervise Aum – and, perhaps most importantly, a budget to match.

Mediated commemoration

In contrast to sparse instances of state-led commemoration, mass media commemoration of the Aum Affair has been both voluminous and consistent. Various media outlets have produced intense bursts of Aum-related stories and special programmes around the anniversary of the Tokyo attack. The contents of these reports have ranged from the history of Aum prior to the attacks and the long-term effects of victims' physical and psychological trauma, to the perceived continuing threat posed by remaining members across the country. Through these commemorative reports, generally speaking, the mass media have reinforced and reproduced the dominant trauma narrative that situates Aum as a dangerous cult that could commit another terrorist attack.

Matsumoto re-remembered

Media commemoration of Matsumoto has been qualitatively distinctive from other media representations of the Aum Affair. While many media reports and re-enactments have tended to focus on the profiles of the perpetrators, media discussions of Matsumoto have usually discussed Kōno Yoshiyuki's experiences as the victim of a false accusation. This has meant that the binary code of Japan as 'good' and Aum as 'evil' has been somewhat attenuated in representations of Matsumoto as a 'difficult past'. For example, marking five years since the Matsumoto attack, both the *Yomiuri* and *Asahi* newspapers ran a series of commemorative reports. These featured interviews with survivors still suffering from the physical and psychological after-effects of sarin poisoning. The stories told of feelings of loss experienced by the victims' families, but, crucially, they included extended interviews with Kōno as the main protagonist of a social drama.[20] The centrality of Kōno as the tragic protagonist was reiterated in the Matsumoto mayor's annual visits to Kōno's unconscious wife in hospital, until she passed away in 2008; local newspapers reported on these annual visitations to Kōno and his wife, even when other forms of commemorative media coverage were absent.[21]

Kōno has been the subject of commemoration in television and film as well. The 2000 feature film *Japan's Black Summer: False Accusation* (*Nihon no kuroi natsu: Enzai*) by the director Kumai Kei reconstructs the night of the Matsumoto attack and the subsequent police investigation (Kumai 2000). In the film, a team of secondary-school reporters interviews a local television station and a character based on Kōno to retrace the circumstances of the attack, to discover why an innocent victim was falsely accused as a potential suspect. Kōno played an advisory role in the making of the film, and some scenes were filmed inside his home and in the streets of Matsumoto, contributing to a sense of realism. Similarly, a 2009 TV documentary-drama by broadcaster Fuji Terebi recreated Kōno and his family's ordeal, featuring interviews with Kōno and his children.[22] In these symbolic

[20] *Asahi Shimbun* (1999), 'Sarin no kyōfu kiezu: Matsumoto sarin jiken, kyō de 5 nen', 27 June, p. 25; *Yomiuri Shimbun* (1999), 'Kyōkō no ato: Matsumoto sarin jiken kara 5 nen (1)', 22 June, p. 28; (1999), 'Kyōkō no ato: Matsumoto sarin jiken kara 5 nen (3)', 24 June, p. 34.; for interview with Kōno, see *Asahi Shimbun* (1999), '"Higaisha shien no jūjitsu o' Matsumoto sarin jiken 5 nen de shinpo', 28 June (Nagano Ed.), p. 27; (2004), '"Mimai uketekureta. Omoi" Kōno san tsuma no nyūin saki ni Oumu', 27 June (Nagano Ed.), p. 32; *Yomiuri Shimbun* (1999), 'Kyōkō no ato: Matsumoto sarin jiken kara 5 nen (2)', 23 June, p. 26.

[21] *Asahi Shimbun* (2004), '"Teisei wa sumiyaka ni" Kōno Yoshiyuki san, shinpo de teigen', 27 June (Nagano Ed.), p. 37; *Yomiuri Shimbun* (2000), 'Matsumoto sarin jiken kara, maru 6 nen', 28 June, p. 32; (2002), 'Matsumoto sarin jiken no Kōno Sumiko san Ariga Shichō ga mimai', 28 June (Nagano Ed.), p. 32.

[22] *Asahi Shimbun* (2009), 'Tsuma yo! Matsumoto sarin jiken: Hinichijō ga nichijō ni natta', 22 June, p. 17.

representations, the primary narrative centred on Kōno's personal biography, not on the broader context of Aum's crimes.

The Tokyo subway attack in mass media

While Matsumoto has been commemorated in various media, the volume of media discourse that it has generated has paled in comparison to commemorative reports of the Tokyo attack. On the first anniversary of the Tokyo attack, many newspapers presented vivid descriptions of the attack as survivors and emergency responders re-narrated the horror and panic of the attack. *Yomiuri Shimbun*'s editorial on the anniversary of the attack emphasised that for both bereaved families and survivors, 'the deep wounds were still raw.'[23] As the years have passed, however, graphic accounts have given way to discussions about the long-term effects of the Aum Affair. An article in *Yomiuri Shimbun* marking the third anniversary stressed that 'bereaved families and the injured have not yet been able to heal their wounds to their body and mind.' The story narrated the sorrow of a widow and mother who was nine months pregnant when her husband was killed: the daughter, now nearly three, only recognises her late father through old photographs.[24] The media have frequently narrated the irreversible damage the attack has inflicted on ordinary people, and survivors and bereaved families have also expressed inextinguishable anger towards Aum. In an article marking the twentieth anniversary of the attack, a victim's mother emphatically stated, 'I cannot forgive Aum. This anger will never change.'[25]

While many newspapers have covered the anniversary of the Tokyo with dutiful regularity, they have also addressed the victims' concerns that their experiences are being quietly forgotten. In 2006, reflecting on the gradual loss of public interest in Aum, the widow and activist Takahashi Shizue lamented that the memory is weathering and being forgotten in spite of the continuing daily struggles of victims.[26] Beyond the media's critical treatment of Aum, then, mass media have acted as a platform upon which victims have articulated these commemorative speech acts by stressing that the Tokyo attack must not be forgotten.[27]

[23] *Yomiuri Shimbun* (1996), 'Chikatetsu sarin 1 nen to anzen shakai', 19 March, p. 3.

[24] *Yomiuri Shimbun* (1998), 'Chikatetsu sarin 3 nen jiken yokugetsu tanjō no Asuka chan, shashin no papa daisuki', 20 March, p. 39.

[25] *Yomiuri Shimbun* (2015), '"Shikkō nogare" mie kakure', 17 March, p. 38.

[26] *Asahi Shimbun* (2006), '"Fūka" mi ni shimiru" Chikatetsu sarin jiken 11 nen', 20 March (Eve. Ed.), p. 15.

[27] *Asahi Shimbun* (1998), 'Fūka sasenu okosasenu 6 eki de kenka', 20 March (Eve. Ed.), p. 27; *Yomiuri Shimbun* (2002), 'Chikatetsu sarin 7 nen "Fūka sasenai" Ireihi de chikau', 20 March (Eve Ed.), p. 18; *Yomiuri Shimbun* (2009), 'Chikatetsu sarin 14 nen Giseisha o tsuitō', 21 March, p. 38.

While many media outlets have, on the whole, reproduced the dominant narratives supported by the police and the PSIA and have often relied on information provided by them, it would be reductive to suggest that the relationship between the media and security agencies has been entirely collusive. In this sense, although elite discourse tends to be self-serving, these 'centres of power' are not necessarily singular. In contrast to state acts of commemoration, which have skirted around the history of police inaction prior to the Tokyo attack, some media reports have contained explicit criticisms of state authorities. Reflecting some of the voices of victims who felt that the police had failed to protect the public by not investigating Aum sooner, commemorative coverage has included criticism and self-criticism of law enforcement in the years prior to the Matsumoto and Tokyo attacks. This has been facilitated in recent years following the retirement of some senior police officers involved in the investigation. For example, one episode in the 2012 documentary series by the public broadcaster NHK titled *Unsolved Incident – File No. 2: The Aum Shinrikyō Affair* (*Mikaiketsu jiken – fairu 2: Oumu Shinrikyō Jiken*) relied on interviews with former police officers to reconstruct how different Prefectural Police forces had investigated Aum but had failed to fully grasp the dangers that Aum posed to the public.[28] In an article marking 20 years after the Tokyo attack, the former Superintendent General of the National Police Agency expressed regret for not taking decisive action against Aum sooner.[29]

Despite these limited critical reflections, the mass media have also been selective about which events they choose to commemorate. Many media outlets remained silent about their own involvement in popularising and legitimating Aum in the early 1990s by inviting Asahara to talk shows, debate programmes, and interviews with celebrities. Commemorative coverage often neglected to mention the infamous 'TBS Video Scandal', in which the national TV broadcaster TBS was indirectly linked to the murders of the Sakamoto family. In October 1989, a week before the murders, Aum's senior disciples entered the TBS headquarters demanding to see Sakamoto's interview footage, which had been filmed for a segment to be aired at a later date. TBS showed them the tape, and, upon Aum's protestations, agreed not to air it. Days later, after talks between Sakamoto and Aum broke down, Asahara gave the order to kill Sakamoto. When details of this encounter emerged in 1996, TBS instigated a cover-up and denied showing Aum the interview footage, until evidence emerged to the contrary (see also Gardner 1999; Hardacre 2007). Although the scandal led to the resignation of

[28] NHK's 'Unsolved Incident' series follows criminal cases of considerable public interest. Other episodes are unrelated to the Aum Affair.

[29] *Asahi Shimbun* (2015), '(Oumu o tou Chikatetsu sarin 20 nen: 4) Moto keishi sōkan Yonemura Toshirō san', 19 March, p. 38.

TBS's CEO and senior staff, this event received only limited attention in subsequent media reports.

Beyond elite commemoration: Grassroots ritualised remembrance

Beyond state commemoration, different civic actors have held various forms of commemorative rituals, such as memorial ceremonies, fundraising concerts, public symposia, and annual press conferences. These commemorative speech acts have tended to vary greatly in scope and content, as some interventions have been explicitly critical of state responses to the Aum Affair.

Outside of the mass media, numerous actors have used various media to commemorate the Tokyo attacks. A year after the attack, the Tokyo Metro Company (then known as *Eidan*) collected video testimonies of station staff to share the memories of the attack among its employees.[30] The Subway Sarin Incident Victims' Society (see Chapter 7) has also self-published books and booklets to communicate their experiences directly to the public. In 1997, marking the second anniversary, the Victims' Society self-published a collection of victims' memoirs titled *The Yellow Collection of Memoranda* (*Kiiroi Shuki-shū*), which was distributed for free by volunteers outside Kasumigaseki Station. The following year, the group published a collection of victims' writings entitled *Still We Keep Living* (*Soredemo Ikite Iku*) (Chikatetsu Sarin Jiken Higaisha no Kai 1998). In direct contradiction to official commemorative narratives which tended to omit references to the police missteps prior to the Tokyo attack, some of the contributions sharply criticised the police for their inaction. In 2007, the group published another collection of writings, this time with contributions from prominent public figures including the former Prime Minister Murayama Tomiichi, journalists, victims, and members of the public. The booklet, titled *What the Subway Sarin Incident Meant for Me* (*Watashi ni totte no chikatetsu sarin jiken*) (Chikatetsu Sarin Jiken Higaisha no Kai 2007) contains a rich tapestry of narratives which details the personal impact of Aum's crimes on individual relationships, careers, and worldviews (ibid.). The book was distributed for free to attendees of a commemorative symposium organised by the group to revitalise and preserve memory narratives from what they perceived to be the inevitable tide of 'weathering'. Continuing in this vein, marking 15 years after the attack, the Victims' Society made and distributed a DVD-only documentary featuring Takahashi Shizue interviewing other victims, their families, experts, and investigators (ibid.). While such forms of mediated commemoration have not necessarily enjoyed large-scale

30 *Yomiuri Shimbun* (1996), 'Chikatetsu sarin 1 nen (2) Joyaku no ishi, kōhai e', 12 March, p. 30.

circulation compared with the national reach of newspapers, television, radio, and magazines, the Victims' Society, under Takahashi's leadership, has continuously engaged in mediated memory work to preserve and disseminate narratives to be shared with the wider public. However, this is not to suggest that victims have universally supported efforts to reproduce memories of the trauma. According to Aoki Yumiko, who edited a number of Aum-related publications including *Still We Keep Living* and *What the Subway Sarin Incident Meant for Me*, there were many survivors who declined to be interviewed or to write contributions for these projects. They could not even look at books on Aum in bookshops and had to avoid anything that reminded them of Aum.[31] For them, it was more important to forget the traumatic past and to move on.

Commemorative ceremonies continue to play a central role in the public remembrance of the Tokyo attack. Every year, the Tokyo Metro Company has observed a minute of silence on the morning of 20 March at 8 a.m. This annual memorial service is attended only by Metro employees; this arrangement arose out of consideration for commuters who might not want to be reminded of the sarin attack as they travelled to work.[32] Instead of holding public ceremonies the company temporarily converts the offices of the six worst affected stations as a sacred space where members of the public can visit to offer prayers and flowers. The station office, cut off from the usual prosaic space of the metro concourse, serves as a temporary memorial space which allows visitors to offer prayers for the dead without affecting the daily running of the stations. When I visited Kasumigaseki Station on 20 March 2015, I was welcomed solemnly by numerous station employees near the Chiyoda Line ticket barriers and was ushered into the room by station staff (Figure 5.1). Camera crews stood in the corridor on the approach to the office, ready to take photographs (with the visitor's consent). Upon entering the room, I was struck by the juxtaposition of sacred Japanese funerary symbols in a room otherwise reserved for mundane office work. At the end of the room was a table covered with a white cloth. A wooden object resembling a tombstone (a rectangular pillar) sat atop the table, with offertory flowers surrounding it. To the left of the entrance was the service desk, again covered in white cloth, where I signed the register: another funerary custom. On the other side of the desk were several staff in uniform who stood and watched solemnly as I offered a bouquet of white lilies, a flower commonly associated with funerals, followed by a silent prayer. To the right of the entrance was another table stacked with bouquets of flowers from previous visitors. From available photographs of the commemoration from previous years, it appears that the design and routine of this custom has

[31] Interview with Aoki Yumiko, 8 July 2016.

[32] *Asahi Shimbun* (1996), 'Chikatetsu sarin jiken asu 1nen Giseisha deta 6 eki de kenka uketsuke', 19 March, p. 34.

Figure 5.1 Metro employees (in black suits) greet visitors at the Kasumigaseki commemorative event, 2015. Media personnel in the left background. Photograph by the author.

remained consistent over the years. This act of offering flowers at Kasumigaseki Station, in the absence of state-led commemorative ceremonies, has become customary in the political calendar for senior politicians. Successive prime ministers and cabinet members have visited the station on the anniversary of the attack as the site has become the de facto official commemorative site (Figure 5.2).[33] Aum and Aleph representatives have also visited Kasumigaseki on a regular basis to issue apologies and to offer flowers to the dead (but only after 2000), adding to its symbolic significance as a temporary, but sacred, site of memory.[34] In 2015,

[33] *Asahi Shimbun* (1998), 'Fūka sasenu okosasenu 6 eki de kenka', 20 March (Eve. Ed.), p. 27; (2000), 'Anohi e mokutō chikatetsu sarin kara 5nen, Chiyoda sen, Kasumigaseki eki', 21 March, p. 1; (2005), '"Sanjō, imamo hakkirito" chikatesu sarin jiken kara 10nen de tsuitō', 21 March, p. 39; *Yomiuri Shimbun* (2010), 'Chikatetsu sarin 15 nen izoku ni "kugiri" nai', 20 March (Eve. Ed.), p. 1; (2015), 'Kyōaku tero wasurenu chikatestu sarin 20 nen', 20 March (Eve. Ed.), p. 1.

[34] *Asahi Shimbun* (2003), 'Chikatetsu sarin jiken kara 8 nen ienu kanashimi, genba de mokutō', 20 March (Eve. Ed.), p. 27; *Yomiuri Shimbun* (2000), 'Chikatetsu sarin jiken "shazai to hoshō o jikko" Oumu ga komento', 20 March, p. 38; (2015), 'Kokoro no kizu nao fukaku "murikai" "fūka" nayamu higaisha', 21 March, p. 39.

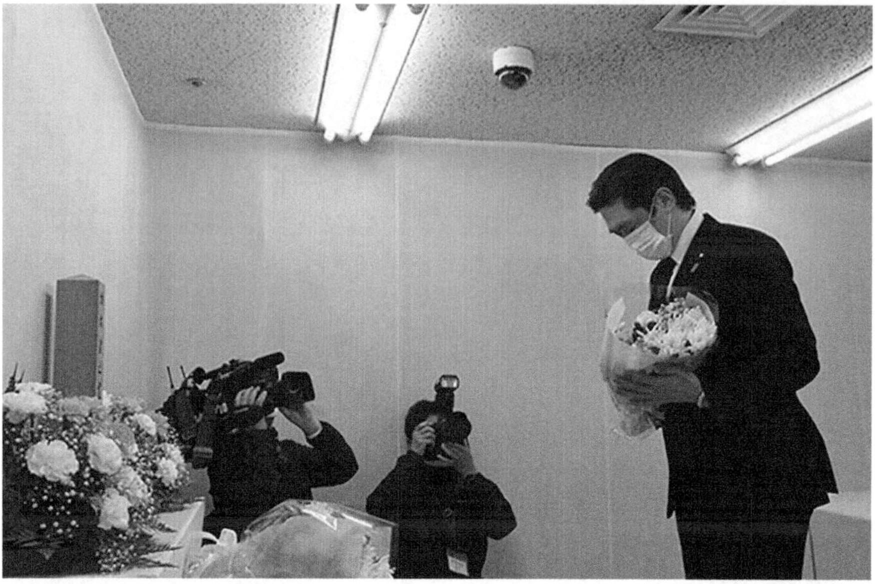

Figure 5.2 Iwai Shigeki, Senior Vice-Minister of Land, Infrastructure, Transport and Tourism, offers flowers at Kasumigaseki Station, 2021. Photograph by the Ministry of Land, Infrastructure, Transport and Tourism. Reproduced under CC-BY-4.0.

on the twentieth anniversary, over a thousand people attended the event to offer flowers.[35]

There has also been an altogether different form of commemoration and therapy organised by the Recovery Support Center (RSC). The RSC is a not-for-profit organisation founded after the Tokyo sarin attack to assist victims of terrorism and natural disasters. The charity offers regular health checks and psychological care to patients suffering from post-traumatic stress disorder (PTSD) at no cost to the patients. In 2005, marking the tenth anniversary of the Tokyo sarin attack, the charity organised an event called Memorial Walking Care, a combination of therapy and commemoration. The event allowed survivors to retrace their footsteps on the day of the sarin attack in the hope of overcoming the traumatic experience by visiting different subway stations (Pendleton 2011). According to the RSC, 55 survivors and their family members participated under the supervision of doctors and nurses.[36] The post-event survey by RSC found that most people reported the walk as a positive experience.[37] It is evident that the event

[35] *Yomiuri Shimbun* (2015), 'Kokoro no kizu nao fukaku "murikai" "fūka" nayamu higaisha', 21 March, p. 39.
[36] Recovery Support Centre (2005), '10nen me no "memoriaru wōkingu kea" zenin kanpo!!' 8 April <http://rsc.or.jp/cp-bin/nikki/nikki.php?logno=200504> Accessed July 2022.
[37] Ibid.

was a significant milestone for many survivors. One survivor, who stepped on the platform of Kodenmachō Station for the first time in ten years, commented, 'there was cold sweat from all over my body, and my heart was pounding, but I think I was able to overcome it. I could remember the day of the incident, and I couldn't help but cry.'[38] The RSC's Memorial Walking Care illustrates the diverse goals of commemorative events: if the commemorative events by the Tokyo Metro and the Victims' Society were intended to preserve the memory of the Tokyo attack at a public, collective level, the memorial walk provided a path for individuals to overcome their trauma and to move forward with their lives at a personal level.

On a smaller scale, separately from the commemoration of the Tokyo and the Matsumoto attacks, relatives and friends of the Sakamoto family have organised regular 'memorial concerts' in their memory in Nagano, Niigata, and Toyama Prefectures, where their bodies were found.[39] These localised, regional practices demonstrate the endurance of commemorative practices outside of elite practices, even if they do not necessarily have a geographically wide-reaching effect.

Erasing Aum's trails: The absence of material objects

One of the most puzzling phenomena surrounding the commemoration of the Aum Affair is the contrast between the relative preponderance of mediated discourses about Aum Shinrikyō and the relative scarcity of permanent physical objects that serve as reminders of the event, such as memorials, museums, and buildings used by Aum. Neither the Matsumoto nor the Tokyo attacks led to notable efforts to construct physical monuments or memorials. In fact, the predominant trend across the country has been for stakeholders to erase visible reminders of the Aum Affair wherever possible.

Perhaps the most telling example of this is the commemorative plaque placed at Kasumigaseki Station. Despite becoming a major memorial site on the anniversary of the attack, the station has hardly any reminders that the attack ever took place, except for a small, black plaque on a wall near the ticket barriers. The black, metal plaque with gold lettering was installed in March 1996 by the Tokyo Metro Company to commemorate the two station employees killed at the station as well as the other victims killed in the attacks (Figure 5.3). Adjacent to either side of the plaque are some potted plants, which provide a sense of spatial distinction by diverting the normal flow of foot traffic away from the area. The plaque constitutes

[38] *Yomiuri Shimbun* (2005), 'Chikatetsu sarin jiken, asu de 10 nen kokoro no kizu, aruite iyasu', 19 March (Eve. Ed.), p. 18.

[39] *Asahi Shimbun* (1996), 'TV shuzai tsūji hyōteki ni', 29 February, p. 38; (2009), 'Satoko san e, omoi imamo', 4 September (Toyama Ed.), p. 27; *Yomiuri Shimbun* (2013), '"Oumu" fūka sasenai tsuitō ensōkai ni maku, ketsui wa fuhen', 4 November (Toyama Ed.), p. 27.

Figure 5.3 Memorial plaque at Kasumigaseki Station, 2016. Photograph by the author.

only an inconspicuous backdrop to the daily function of the station as a major transport hub. Although there have been some discussions about constructing permanent monuments in memory of the Tokyo attack (Pendleton 2014), such plans have not been realised, possibly due to limitations of cost, space, and public support.

Elsewhere, there have been concerted efforts to remove any physical evidence of Aum's former presence. In Matsumoto, a company dormitory building in which multiple employees died was dismantled, as was Aum's building at the heart of the legal dispute which led to the attack on Matsumoto.[40] In its place, there is a small public park with little visible evidence that the attack ever took place.[41]

The near-total elimination of material reminders of Aum is most conspicuous at Kamikuishiki village, where Aum built its largest building complex. The site was also home to *Satyam* (*satian*) No. 7, the notorious building which was constructed to mass manufacture up to 70 tonnes of sarin (the chemical plant was never completed). After Aum was declared bankrupt in early 1996, a trustee took control of its assets, after which point public authorities tore down all the building

[40] *Yomiuri Shimbun* (1999), 'Kyōkō no ato: Matsumoto sarin jiken kara 5 nen (1)', 22 June, p. 28.
[41] *Asahi Shimbun* (2012), '"Naze" gimon imamo Matsumoto sarin jiken kara 18 nen', 28 June, p. 27.

structures at the Kamikuishiki commune except *Satyam* No. 7, which was kept for several more years as evidence. The erasure of Aum from the local landscape was a long-awaited victory for Kamikuishiki's villagers, who had campaigned against Aum for years, and had united under the motto 'Not a single [Aum] believer or a building left in the village'.[42]

Local authorities eventually turned the former commune site into a publicly maintained park, where a memorial was erected to commemorate the dead; however, the memorial stone itself only reads 'cenotaph' (*ireihi*), with no explanation of the purpose of the memorial. There are conflicting accounts of why the meaning of the cenotaph remains so ambiguous. Some have reported that the lack of explicit references to the Aum Affair was to dissuade remaining Aum believers from visiting the memorial site.[43] One villager has contradicted this account, suggesting that the cenotaph was intended for Aum believers who died or were killed in Kamikuishiki, not specifically for members of the public killed by Aum.[44] The lone memorial, devoid of epigrams denoting its significance, illustrates the precarious interaction of the opposing social pressures to remember and to forget.

While the demolition of Aum's buildings effectively erased visible traces of Aum, for Kamikuishiki, the village's association with Aum's infamy proved much more difficult to efface.[45] One inventive, but ultimately unsuccessful, attempt to reverse this fortune was the construction of a theme park several kilometres away from Aum's commune. The theme park, named Gulliver's Kingdom (*Gulliver Ōkoku*), was based on Jonathan Swift's *Gulliver's Travels* and featured a 45m-wide giant statue of the eponymous character lying on the ground. The park opened in 1997 but closed in 2001, as it struggled to stay afloat amidst an economic downturn. The unsuccessful attempt to reverse Kamikuishiki's fortunes ultimately ended in the dissolution of the local authority and the erasure of the village itself. In 2006, as part of a national restructuring policy of municipal councils, the northern half of the village was absorbed by Kōfu City while the southern half was incorporated into the town of Fujikawaguchiko (Pendleton 2014: 80–81).

In recent years, there have been some attempts by residents of Kamikuishiki to reverse the process of social amnesia and to restore and preserve the region's difficult past. Takeuchi Seiichi, who was a leading figure in the village's anti-Aum movement, expressed regret in 2010 that nearly all traces of Aum had been effaced. He commented, 'we should have left even just the Satyam No.7 [the planned sarin

[42] *Asahi Shimbun* (2015), 'Oumu no kioku kyōsei sōsa 20 nen (4) kataritsugi, kōsei ni nokosu sekinin', 23 March (Yamanashi Ed.), p. 37.

[43] *Yomiuri Shimbun* (2002), 'Ōsawa Masachi san to iku Kamikuishikimura: Kioku ga tsuzukanai jidai', 20 March (Eve. Ed.), p. 15.

[44] *Yomiuri Shimbun* (2015), 'Oumu jiken 20 nen "tatemono nokosazu" shiryō wa nokori', 21 March (Yamanashi Ed.), p. 33.

[45] *Yomiuri Shimbun* (2008), '(Toikatari) Oumu no kioku no yukue', 17 March, p. 38.

plant] for future generations as a historical and moral lesson of the evil crimes.'[46] Other villagers have also proposed the creation of private and public archives to preserve and pass on the difficult past experienced by the local community, though there is currently no public archive of this kind.[47]

The impetus to erase all traces of Aum has extended to existing locations of Aum communes around the country. Since 1995, numerous resident groups and municipal authorities have made sustained efforts to drive out Aum believers through protests and social ostracism. Residents living near Aum's communes have organised demonstrations calling for the group's expulsion from their community, fearing another terrorist plot. In some areas, local committees set up surveillance tents outside Aum buildings and demanded to inspect any goods entering the premise. The groups enforced a rule of 'no engagement' by banning residents from speaking to Aum members, and vice versa.[48] This is similar to a historic form of community-wide ostracism known as '*mura hachibu*'. Only in rare cases has this tension between residents and Aum members resulted in reconciliation, a phenomenon that documentary film-maker Mori Tatsuya has captured in his documentary film *A2* (see Chapter 6).

Municipal governments sided with local residents in such disputes, even at the risk of breaking the law. Concurrent with the government's application of the ORA to Aum, many municipal governments enacted a policy of refusing resident registration records (*jūminhyō*) submitted by Aum believers. Resident records are vital for exercising civil rights and legal duties, such as submitting tax returns and voting in elections. The refusal to accept submitted resident records lacked a legal basis. In 1989, when the same tactic was used by Namino village, Kumamoto Prefecture, the dispute resulted in a costly lawsuit and a settlement that resulted in the village purchasing the estates from Aum for ¥920 million (approx. US$9.2 million).[49] Despite this precedent, many municipal governments followed Namino's example, spurred on by community demands to keep Aum out at whatever cost. Aum promptly sued these councils to annul the decisions and claim damages. The Supreme Court ruled in 2001 that the annulment and refusal of Aum believers' resident records was illegal.[50] Most district courts also ruled in

[46] *Asahi Shimbun* (2010), 'Yamanashi, Kamikuishiki kesenu kioku jūmin to moto shinto, tagai ni kizukai', 18 March, p. 39.

[47] *Asahi Shimbun* (2015), 'Oumu no kioku kyōsei sōsa 20 nen (4) kataritsugi, kōsei ni nokosu sekinin', 23 March (Yamanashi Ed.), p. 37; *Yomiuri Shimbun* (2008), '(Toikatari) Oumu no kioku no yukue', 17 March, p. 38; (2015), 'Oumu jiken 20 nen "tatemono nokosazu" shiryō wa nokori', 21 March (Yamanashi Ed.), p. 33.

[48] This form of ostracism probably did not inconvenience Aum members, for whom contact with the outside world was seen as ritually polluting.

[49] *Asahi Shimbun* (1994), 'Oumukyō gawa ni 9 oku en shiharai Kumamoto Naminoson ga wakai', 13 August, p. 22.

[50] *Yomiuri Shimbun* (2001), 'Jūmin tōroku torikeshi mitometa kettei o haki Oumu mōshitate mitomeru', 15 June 2001, p. 38.

Aum's favour and all municipal governments were eventually forced to accept and process resident records.[51]

Perhaps the only exception to the prevailing impulse to erase and forget physical manifestations of Aum's actions has been the remembrance of the Sakamoto family, whose friends and family have been committed to preserving their legacy. In 1997, eight years after their 'disappearance' and two years after the discovery of their bodies, friends and family raised funds to construct three identical cenotaphs at each of the locations where their bodies were buried. The memorial, composed of a small stone ring sitting atop two larger ones, represents the symbolic reunion of the family across disparate spaces. The memorials have acted as sites for friends, family, and the local community to remember the victims through regular remembrance ceremonies, albeit on a much smaller scale than the commemorative event at Kasumigaseki Station.[52]

Conclusions

The commemoration of the Aum Affair has been a complex and at times divisive issue, as some stakeholders' interests to remember the Tokyo attack in particular ways have clashed with others' wishes to forget the event whenever and wherever possible. For the political elites, legislation has been used to inscribe institutional responses to the Aum Affair with reference to the nation-state's norms and values. Notwithstanding the public debates over the legal reforms, during which some media outlets were critical of government plans, mass media outlets have commemorated the Aum Affair in relative consonance with the state by representing Aum's successor organisations as perennial threats to the body politic. At the same time, mass media have provided some discursive space for victims to express their views about the 'weathering' (*fūka*) of memories of the Aum Affair that diverge from predominant, elite representations that are critical of state responses.

Different civil actors have used diverse methods to commemorate the Aum Affair. While some have sought to fight the perceived 'weathering' of public memory through grassroots commemorative speech acts through self-publishing,

[51] For reports of different court judgements, see *Yomiuri Shimbun* (2001), 'Oumu shinja no jūminhyō fujuri soshō Suitashi ga kōso', 24 October (Osaka, Eve. Ed.), p. 12; (2001), 'Tennyū fujuri no torikeshi meijiru Oumu shinja shōso', 12 December (Eve. Ed.), p. 19; (2002), 'Oumu shinja no tennyū, Adachiku ga juri e', 31 October (Tokyo Ed.), p. 32; (2002), 'Oumu shinja tennyū todoke fujuri Miwachō mata haiso', 27 November (Ibaraki Ed.), p. 32; (2003), 'Oumu moto shinja tennyū todoke soshō kōsoshin Koshigayashi no shuchō mitome, baishō seikyū o kikyaku', 28 August (Saitama Ed.), p. 30.

[52] *Yomiuri Shimbun* (2000), 'Itai hakken kara 5 nen Niigata no sanchū de Sakamoto bengoshi no tsuitō ensō', 25 August (Kanagawa Ed.), p. 28; (2009), 'Sakamoto bengoshi jiken 20 nen', 8 September (Toyama Ed.), p. 26; (2013), 'Tsuitō konsāto hagukunda machi', 24 November (Toyama Ed.), p. 31.

others have sought to erase remaining reminders of Aum altogether by destroying physical structures associated with Aum's negative legacies and seeking to drive out remaining Aum members from the local community. This adversity to physical reminders of the Aum Affair resurfaced most recently during the disputes over the custody of Asahara's ashes after his execution in 2018. Following the execution, the government announced that his ashes and belongings would be handed over to Asahara's fourth daughter Satoka, who had previously publicly denounced Asahara and cut legal ties with her family (see Chapter 8). Days later, releasing a statement through her legal representative Takimoto Tarō, she expressed her wishes for the remains to be scattered over the Pacific Ocean to prevent his burial site from becoming a sacred site for remaining worshippers, and requested state assistance for a burial at sea (although it bears mention that his remaining followers never specified what they intended to do with Asahara's ashes had they had access to them). Asahara's surviving family members including his wife and other children have disputed whether Asahara explicitly designated Satoka to inherit his remains. The case was further complicated by the absence of formal documentation signed by Asahara himself, which would normally specify the recipient of the body and personal belongings. His third daughter argued that the absence of such documentation was evidence that he was not mentally fit to be executed. In a blow to the Ministry of Justice, the family court concluded in 2020 that Asahara's remains should be given to his second and third daughters, ruling that there was insufficient evidence that he had explicitly directed his remains to be given to Satoka.[53] The fourth daughter appealed this decision, but the Supreme Court upheld the ruling in 2021, awarding custody to the second daughter.[54] The ruling is significant, as the courts have repeatedly ruled against the Ministry of Justice's argument that Asahara had orally specified his fourth daughter to be the custodian of his remains. This raises further questions about the state of his mental health at the time of the execution. How this dispute might continue, however, remains to be seen.

[53] *Asahi Shimbun* (2020), 'Matsumoto moto shikeishū no ikotsu, jijo ni hikiwatashi', 17 September.
[54] NHK (2021), 'Oumu Shinrikyō Matsumoto Chizuo moto shikeishū ikotsu Jijo hikitori kakutei; Saikōsai', 5 July, <www3.nhk.or.jp/news/html/20210705/k10013120881000.html> Accessed September 2021.

6

Public Intellectuals and the Struggle Over Mind Control[1]

The Aum Affair reverberated across all aspects of civil society. On public transport, trash cans initially disappeared before eventually being replaced with cans with see-through casing. As Japan entered the panoptic age, CCTV cameras were installed in public spaces in greater numbers than ever before. Religions, whatever the tradition, found themselves navigating a perilous landscape in which any perceived infractions of social norms risked being tarred with the same brush as Aum amidst a general apathy – or even antipathy – towards organised religion. In short, what occurred in Aum's wake was a 'securitisation' of minority religions as dangerous 'cults', reinforced by widespread negative cultural stereotypes of charismatic leaders, zealous followers, and litigious organisation representatives.

The Aum Affair dramatically and permanently altered the contours of academic and public debates about religion. In the aftermath of the attack, many academics and scientists played important roles as public intellectuals in communicating the causes and consequences of Aum Shinrikyō in public debate, as experts from fields as diverse as social psychology, sociology, medicine, chemistry, criminology, security studies, history of religion, and religious studies took part in these extensive media debates. At the same time, the Aum Affair exposed a rift between public discourse and academic discourse, raising meta-discursive questions about the relationship between the two domains. On the one hand, anti-cult activists and public intellectuals successfully disseminated theories about 'brainwashing' and 'mind control' in public discourse to explain the submissive behaviours of Aum's most senior adherents. On the other hand, academics were

[1] Parts of this chapter appeared as 'Cultural Trauma, Counter-narratives, and Dialogical Intellectuals: The Works of Murakami Haruki and Mori Tatsuya in the Context of the Aum Affair' as an article co-authored with Patrick Baert in *Theory and Society* (2016), originally published under a Creative Commons Attribution 4.0 International License (https://creativecommons.org/licenses/by/4.0/).

generally sceptical that religious leaders could manipulate followers into submission through such psychological techniques. Nevertheless, many academics – especially scholars of religion – struggled to make an impact on these debates as it emerged that some academics had previously made remarks that appeared to endorse Aum. As a result, public discourse surrounding 'cults' – fuelled by a moral panic towards minority religions – became increasingly decoupled from academic debates, which urged caution before branding certain religious movements as dangerous and anti-social.

This is not to suggest, however, that the validity of the mind control thesis was universally accepted at face value in public discourse. Even amidst the media hysteria and 'moral panic' surrounding Aum, there were some public intellectuals who questioned these mainstream depictions of Aum as a murderous brainwashing cult plotting to take over Japan; instead, they offered more nuanced interpretations of Aum's growth and eventual turn to violence. This chapter focuses on two of these figures, the novelist Murakami Haruki and the filmmaker Mori Tatsuya, whose works explicitly complicated and destabilised simplistic understandings of the Aum Affair by talking to participants directly affected by it. While coming from relatively privileged cultural positions, both Murakami and Mori spoke in opposition to the dominant narrative of Aum as an imminent threat to society and its members as brainwashed followers. Instead, both figures produced 'centrifugal' narratives that ran against the grain of state and mass media representations of the Aum Affair, introducing the public to the voices of those who had hitherto remained at the margins of these public debates by including both sarin attack survivors and Aum members.

To understand the significance of Murakami and Mori's public interventions in relation to the wider cultural debates surrounding Aum, this chapter introduces the dichotomy of 'authoritative intellectuals', who pose narratives from a position of cultural, academic, and political authority, and 'dialogical intellectuals', who rely on dialogue with local participants to produce polyphonic narratives without necessarily appealing to their own intellectual authority. Whilst authoritative intellectuals have a preference towards unifying, 'monological' narratives – whether for or against elite 'official' speech genres – dialogical intellectuals are predisposed to the creation of 'polyphonic' narratives. This chapter argues that both Murakami's *Underground* series and Mori's series of movies and non-fiction works are examples of dialogical intellectual works which value the presentation of diverse worldviews as a goal in itself.

Public intellectuals and collective memory

Public intellectuals have historically occupied a central position in the creation and dissemination of trauma narratives. A public intellectual can be defined as anyone who speaks to a public audience on a range of issues considered to be of social and political importance. In the Western world as well as in modern Japan, public intellectuals have tended to be comprised of male, highly educated cultural elites from professions such as artists, writers, novelists, journalists, scientists, and academics. For example, contemporary Japanese novelists such as Ōe Kenzaburō, Takahashi Genichirō, and Ikezawa Natsuki have written and spoken extensively on issues including social crisis, war memory, and natural disasters through various media using accessible language.

Whatever their professional background, intellectuals often play a pivotal role in narrating the moral significance of events to wider public audiences (Eyerman 2011). Through various media – such as artwork, reportages, newspaper opinion pieces, film and television – public intellectuals function as an important 'carrier group' for narrating the traumatic impact of particular events on affected communities.

This is not to say, however, that all public intellectuals engage in public discourse using the same strategies. This chapter develops a dichotomy of 'authoritative intellectuals' and 'dialogical intellectuals' who participate in civil discourse through different methods of knowledge production and performative strategies. Authoritative intellectuals narrate trauma from an assumed privileged social position, speaking from 'above' society. Often benefiting from a privileged *parcours* and from having been trained in high-status disciplines such as philosophy, mathematics, and increasingly, the natural sciences, they presume superior knowledge of history and politics, or they may even claim to have philosophical insights into the human condition which explain the causes and consequences of traumatic events to the general public. Generally, authoritative intellectuals are averse to associating with external sources of authority such as the state or party (Baert and Shipman 2012: 189), although they may rely on other forms of cultural capital such as professorial titles and artistic prizes as sources of authority and respect. Authoritative intellectuals often provide 'monological' trauma narratives; these are close-ended interpretations, often involving moral judgements whereby the intellectual speaks as an objective arbiter of truth (Baert 2015).

By contrast, dialogical intellectuals rely not so much on their intellectual authority as the process of creating knowledge through conversations with local actors as the foundation for their intellectual claims. Unlike authoritative intellectuals, dialogical intellectuals operate 'alongside' the public, engaging in dialogue with participants directly to produce knowledge. Dialogical intellectual action can take three primary forms. Firstly, they can engage in dialogue and direct exchange of knowledge with local actors and communities, resulting in mutual understanding and education. Secondly, the intellectual work itself can be dialogical in content and argument, as it seeks to produce polyphonic, open-ended interpretations of a particular social phenomenon. For example, the work could consist of interviews which contain contradictory or inconsistent accounts and perspectives without resolving the accuracy or truthfulness of those statements. Thirdly, the intellectual product can be a record or collection of dialogue among local participants, which is disseminated for public consumption. In this example, the intellectual situates herself as a participant observer standing alongside local actors collecting and disseminating dialogical encounters without necessarily taking part in the conversation. As discussed below, Murakami engages in the second type of dialogue, while Mori displays both the second and third types of dialogue. Because of their mode of public engagement, dialogical intellectuals can create dialogical and polyphonic trauma narratives which, instead of imposing authoritative interpretations, can help to introduce nuance, uncertainty, and contradictions to trauma narratives, while potentially helping to alleviate the polarizing distinction between sacred and profane, pure and impure, and victims and perpetrators.

The distinction between 'monological' and 'dialogical' trauma narratives is an obvious analogue to Bakhtin's distinction between the 'epic' and the 'novel'. However, the dichotomy extends well beyond the content of public intellectuals' interventions. These public intellectuals differ not just on the basis of the content of their outputs, but also on the basis of their *investigative strategies* for collecting information, as well as their *performative strategies* for communicating their ideas to the public. For example, authoritative intellectuals may make claims based on their areas of expertise without personally collecting primary data such as interviews. They may prefer to give public lectures, write in newspaper columns, or appear on television, in short, speaking *to* an audience. In contrast, dialogical intellectuals may choose to conduct interviews and ethnographic fieldwork as the basis for their work, and to perform using a different strategy, such as by publishing interview transcripts, co-authoring publications with informants as collaborators, and by engaging in more interactive media outlets such as social media. As such, it is important not simply to highlight the content of intellectual interventions, but also the social processes through which such works are created and disseminated.

Besides the investigative, performative, and narrative dimensions of public intellectuals, the social location of their utterances vis-à-vis official, centripetal speech genres and vernacular, centrifugal speech is also important. Within any given discursive landscape, public intellectuals often navigate the intermediary space that is neither completely 'official' nor 'vernacular'. To reach out to large public audiences, public intellectuals must escape the narrow confines of specialised professional jargon that is characteristic of elite academic speech genres; at the same time, they must command some degree of authority to demonstrate that they are worth being listened to. Moreover, independence – or the perception of independence – is crucial to their credibility. Public intellectuals often appeal to their own autonomy and separation from quotidian interests and ideological biases. This means they usually resist co-option or suppression by 'official' elite representations – without becoming yet another 'lay' voice at the margins.

As a result, both authoritative and dialogical intellectuals produce narratives that mix 'centripetal' and 'centrifugal' dimensions. On the one hand, authoritative intellectuals are more likely to produce 'centripetal' discourse that commands respect for their intellectual authority. At the same time, they must be sensitive to public moods and topical themes and eschew technical jargon to reach the public. On the other hand, dialogical intellectuals are better placed to produce 'centrifugal' narratives that disrupt and challenge established systems of meanings as they seek to introduce a multitude of voices into public discourse. Nevertheless, dialogical intellectuals are also constrained by the need to appeal to some sense of intellectual authority – for example, claiming mastery of an academic field or medium of art – and therefore cannot eliminate 'centripetal' elements from their interventions entirely. Of course, this is not to suggest that authoritative intellectuals are incapable of challenging elite narratives, or that they do not engage in dialogue. The very act of narration, whether authoritative or dialogical, can help to disrupt established discursive structures that impose silence on suffering past and present (Kurasawa 2009; Eyerman 2004: 162–3). For example, Edward Said was committed to supporting Palestinian independence as an intellectual, activist and citizen, engaging dialogically with Palestinians throughout his career. Nevertheless, he largely adhered to a monological form of intellectual intervention by writing essays and opinion pieces and delivering public lectures (Said 1994; 1995). In such cases, authoritative intellectuals may challenge the centripetal narratives of 'official' discourse by presenting an alternative centripetal narrative that focuses on the intellectual and moral authority of the speaker: in Said's words, by 'speaking truth to power'. If the aim of authoritative intellectuals is to replace what lies at the political centre of social discourse, the aim of dialogical intellectuals is to subvert the very *structure* and *flow* of social discourse by introducing heterogenous interpretations and perspectives.

The following sections discuss how Murakami Haruki and Mori Tatsuya produced dialogical trauma narratives through the medium of print media and film respectively. Although they hail from contrasting social and professional backgrounds, their dissatisfaction with dominant cultural representations of Aum led them both to engage directly with individuals personally affected by the Affair, including victims of the attack and both current and ex-members of Aum. As a result, they disrupted the exclusionary boundary between 'victims' ('Japanese society') and 'perpetrators' ('Aum'), with two major effects. Firstly, they located the social problems that led to Aum within Japanese society, rather than isolating Aum as a foreign enemy threatening civil society. Secondly, by trying to find what Aum members had in common with the wider society, they suggested new interpreting categories that transcended those of 'victims' and 'perpetrators' without underplaying or condoning Aum's violence.

Authoritative intellectuals and the rise of mind control as paradigm

Throughout the initial period of intense media coverage after the Tokyo attack, public intellectuals played an instrumental role in attributing moral meanings to the perceived social crisis. Some authoritative intellectuals such as the philosopher Umehara Takashi provided relatively straightforward readings of the Aum Affair, attributing the causes of Aum's violence to Asahara's personal grudge against Japanese society (Umehara and Yamaori 1995). A different subset of authoritative intellectuals displayed partisan interests by collaborating with anti-cult movements to propagate an explicitly 'anti-cult' public agenda.

This team of 'anti-cult' public intellectuals championed mind control theory, drawing on pre-existing theories propounded by American anti-cult movements. Steven Hassan, a former Unification Church member who became an anti-cult activist and an 'exit counsellor' – a self-styled expert who encourages 'cult' members to quit movements through intensive counselling sessions – had an indirect but formative impact in bringing mind control theory into the popular lexicon. The Japanese translation of Hassan's book *Combatting Cult Mind Control*, published in Japan as *The Horrors of Mind Control* (*Maindo Kontorōru no Kyōfu*) in 1993, became a standard reference point for intellectuals to explain how 'cults' manipulated believers into subservient subjects (Hassan 1993; Watanabe 1999). Hassan argued that, while brainwashing and mind control are similar concepts, mind control is more pernicious because it is non-coercive and difficult to differentiate from normal social interaction. Although both concepts aim at permanently altering a person's identity and beliefs, brainwashing is coercive in nature, often conducted under physical constraint. By contrast, mind control is a subtler form of social control because many do not realise they are being manipulated (Hassan 1993: 107–9).

In his book, Hassan (1993) presents four types of mind control. First, 'behavioural' control restricts the daily regimen of individual members, including diet, clothing, and social interactions. Second, 'informational control' exposes members only to pre-approved information with limited access to outside information. Third, 'thought control' restricts members' thoughts with reference only to the group's moral and linguistic system, making any criticism of the group impossible. Last, 'emotional control' defines certain needs as evil or unnecessary and instils a fear of outsiders and leaving the movement. Hassan argues anti-social 'destructive cults' can be distinguished from religions proper by whether they engage in these modes of mind control. Subjects under the influence of mind control would need to undergo 'exit counselling' to overcome these obstacles and begin to think rationally for themselves. Hassan distanced his own approach from coercive practices of 'deprogramming' as advocated by activists such as Ted Patrick, in which anti-cult groups would kidnap and imprison adherents and forcibly de-convert them (though Hassan was himself involved in coercive deprogramming in his early career). Hassan travelled to Japan to expound his ideas to the public in the aftermath of the Aum Affair (Watanabe 1999). In an interview with the newspaper *Asahi Shimbun*, Hassan urged the public not to demonise low-ranking members; in his view, they had been manipulated into their beliefs and blanket criticism would only further strengthen the bonds between believers.[2]

Hassan himself did not become a popular figure on the Japanese media circuit. However, many public intellectuals quoted and reproduced Hassan's claims extensively throughout the public debates on Aum. The 'breakout star' from these debates was undoubtedly Egawa Shōko, a freelance journalist who had been consistently critical of Aum as an anti-social cult since the late 1980s and had continued to write on Aum during the 1990s despite low levels of public interest (Egawa 1991; 1995). Drawing on her extensive knowledge of the group's history and practice, Egawa received universal acclaim for her incisive critique of Aum's recruitment strategies, strenuous training methods, and members' blind obedience. In her commentaries, Egawa frames Asahara as a false prophet who tricked vulnerable youths for money and personal vainglory, making them into obedient 'robots' by using various mind control techniques (Egawa 1995: 500–03). Egawa received the prestigious Kikuchi Kan Prize in 1995, awarded by the literary magazine *Bungei Shunjū* to people that have made significant contributions to Japanese culture.

Similarly, anti-cult lawyer Takimoto Tarō, the representative for Aum Shinrikyō Victims' Society (renamed to Aum Shinrikyō Families' Society after the Tokyo attack; see Chapter 7), composed mainly of Aum members' parents, also played an active part in explaining Aum's internal structure and practices to the general public. On television, Egawa and Takimoto both played the role of prosecutor, cross-examining senior Aum members who appeared on television daily to deny responsibility and accuse the state of religious persecution (Gardner 1999: 222). It is worth noting here that both Egawa and Takimoto were targets of '*poa*'.[3] Yet, they largely refrained from speaking as 'victims' or 'survivors' of the Aum Affair, instead positioning themselves as authoritative sources of knowledge on Aum. Some academics, such as the social psychologist

[2] *Asahi Shimbun* (1995), 'Ippan shinto to hanzai, musubitsukenaide', 1 May, p. 22.

[3] Egawa and Takimoto both had personal stakes in confronting and seeking to dismantle Aum. Egawa was friends with Sakamoto and she had introduced him to a client in dispute with Aum (Egawa 1995: 63–4), while Takimoto was several years Sakamoto's junior at Yokohama Law Firm.

Nishida Kimiaki, theologian Asami Sadao (the translator of Hassan's influential text), and computational linguist Tomabechi Hideto, were strong proponents of brainwashing/mind control theories.[4] These intellectuals performed a pivotal role in challenging Aum's senior disciples who frequently appeared on television to feign innocence and accuse the government of religious persecution. In late 1995, these anti-cult intellectuals formed the advocacy group Japan De-Cult Council, bringing together figures including Takimoto, Nishida, and Asami.[5] The advocacy group later changed its name to Japan Society for Cult Prevention and Recovery in 2004.[6] Although the group does not endorse coercive deprogramming or exit counselling, such practices remain widespread today (Richardson 2011: 326). In a particularly egregious case, Gotō Tōru, a Unification Church member, was imprisoned by his family in solitary confinement and subjected to deprogramming by a Christian pastor for 12 years (Human Rights without Frontiers 2011). However, because these cases are often treated as familial disputes, the police have been reluctant to investigate these cases and they have rarely resulted in criminal prosecution.

In this context of general anxiety and antipathy towards cults, anti-cult intellectuals and activists have generally maintained their antagonistic stance towards Aum as well as other religions accused of being cults more broadly. In the afterword to an edited collection of ex-believers' testimonies, Takimoto expands his object of criticism beyond Aum to include a more expansive category of 'destructive cults', which, in his view, were on the rise in contemporary Japan. He alleges that these groups 'accumulate and systematically use mind control techniques, frighten those trying to leave, exploit labour, collectively use psychological harassment, use violence, lynch, wiretap, and sue frequently' (Kanariya no kai 2000: 259–60). In a newspaper comment marking the tenth anniversary of the Tokyo sarin attack, Takimoto reiterated his position that 'Aum must be eradicated.'[7] Reasserting the similarities between Aum and

[4] Nishida and Asami have consistently used 'mind control', while Tomabechi has used 'brainwashing' as a catch-all term in his publications.

[5] Takimoto has resigned as the Director of the Japan Society for Cult Prevention on two separate occasions. Takimoto resigned first resigned in 2015 after he was fined and disciplined for breaking into a Unification Church facility. He was reappointed as a director in 2018. In September 2021, Takimoto resigned again after he lost a libel case raised by Asahara's son, after Takimoto wrongfully named him as the culprit behind a death threat: Japan Society for Cult Prevention and Recover (2021) 'Takimoto riji jinin no oshirase (2021.9.6)' <www.jscpr.org/archives/1052> Accessed May 2022.

[6] Japan Society for Cult Prevention and Recovery. 'What is The Japan Society for Cult Prevention and Recovery: JSCPR.' <www.jscpr.org/english> Accessed May 2022.

Japan Society for Cult Prevention and Recovery. "Nihon Datsu Karuto Kyōkai towa". <www.jscpr.org/aboutjscpr> Accessed May 2022.

[7] *Yomiuri Shimbun* (2005), 'Chikatetsu sarin jiken kara 10 nen Takimoto Tarō shi vs. Yumiyama Tatsuya shi', 15 March, p. 15.

Nazis as totalitarian movements, Takimoto argued that 'like Nazis in Germany, the nation must not give recognition to a religious group that has committed indiscriminate murder under a set of beliefs. The [current] situation, in which reparations for victims gives an excuse for the group to survive, is a contradiction similar to permitting Nazis to survive so that they pay reparations for the Holocaust.'[8] The mass media have largely accepted and reproduced these narratives without challenging or criticising their overtly partisan interests against certain new religions, consistently providing them with airtime and column inches amidst heightened levels of public interest in new religions. The strong moral drive of the argument, which isolated Aum as an enemy and a cultural 'Other' invading the core of civil society, became so predominant in media discourse that it 'all but drowned out alternative voices and perspectives' (Reader 2001: 229).

Authoritative intellectuals questioning the mind control narrative

Although authoritative intellectuals speaking from an explicitly 'anti-cult' perspective dominated public discussions, religious scholars in Japan – much like their counterparts in North America and Europe – were sceptical of the idea that 'cults' could psychologically manipulate members to become as docile and obedient as proponents of mind control claimed (Anthony and Robbins 2008; Barker 1984; Shupe et al. 2008; Ushiyama 2019a). In the months after the Tokyo attack, various religious scholars challenged the simplistic frame of Aum as a 'death cult' and sought Aum's origins in changes in youth culture (Inoue et al. 1995). Some disagreed with the characterisation of Aum as a 'foreign species' and a cultural anomaly by arguing that Aum was indeed 'born of and nourished in the soil of contemporary Japan' (Shimazono 1995: 382).

Given Aum's unique history as a religious movement, one might expect that religious scholars, such as historians, sociologists, and philosophers of religion, as well as religious practitioners, would play a leading role in offering authoritative trauma narratives. However, religious scholars were relatively marginal in these public debates: 'alternative accounts of Aum [to the mind control narrative] ... had little if any impact upon television coverage' of the Aum Affair (Gardner 1999: 222). To understand why, it is necessary to look at the wider socio-cultural environment in which religious scholars faced a public crisis of confidence.

[8] *Yomiuri Shimbun* (2005), 'Chikatetsu sarin jiken kara 10 nen Takimoto Tarō shi vs. Yumiyama Tatsuya shi', 15 March, p. 15.

From the moment that Aum's culpability became public knowledge, religious scholars faced public criticism on two fronts. Firstly, they had appeared to be entirely oblivious of the rise of Aum throughout the late 1980s and early 1990s, despite Aum's involvement in a number of social controversies, thereby putting their supposed 'expertise' of new religions into question (Dorman 2012b: 158). Secondly, and more seriously, it emerged that some writers with backgrounds in religious studies had spoken out in favour of Aum in the past, forming an impression among the public that religious scholars were too lenient about, or possibly even in collusion with, anti-social religious movements.

There were two figures who faced intense criticism for their prior comments on Aum: Nakazawa Shin'ichi and Shimada Hiromi. A philosopher of religion, Nakazawa Shin'ichi was a former graduate student at Tokyo University who had studied Tibetan esoteric Buddhism. As an ascetic, he had personally trained under a Tibetan *lama* and published *The Rainbow Ladder* (*Niji no Kaitei*) in 1981, a text that later became foundational for popularising Tibetan Buddhism among aspiring practitioners in Japan, including individuals who eventually joined Aum (Sanpo and Nakazawa 1981). Furthermore, and more problematically, Nakazawa had engaged in several magazine interviews with Asahara during the early 1990s, in which he had praised Asahara as a true practitioner of Buddhism (Hirano and Tsukada 2015). Separately, the sociologist of religion Shimada Hiromi had spoken positively about Aum prior to the Tokyo sarin attack. As a graduate student in sociology of religion, also at Tokyo University, he had studied a rural commune-based movement called Yamagishi-kai as a covert member (Shimada 2012). His interactions with Aum started when he was invited by an acquaintance to contribute a piece to a contemporary affairs magazine, which resulted in him conducting an interview with Asahara.[9] Although he did not study Aum systematically, Shimada continued to write about Aum, countering accusations that it was a dangerous cult (Hirano and Tsukada 2015). At the start of 1995, reacting to the first media reports of suspected links between Aum and sarin production, Aum invited Shimada personally to inspect the Kamikuishiki headquarters. Shimada accepted the invitation and visited the sarin chemical plant, which had been hastily disguised as a shrine to Shiva days before his visit. Shimada went on the public record to deny that he saw any evidence of sarin production, and that another group was likely to be behind the Matsumoto sarin attack the previous year (Reader 2000b: 371).

Although these instances of praising or defending Aum were by no means widespread, Nakazawa and Shimada's actions significantly weakened the epistemological authority of religious experts in commenting on the Aum Affair and about controversial new religions more generally. Consequently, scholars who

[9] Author's interview with Shimada Hiromi, 18 March 2015, Tokyo.

'discuss[ed] movements such as Aum in any terms other than those of cultic deviance and evil' were viewed as 'little more than apologists' (Reader 2001: 232). This, in turn, created a discursive space in which anti-cult intellectuals and activists could take centre stage without encountering strong resistance or criticism from scholars.

Although religious scholars had a relatively marginal role in informing public opinion, there were some examples in which other public intellectuals offered alternative trauma narratives from an authoritative position. Furihata Ken'ichi, a journalist and editor at *Asahi Shimbun* who had extensively covered the Aum trials, characterised Aum as a uniquely Japanese phenomenon that arose out of various structural ailments in contemporary society. In his view, the believers' willingness to carry out horrific crimes should be explained as 'obedience to authority', but not necessarily mind control (Furihata 2000). Reiterating media characterisations of Aum as a social illness, Furihata situates Aum as a pathological iteration of rigid, irrational, vertical structures which have characterised Japanese organisations at various historical junctures. Furihata argues that a parallel to Aum's 'totalitarian' organisational structure could be found in fascist Japan; just as Aum members valorised total devotion to Asahara as an end in itself, the Imperial militarist regime justified and aestheticised absolute obedience to superiors' orders as a virtue, emphasising the primacy of putting the collective above the individual. Even after Japan's defeat, the vertical organisational structure – and with it, moral justifications for group unity and absolute loyalty – survived through corporations, which produced their own 'soldiers' and 'warriors' (ibid.: 221–5). Once the post-war period of high economic growth ended and uncertainties grew about where Japan was heading, the 'spectre' of totalitarianism reappeared and reproduced itself under the guise of Aum Shinrikyō (ibid.: 224). Echoing Erich Fromm's (2001) thesis in *Fear of Freedom* that totalitarianism is the result of existential angst created by modern individualism, Furihata suggests that Aum's members had not been 'mind controlled' but rather had ceded the will to think independently and refused to reflect on the moral consequences of their actions (Furihata 2000: 225–30). Furihata accepts mind control as only a partial explanation for the escalation of violence (ibid.: 242–4), stating, 'I do not consider this group as simply an enigmatic and incomprehensible [*makafushigi*] cult. I don't consider the people who belonged to the religious organisation to have been particularly peculiar either. But they were a little selfish and pretentious, suggestible but also conceited, and unable to be independent, in the true sense of the word' (ibid.: 245).

Furihata also takes a critical stance towards public attitudes towards surveillance and national security in the post-Aum landscape. He warns that in the post-Aum climate, people have become too dependent on state power to ensure public security, at the expense of fundamental civil rights and liberties (ibid.: 16–17).[10]

Furihata's authoritative counter-narrative highlights how authoritative counter-narratives who questioned the mind control narrative emerged not from religious scholars, but from journalists, who were arguably seen by the public as having a critical distance from new religions. In this cultural context, where opposition to mind control was – and to an extent still is – a minority position, Murakami and Mori are notable for taking up a dialogical approach to create alternative trauma narratives.

Murakami Haruki's *Underground*

Murakami Haruki was already an established author by the late 1990s, having published a string of commercially successful novels since the late 1970s. Compared to his fictional works, which often featured young protagonists, sometimes in surreal settings, the two-volume work, *Underground* (Murakami 1997) and *Underground 2* (Murakami 2001) marked a radical change in tone and subject matter. The *Underground* series is an edited collection of interviews carried out by Murakami with victims and families of victims of the Tokyo sarin incident (in the first volume) and current and ex-Aum members (in the second volume). Explaining his decision to write his first non-fiction work, he states that it was necessary to revisit a question that, to him, was never answered satisfactorily: 'what actually happened in the Tokyo subway the morning of 20 March, 1995?' (Murakami 2003: 196).[11] Keeping his distance from existing narratives, he seeks 'words coming from another direction, new words for a new narrative. Another narrative to purify this [existing] narrative' (ibid.: 196) by interviewing individuals with first-hand experience of Aum and the Tokyo attack. Methodologically, he begins by collecting the experiences of those whose lives were directly affected by the terrorist attack, rather than relying solely on his areas of expertise. As Murakami states,

> At the beginning of every interview I would ask the interviewees about their background – where they were born, their upbringing, their family, their job (especially their job) – in order to give each a 'face', to bring them into focus. What I did not want was a collection of disembodied voices. Perhaps it's an occupational hazard of the novelist's profession, but I am less interested in the 'big picture' as it were, than in the concrete, irreducible humanity of each individual. (Ibid.: 6)

[10] *Asahi Shimbun* (2005), 'Kenryoku ni yudaneta "anzen" Chikatetsu sarin jiken kara 10 nen', 20 March, p. 39.

[11] All direct quotes are from the 2003 English translation (Murakami 2003).

The result is a complex and nuanced collection of individual stories that do not necessarily present a coherent or singular picture. In the first volume, he is concerned with the victims: he interviews those commuters who survived the attack, as well as grieving families and family members of survivors. Individual memories of the event vary greatly. Some suddenly experienced their vision darkening and found it hard to breathe; others smelled a noxious smell and reacted immediately to escape. While some suffered from lasting psychological and physical trauma, others moved on quickly to resume their ordinary lives, seemingly relatively unaffected by the attack. Some experienced irreversible loss. In one interview, a widow relates the shock of losing her husband while heavily pregnant with his baby (ibid.: 165–74), while in another interview the brother of a woman who was severely disabled by the attack recalls the sorrow of looking after his sister in a near-vegetative state, but celebrates her gradual recovery (ibid.: 76–83). Throughout the volume, Murakami favours fragmented individual narratives over a singular trauma narrative. He states, '[w]hat transpired was more profound, more compounded with meanings than anything I could have imagined' (ibid.: 205). Unravelling and isolating the individual psychological traumas of victims from the singular orthodox trauma narrative, Murakami attempts to represent the actual suffering of individual victims as told to him, rather than understanding the symbolic wound that 'Japan' collectively suffered as a nation.

Although Murakami displays the second dimension of dialogical intellectual action – producing a work which is dialogical in content – and uses dialogue with local participants to deconstruct the orthodox trauma narrative, he is not a purely dialogical intellectual. He also acts authoritatively as he constructs and advocates a new, alternative trauma using his cultural authority and expertise. In the afterword, employing his command of psychoanalysis and literary criticism, he offers a new trauma narrative, placing Aum not as an outsider, 'an alien presence viewed through binoculars on the far shore' (ibid.: 197), but as a return of the repressed subconscious of the Japanese psyche ('the underground'), which attacked the conscious, surface world (ibid.: 197–9). Although Aum constructs a different cognitive, linguistic, and symbolic universe to that of Japan, Murakami sees certain resemblances between the Japanese psyche and Aum's beliefs; similar to Furihata's comparison of Aum and Japanese corporations, Murakami points out that blind obedience to an existing structural order is not unique to Aum, but is present in Japanese society as a whole (Ibid.: 206–8).

The second volume, *Underground 2*, originally serialised in the literary magazine *Bungei Shunjū* in 1998, directly follows the concerns he raised in the first volume, as he tries to understand why Aum Shinrikyō came into being: his intention is to open up the '"black box" … which suddenly, from out of nowhere, made an assault on the everyday' (ibid.: 213). Though he does not interview the actual perpetrators of the attack, Murakami speaks to rank-and-file believers, many of whom were full-time devotees (*samana*) at the time. Many of them had already left the group, but some of his interviewees were still members at the time of the interview (some also quit Aum following the interview). As with the first volume, he adheres to a novelistic and polyphonic approach that values diversity. His goal is to convey 'not one clear viewpoint' but to gather 'flesh-and-blood material from which to construct *multiple* viewpoints' (ibid.: 215, emphasis in original). Instead of condoning or condemning members' actions, Murakami listens to their motivations for joining, enquires what life was like at the commune, challenges their views on guilt and responsibility, and asks why they left (if they did and, if not, why not).

The interviewees' accounts confirm that Aum relied on training techniques that its critics identified as mind control, including solitary confinement, and forcible administration of LSD in an initiation ritual (ibid.: 251–60; 298–304). Multiple accounts corroborate Aum's sinister characteristics; a young woman recalls that she refused sexual advances by Asahara, and later had two years of her memory erased by electro-shock (ibid.: 285–94). Still, Murakami breaks down the stereotypical image of the 'crazed' cult worshipper by introducing the interviewees as varied and interesting characters. Some were never fully convinced of Aum's claims in the first place and had doubts about Asahara's teachings, while others, who were not involved in Aum's militarisation programme, still held mixed feelings towards their guru despite admitting that the Tokyo sarin attack was abhorrent (ibid.: 239–50). Unlike the sensational media reports which emphasised brainwashing practices and torture methods, the interviews show Aum to be far less restrictive and 'cult-like' in some respects. One believer commented that it was possible to suggest changes to the guru's initial orders (ibid.: 244), while another wryly remarked that Aum was '[n]ot much different from the secular world', as Asahara treated Tokyo University graduates and beautiful women better than other members (ibid.: 255).[12]

As with the first volume, Murakami's dialogical method deconstructs and challenges the orthodox trauma narrative before he offers a new, authoritative interpretation of why so many intelligent youths with bright prospects joined Aum. According to Murakami, the Aum elites, with high levels of education and technical expertise, 'couldn't help having grave doubts about the inhumane, utilitarian grist mill of capitalism and the social system in which their own essence and efforts – even their own reasons for being – would be fruitlessly ground down' (ibid.: 307). The sense of *anomie* and powerlessness of those individuals on

[12] The comment about Tokyo University students and beautiful women is included in the Japanese version, but is missing from the English translation. Although this might be a good representation of how ordinary *samana* perceived the hierarchy, the statement is not entirely accurate. Aum had several high-ranking members who hailed from low socio-economic backgrounds and had few educational qualifications, including Niimi Tomomitsu and Okasaki Kazuaki.

the corporate ladder pushed them to Aum, a (false) sanctuary that provided the possibility for self-improvement, on the condition that they followed Asahara's words as truth and abandoned the capacity for self-criticism. As he suggests in the conclusion of both volumes, Aum is an unwanted outcome – the return of the repressed – of an excessively materialist society which excludes those who do not endorse capitalism, but it is not a foreign enemy to be rejected. The people who joined Aum are 'not abnormal; they're not disadvantaged; they're not eccentrics. They are the people who live average lives ... who live in my neighbourhood' (ibid.: 309).

The *Underground* series was reviewed positively by critics, although some critics such as Ian Hacking (2000) questioned whether it was ultimately successful in uncovering anything specifically 'Japanese' about the terrorist attack.[13] There are also methodological weaknesses in Murakami's works, as the interviewees for both volumes were arbitrarily and unsystematically selected by his assistants and editors. The abstractions he makes from interviewing low-ranking believers are also problematic, as many of them were ignorant of the militarisation process. As such, his interviews provide relatively little insight into what life was like for higher-ranking disciples chosen to participate in Aum's criminal activities. The result is a disjuncture between the dialogical content of his interviews, and the monological conclusions he draws; if some believers were capable of being detached from Aum's apocalyptic claims, why did the high-ranking members seem so obedient in carrying out such abhorrent crimes? Whilst privileging the interpretive authority of low-ranking members for making sense of their own biographies, Murakami neglects to consider the possible variance between low-ranking and high-ranking disciples who were engaged in very different types of devotional work: ordinary members were engaged in mundane tasks such as construction, recruitment, and cooking, as opposed to illegal, 'secret work' of weapons development research, kidnapping, and murders in which Asahara's aides were selected to participate.

Mori Tatsuya's *A*, *A2*, and *A3*

Mori Tatsuya's public interventions differ significantly from Murakami's, both in context and content, despite their similar methodologies of talking to 'perpetrators'. Unlike Murakami, Mori was unknown in public discourse before his directorial debut with the documentary film, *A* (Mori 1998). *A* follows the daily life of a young believer called Araki Hiroshi, who is entrusted with the

[13] *Asahi Shimbun* (1997), 'Andāguraundo Murakami Haruki cho (Shohyō)', 6 April, p. 14; *Yomiuri Shimbun* (1997), '"Andāguraundo" Murakami Haruki cho. Monogatari no sekai ni gedokuzai o hanatsu', 23 March, p. 13; (1999), '"Yakusoku sareta basho de" Murakami Haruki cho. Intabyū de ukabu setsujitsu na kotoba', 17 January, p. 9.

organisation's public relations after the arrests of the leadership. Gaining the trust of Araki and his fellow members, Mori captures the daily life inside the organisation, thereby dispelling some myths surrounding Aum believers and challenging the Manichaean frame separating Aum and Japanese society. As Mori states in a subsequent commentary book (Mori 2002), he envisaged revealing a side of Aum that was previously inaccessible through conventional television coverage.

Unlike Murakami, whose international career as a novelist had given him access to a large publishing house and, later, a serial in a premier literary magazine, Mori initially struggled to find an outlet for his vision. As a freelance television director, he initially pitched the idea of a television documentary to various producers, arguing that it was necessary to go beyond the hackneyed trope of Aum as a 'dangerous cult' to better understand the motivations behind the group's actions. However, according to Mori, no television production company was willing to commission the project, as they deemed it too controversial, and simply did not fit well with the condemnatory tone required of Aum-related coverage (Gardner 1999; Mori 2002). Denied access to television as a medium of expression, Mori opted to self-finance the project as an independent film, and eventually completed the film with the help of the producer Yasuoka Takaharu, who frequently doubled as second cameraman.

Throughout the film, Mori challenges the supposed objectivity of the camera, that whatever is captured on film must be 'true' and 'factual'. Speaking from experience, Mori argues in his accompanying commentary book that any video footage can be edited in post-production to induce multiple impressions (Mori 2002: 215–16). In his experience, all camera footage, presented as 'fact', is merely a manipulated representation of reality. By rejecting the false objectivism of the camera, Mori adopts a perspectival shift which is central to the film. Itself a subject with limited horizons, Mori's camera captures life in Aum from *within* the organisation, as well as *on the level* of its participant subjects. Rather than seeking to produce an 'objective' bird's-eye view depiction of Aum, Mori implicitly endorses Weber's spirit of *verstehen* through an attempt to understand how Aum members see the world. Although Mori does not fully embed himself into Aum's lifestyle, he builds up enough trust with believers to engage in candid conversations about why they continue to believe in Asahara as an omniscient guru, and whether they still believe in Aum's doctrines. By treating Aum believers as legitimate sites of knowledge and information, Mori shows Aum believers to be reflexive and much less 'brainwashed' than media reports suggest.

The deliberate perspectival shift also enables Mori to reveal disingenuous and questionable practices by some media personnel behind the camera. In a scene near the beginning of the film, a reporter from a national television network approaches Araki for permission to film. As Araki asks whether he is being filmed at the moment and denies permission for the footage to be used, the reporter replies that she does not know if he is being filmed and asks whether they can use the footage anyway if the camera was running, citing 'journalistic freedom' (*shuzai no jiyū*). In another scene, outside the Kamikuishiki headquarters, a news reporter approaches Araki, claiming he has secured permission to film inside Aum's buildings from the bankruptcy trustee (an external auditor appointed to manage Aum's finances after it was declared bankrupt), and that Araki's consent is unnecessary. As Araki rebuffs the claim to say the news crew cannot film without the permission of Aum residents living in the commune, the reporter changes his tune to admit he was there to secure Araki's permission, and that the trustee's agreement was insufficient by itself.

In a sequence that has gained a central significance in the film, Mori unexpectedly captures a scene of false arrest. In this scene, a group of believers leave the commune and go into the street, whereupon several policemen interrogate Araki and his companions. As they refuse to show identification and attempt to walk away, a police officer tackles a member down to the ground, himself falling to the ground in the process. The officer claims to be hurt, and as the member lies apparently concussed on the ground, he is arrested promptly for assault and obstruction of justice. On the sidelines, members of the public watch the incident and later try to talk Araki and others out of Aum. In the following scene, breaking his principle of non-interference, Mori hands the tape over to Aum's defence lawyer as evidence; the man is later released without charge.

Throughout the film, Mori questions the dualistic codes imposed upon Aum – of society as good, civil, morally upright, and rational, and Aum as evil, barbaric, immoral, and irrational – without condoning or defending Aum's crimes. Mori shows Aum first and foremost as a religious organisation; devoted to a moral order different to Japan's, but hardly resembling a dangerous terrorist group intent on destroying Japan at all costs. Although the film itself lacks a clear narrative direction and thus does not impose an authoritative interpretation of the Aum Affair, Mori provides an exegesis of his motivations behind the film in his commentary book. Like Murakami, Mori questions the boundary drawn between Japanese society and Aum by asking whether the Japanese people might be as obedient to rules and norms as some Aum believers are, as Japanese society hatefully and vengefully attacks Aum – the evil 'perpetrators' – on behalf of the reified 'victims' (Mori 2002: 157; 175–6).

In terms of cultural impact, Mori was largely excluded from mainstream media outlets, probably as a result of his provocative message that was much more directly critical of the police and the media than other existing counter-narratives. Mori's limited financial resources also meant *A* was shown only at a small number of independent cinemas. Attendance was approximated at 10,000 people nationwide as of 1999 (Mori and Yasuoka 2001: 11). While some critics reviewed the film positively (Gardner 1999: 231–2), mainstream media also criticised Mori as being too sympathetic to Aum (Koike 2011). Unsurprisingly, Takimoto Tarō criticised the film, claiming Mori was too kind to Aum believers and neglected to capture the suffering of Aum's victims; the film did not properly address Aum as 'perpetrators' and Japanese society as 'victims', and neglected to address questions of 'mind control' (Gardner 1999: 233–4; Mori 2012 (v. 2): 110–16).

Undeterred by these criticisms, Mori made a sequel titled *A2*, which was released in 2001. Whereas the first work fits with the second dimension of dialogical intellectual action as content and argument, *A2* serves also as an illustration of the third dimension of dialogical intellectual action as a record of dialogue among local participants. Throughout *A2*, Mori shuttles back and forth between Aum and the surrounding world as a participant observer.

A2 features less of Mori as a talking participant and foregrounds the conversations between Aum members and local residents. *A2* focuses on the interaction between Aum members living in a small shared house and local resident groups campaigning for their eviction, exploring the potential for reconciliation and mutual understanding through these daily conversations. In one instance, a local community-based Aum surveillance group – similar to a 'neighbourhood watch' group – agrees to disband after befriending and reconciling with Aum members, concluding that they no longer pose a threat to the community. While the residents dismantle the surveillance tent next to the commune building, they seem to give a qualified endorsement of the adherents' religious commitments. Nonetheless, reconciliation with Aum members seems a distant possibility for the rest of Japanese society. In one scene, a real estate broker comes under public scrutiny for employing Aum believers. As crews wait outside, an Aum representative heads to the company to apologise to company executives and local government officials, promising that the members will quit and never return to their town. As a reporter approaches the representative and Mori for comment, Mori leaves the site, apparently exasperated. *A2* received a wider theatrical release than *A* did, was critically acclaimed, and won an award in the Yamagata International Documentary Film Festival, subsequently securing Mori's position in the Japanese civil sphere as a progressive public intellectual (Gardner 2002a: 340; 343).

Like Murakami's interviews, Mori's exploration of the daily lives of Aum believers is not without limitations. Like an early 20th-century ethnographer on fieldwork, Mori is reliant on informants who guide and define what and whom he is allowed to see. However, unlike an ethnographer, who can question and exclude things or information which he or she sees as untrue or irrelevant, Mori's suspension of his epistemological authority limits his critical capacity to challenge the veracity of his interviewee's claims. Moreover, like Murakami's interviewees, Mori's informants are all low-ranking ones who were not involved in the militarisation process, and his ahistorical method reveals very little about Aum's gradual turn to terrorism prior to the Matsumoto and Tokyo attacks. The decision to talk with Aum members also came at the cost of excluding dialogue with the victims, whose perspectives are patently absent from *A* and *A2*.

Since directing *A2*, Mori has turned to writing non-fiction. *A3* (Mori 2012) is a series of essays originally serialised in the Japanese edition of *Playboy* magazine between 2005 and 2007. The book challenges the demonisation of Asahara as a psychopathic and manipulative leader and seeks to uncover the 'true' version of Asahara. He continues to employ a broadly dialogical method, interviewing people who knew Asahara during childhood or in the years before he established himself as a guru. Speaking to and exchanging letters with Asahara's closest aides in jail, he contests the orthodox representation of Asahara as the source of evil and a master manipulator, instead suggesting that Aum's turn to violence was the result of complex social dynamics within the organisation. Mori argues that Aum turned violent not because Asahara brainwashed and controlled his disciples to enact his destructive vision, but because his disciples, eager to please Asahara, presented him with possible solutions to his paranoid fears and delusions, and executed them with his approval and consent.

In the book, Mori focuses on Asahara's mental condition during the trials. During the trial hearings, Asahara's behaviour became increasingly erratic, speaking broken English and gibberish on occasion before eventually falling silent. Towards the end of the trial, his defence argued the trial should be halted on the basis that Asahara was not mentally fit to stand trial. Several psychiatrists appointed by the defence team concurred that Asahara was in a state of mental confusion and required treatment. The court-appointed psychiatrist, however, reached the opposite conclusion: that Asahara was faking illness and that he was fit to stand trial. In a further turn of events, after the initial verdict, the Tokyo High Court dismissed the appeal on purely procedural grounds (for the defence's failure to file documents on time). Subsequent special appeals to the High Court and the Supreme Court were also dismissed, thereby finalising the first trial's death-sentence verdict without the case advancing to a higher court of appeal. Following these developments, Mori criticises the series of judicial decisions as politically motivated, and reflective of Japan's moral impulsion to sentence Asahara to death regardless of his current mental condition (Mori 2012 (v. 1): 329–39). Although Mori continues to rely on dialogical methods to inform his views, unlike *A* and *A2*, *A3* is driven by an authoritative counter-narrative which directly challenges the image of Asahara as the evil mastermind. *A3* won the 2011 Kōdansha Non-Fiction Award, and Mori continues to write mainly non-fiction books on an array of social issues such as the critique of Japanese media, the death penalty, and the discrimination of minority groups.

Mori has continued to speak publicly about the Aum Affair on a number of occasions since then. In 2018, amidst media speculations that Asahara and his accomplices were likely to be executed before Emperor Akihito's abdication in

2019, Mori founded the group Society for Pursuing the Truth of the Aum Affair (*Oumu Jiken Shinsō Kyumei no Kai*) alongside sociologist Miyadai Shinji. The Society attracted the support of several dozen public intellectuals, journalists, and writers who – like Mori – were convinced that Asahara's mental condition required medical treatment, and that due process was being sidelined in favour of a speedy execution. The website – which closed after the executions were carried out – reproduced sections of texts taken from reports written by psychiatrists appointed by the defence to argue that Asahara was likely suffering from mental illness caused by prolonged confinement. Despite their protestations, the government carried out the executions in July 2018. In August 2018, the Society held its first and final symposium, inviting speakers to reflect on the executions. Among the speakers was Kōno Yoshiyuki (see Chapters 3 and 7), a survivor of the Matsumoto sarin attack.[14] Although the Society for the Pursuit of Truth of the Aum Affair lasted for a mere few months before disbanding, the event was demonstrative of Mori's transformation from a dialogical listener to a more authoritative opinion leader in seeking to shape public understandings of the Aum Affair.

Conclusions

Whether or not Murakami and Mori's polyphonic narratives as dialogical intellectuals have been successful in changing prevailing social attitudes towards Aum is debatable. On the one hand, Murakami's case demonstrates how a high-status writer and novelist with privileged access to national media outlets can pose centrifugal, polyphonic counter-narratives that challenge established frames of meaning to a mass audience. Published by Kōdansha, one of Japan's largest publishing houses, *Underground* was a national bestseller that sold 270,000 copies within the first two months of its release (Kavitha and Murakami 1997), and the sequel *Underground 2: The Place That Was Promised* was also a bestseller.[15] The commercial success of the works suggest that Murakami's works resonated with the public to a certain extent. On the other hand, Mori's unsuccessful bid to create a television documentary illustrates how Mori's creative vision – to portray Aum in a more nuanced way beyond the sensationalist caricatures – conflicted with mass media interests that defined the discursive rules of what could and could not be said publicly. Barred from using television as a medium of expression, Mori was forced to turn to independent film-making, and the resulting productions were watched by a much smaller audience: in Mori's words, he was completely

[14] Talks by the individual speakers are available on YouTube: www.youtube.com/channel/UCOMM-Q4hwpHV5X15RdGzaWA Accessed May 2022.

[15] *Yomiuri Shimbun* (1998), 'Shūkan besuto serā. Tankōbon, bungei 1i wa "Tariki"', 5 December (Eve. Ed.), p. 6.

ignored by the mass media.[16] Nevertheless, this fortuitous turn also paved the way to his emergence as a maverick film-maker, enabling him to write for established newspapers and magazines in his later career.

Whatever the cultural impact of these counter-narratives, however, it is difficult to deny that authoritative anti-cult intellectuals' explanations of mind control as the central mechanism by which religious followers lose autonomy, as well as representations of 'cult' leaders as essentially malevolent and self-interested villains, have been reproduced not only in media discourse but also in other areas of public life. For instance, many universities in Japan today regularly warn students against 'cults' recruiting new members on campuses through public service announcements, leaflets, and classroom seminars.[17] In other words, these universities actively discourage students from joining controversial religious movements on the grounds that they pose a danger to mental, financial, and familial well-being. After the perceived blunders of Nakazawa and Shimada, which turned public opinion against religious scholars, few scholars have explicitly challenged these generalised cultural biases against minority religions in the post-Aum world, as compared with religious scholars in European and North American contexts who, in general, have been unafraid to criticise policies which single out certain new religions as harmful. To this end, the representation of Aum as a 'destructive cult', embedded in wider anxieties about religions as potential threats to civil society, remains central to the 'official' and 'elite' centripetal discourses supported by anti-cult activists, mass media, security agencies, universities, and some public intellectuals.

Despite the modest public impacts of Murakami and Mori's dialogical trauma narratives, indirect effects of their works may be found in other cultural products. As the following chapters will discuss, in parallel with, and following the release of their works, there has been an emergence of narratives that take a distance from, or directly question, the dominant centripetal, meta-narrative of the Aum Affair as a traumatic moment for the nation. For instance, the Subway Sarin Incident Victims' Society has published several works narrating victims' experiences to mark anniversaries of the Tokyo attack (see Chapter 7). In 2010, book editor Aoki Yumiko, who had previously worked with the Victims' Society, published an edited collection of autobiographical interviews with ex-members titled *Having Lived Aum* (Oumu o Ikite),[18] which followed a methodology similar to Murakami and Mori's (Aoki 2010). Publishing the autobiographical accounts with minimal comment, the volume dispels the myth that there is a 'typical' background of Aum

[16] Author's interview with Mori Tatsuya, 20 July 2016, Tokyo.

[17] Ibid.

[18] The 'ikite' ('having lived') in the title describes the experience of Aum in the continuous tense, suggesting a degree of continuity of their lives in the past to the present. Moreover, the particle 'o', rather than 'ni' or 'de' denotes that they had lived 'as' Aum, rather than 'in' Aum.

believers and their subsequent trajectories, including their motivations for their continued membership or disaffiliation. Whether or not Murakami or Mori had a direct impact on these works, it is evident that there are many narratives, from the perspectives of both 'victims' and 'perpetrators' that make sense of the Aum Affair beyond the ossified meta-narrative of Aum simply as an external enemy attacking the Japanese state and civil society. The following chapters discuss and explore some of the most important interlocutors in these discursive battles.

7

Performing Victimhood: Pursuing Justice After Tragedy

For the survivor who chooses to testify, it is clear: his duty is to bear witness for the dead and for the living. He has no right to deprive future generations of a past that belongs to our collective memory. To forget would be not only dangerous but offensive; to forget the dead would be akin to killing them a second time.

Elie Wiesel 2006 [1972]: xv

There are many academic, medical, and legal definitions of what it means to be a 'survivor' or a 'victim', but few capture the survivor's role in the construction of collective memory so succinctly and beautifully as Elie Wiesel does in his explanation of why he wrote *Night*, an autobiographical account of his survival as a teenager imprisoned in Auschwitz and Buchenwald. Wiesel employs the normative-legal language of 'duty' and 'rights' to delineate what a survivor must do; they have a duty to pay respects to the dead, but they also have 'no right to deprive future generations' of their experiences, which form part of 'our collective memory'. Moreover, he situates witnessing as a moral imperative, not simply because of the danger of forgetting past atrocities, but also because it would be 'offensive' to the dead. In this view, the survivor-witness situates their commemorative speech acts as a bridge between the past ('the dead'), and the future ('the children who will be born tomorrow') (Wiese 2006 [1972]: xv). The survivor, speaking for those who can no longer speak for themselves, responds to tragedy out of a sense of 'responsibility'. The witness 'does not want his past to become their future' (ibid.: xv).

In this short extract, Wiesel captures many of the characteristics that the victim or survivor holds as a 'memory agent'. The victim-survivor is someone who has direct knowledge of past events that enables her to communicate her experiences to future audiences. This direct experience – and the direct connection with those who perished – accords her with a moral authority above that of witnesses, perpetrators, or those with secondary knowledge of events.

Victims can communicate what others cannot: how it *felt* to be victimised at that moment in time and what the physical and psychological effects of those traumatic experiences are. In the commemoration of narratives of violence and loss, the authenticity and the moral authority of the 'victim' plays a crucial role in giving emotional weight to the event being remembered.

Yet, one must be cautious not to take the meaning of 'victim' to be transparent and self-evident. In Wiesel's case, the distinction between the victim ('Jews') and perpetrator ('Nazis') is clear-cut. However, such distinctions are not always so easy to make. For instance, when a domestic violence survivor kills their attacker, or when the victim belongs to the perpetrating group (such as a dissident believer of a religion killed in an internal dispute), such moral distinctions become more difficult to delineate. Moreover, while Wiesel situates testimony as a central component of what a victim must do, this depends on the willingness of victims to speak out, as well as what goals victims seek through the act of testimony.

Using Wiesel's remarks as a springboard, this chapter proposes a new sociological and context-sensitive conceptualisation of victimhood. It suggests that victimhood is not an automatic social attribute, but an identity that is enacted through 'social performances' and 'performative utterances' through different channels such as commemorative ceremonies, memoirs, press conferences, interviews, fundraising, and activism. To paraphrase Neil Smelser's (2004b: 37) aphorism that 'traumas are made, not born' through linguistic mediation, victims are also made, not born. In particular, this chapter focuses on the cultural politics of victimhood that emerged after the Tokyo sarin attack, resulting in the shifting of symbolic boundaries which redefined what it means to be a 'victim' of Aum Shinrikyō's violence. The Aum Affair is a pertinent reminder that religious violence can create multiple categories of victims only some of whom become acknowledged publicly *as* victims. The central aim of this chapter is to answer the following questions.

Firstly, who were the 'victims' that engaged in public commemoration in the aftermath of the Aum Affair? Aum's crimes, including the unlawful disposal of human remains, attempted murder, murder, and the two terrorist attacks, resulted in a plethora of potential 'victims' who were harmed by Aum. Yet, only some of those victims, such as survivors and bereaved families of the sarin attacks, subsequently chose to engage in testimony and activism. There were numerous other 'victims' of the Aum Affair who were conspicuously absent from memory discourse about the Aum Affair. Former members who suffered abuse as *samana*, relatives of members who died under extreme training, and relatives of members and ex-members who were killed under Asahara's orders were just some of Aum's 'victims' who largely refrained from entering public debates about Aum's crimes. To consider the relative presence and absence of these voices in commemorative speech acts, one must look for the social 'selection mechanisms' through which victimhood emerges as a social identity, both in terms of the specific contexts in which harm occurred that enabled the articulation of victimhood, as well as within the broader social-cultural schemas that enabled some actors to come forward to claim victimhood and others to abstain from or be excluded from this process entirely.

Secondly, out of those figures that engaged in public discourse about Aum, what kinds of goals did they pursue, and why? Many victims of Aum's violence narrated their experiences in terms of trauma, hurt, loss, shock, and anger. Yet, it would be myopic to reduce their social activism merely to 'narrating trauma'. While there is no doubt many of those affected by Aum's violence were psychologically traumatised, framing their experiences merely in these psychoanalytic terms fails to capture not only the variety of these experiences, but also the multitude of goals that different victims have sought through their public interventions. The fact that victims demand justice is a truism; a more important sociological question is what *kind* of justice these victims demand. Justice does not have a single meaning. It can mean punishment for offenders including capital punishment, restitution, equality before the law, new legal frameworks for preventing future transgressions, and reconciliation through mechanisms of redress.

This chapter investigates the actions of three victims who, as 'moral entrepreneurs' and 'memory activists', shaped cultural interpretations of the Aum Affair through public testimony and social activism. Although they all pursued justice, their interpretations of justice differed significantly, leading to a polyphonic articulation of victimhood in public discourse. First, Nagaoka Hiroyuki, father of an ex-believer and survivor of Aum's murder attempt, had spoken on behalf of family members of believers for clemency and forgiveness while negotiating the difficult and ambiguous symbolic space between 'victim' and 'perpetrator'. Second, Takahashi Shizue, who was widowed by the Subway Sarin Incident, became a prominent proponent for state restitution, and has occasionally defended capital punishment as a mechanism for retributive justice. Third, Kōno Yoshiyuki, survivor of the 1994 Matsumoto Sarin Incident and a victim of false accusation, has defended the constitutional rights to freedom of religion, has criticised discriminatory practices by local state bodies against Aum believers, and has explored possibilities for reconciliation between Aum members and local communities.

Given that thousands of people were directly or indirectly 'victimised' by Aum's actions, the focus on only three individuals may appear too narrow. After all, as Murakami Haruki's interviews revealed, there were many others who spoke out about their experiences, albeit on the condition of anonymity. There are certainly many others who have contributed to public debates about Aum as victims. These figures include Kariya Minoru, the son of public notary Kariya Kiyoshi who was kidnapped by Aum and died after being drugged; Sakamoto Sachiyo, the mother of the murdered lawyer Sakamoto Tsutomu, and Asakawa Kazuo, whose sister Sachiko was severely paralysed by the Tokyo sarin attack and passed away in 2020. Without downplaying the importance of their interventions in their own right in public discourse, the discussion of victimhood is restricted here to the three individuals for three reasons. Firstly, the three figures discussed here have been far more prominent than others in public debate, owing to their public positions as representatives of Aum's victims. Nagaoka has represented the Aum Families' Society (formerly Aum Victims' Society) since 1989, a group for parents of Aum believers and ex-members. Takahashi has been the representative for the Subway Sarin Incident Victims' Society since its inception in 1996. Kōno has been associated with Recovery Support Center, a charity supporting trauma victims including survivors of the sarin attacks, first as a consultant and then as a deputy director. He has also acted as an external auditor for Hikari no Wa. For this reason, they have enjoyed a level of cultural status and public credence in speaking as and for 'victims' in public discourse. Secondly, various dramatisations and mediatisations of their personal experiences have themselves become integral to, and emblematic of, trauma narratives about the Aum Affair. For example, the national TV broadcaster Fuji Terebi aired biographical documentary-dramas of Nagaoka, Takahashi, and Kōno to mark anniversaries of the Tokyo and the Matsumoto sarin attacks in 2015, 2010, and 2009 respectively. The public broadcaster NHK also produced a documentary on Takahashi marking the 10th anniversary of the Tokyo attack, while Kōno's ordeal as a victim and suspect was recreated in a 2000 feature film. Thirdly, the public performances of victims such as Kariya, Sakamoto, and Asakawa fit relatively well with the notion of victimhood as articulated by Takahashi, which means that extended discussions of these figures are not essential for understanding the different models of victimhood. The purpose of this chapter is to show the potential variations of victimhood, not simply to record and reproduce what different actors have said; their public interventions, for the purposes of this chapter, do not constitute a novel or unique mode of victimhood when compared to other victim actors whom this chapter discusses.

Victimhood and trauma re-examined

Before starting the empirical discussions of the individual figures, it is vital to re-examine some of the theoretical foundations and assumptions that have informed studies of victimhood. Trauma theory, based on Freudian psychoanalysis, has historically dominated scholarly debates of victimhood in the aftermath of violence and loss (Radstone 2007). In this approach, victims of horrific events, including war, genocide, torture, violent crime, child abuse, and sexual assault, are mentally overwhelmed by the experience, which results in 'delayed, uncontrolled repetitive appearance of hallucinations and other intrusive phenomena' (Caruth 1996: 11). These vivid episodes exist in 'symbolic excess'; the trauma cannot be represented through language or any other symbolic manipulation. This results in an 'acting out', in which the repressed traumatic experience intrudes upon the subject latently and repeatedly in uncontrollable episodes. Through psychiatric care and the benefit of temporal distance, traumatised subjects 'work through' their trauma, in order to overcome it through narration. This allows subjects to transition from a state of 'melancholy' to a state of 'mourning' (Freud 1917; Friedlander 1992; LaCapra 2001). Trauma theory has been pivotal for understanding individual and collective responses to horrific violence from its initial response to subsequent commemoration (Erikson 1976; Taylor 2003).

Another important contribution of trauma theory is the role of the victim in 'speaking the truth', a function that Wiesel describes as a unique 'duty' for victims. In this view, narrating trauma is not merely a healing process for individual subjects; it is an inherently social task tied to political and ethical responsibility (LaCapra 2001: 152). This is also the model that Elie Wiesel champions and advocates. The victim narrates their experiences as a truth-telling exercise in defiance of powers that may commit the same atrocities all over again. The implication is that victims have a claim to authentic experience that other acts such as perpetrators and bystanders do not. Victims possess a special kind of experience that is at risk of being erased, silenced, or sanitised were victims not to speak out.

This model of the traumatised victim as a 'truth-teller' in defiance of political adversity provides a powerful heuristic for understanding the psychological motives of victims of horrific experiences, given that many victims of war, terrorism, and genocides are at the mercy of political forces beyond their control and frequently engage in concerted commemorative efforts to prevent future tragedies. Yet, the psychoanalytic approach alone is deficient in fully addressing the complexities of social struggles that occur around victimhood.

Firstly, because trauma theorists locate psychological trauma as a defining characteristic of victimhood, they provide an ahistorical and decontextualised model of victimhood, which assumes the relationship between victim and perpetrator to be transparent and self-evident. The victim receives the trauma and the perpetrator inflicts the trauma.[1] This ignores historical and cultural patterns in which actors apply codes of who counts as 'victims' and as 'perpetrators'. In other words, individuals and groups are recognised as victims and perpetrators only to the extent that socio-cultural patterns enable these identifications and claims

[1] This does not preclude the possibility for perpetrators themselves to be traumatised: this is discussed in the following chapter (Chapter 8).

of victimhood to be accepted as legitimate. As the sociologist Bernhard Giesen points out, the 'very notion of victims presupposes agencies that intervene and change human lives, that define and recognize victimisation' (Giesen 2004: 46). For example, female victims of rape across different cultures and across time have been blamed for 'tempting' or 'seducing' their attackers and have been further vilified as a result without social or legal recognition as legitimate 'victims', regardless of their experience of psychological trauma. Moreover, as Giesen (2004) has argued, victimhood does not simply connote a relationship of received harm; it is a symbolic state in which the sovereignty of the self has been desecrated. This stands in contrast to other terms such as 'martyrs', in which the subject preserves their individual autonomy and freedom, even in death. Victimhood is therefore not an ontological and transparent category, but an identity that is claimed and constructed through performative utterances.

The second problem lies in trauma theory's simplistic attribution of victims' motives to speak out or to stay silent. In the psychoanalytic binary between 'acting out' and 'working through', silence or refusal to testify are assumed to be symptoms of unassimilated trauma ('melancholy'). This (mis)placement of trauma as the ultimate cause of the victims' silence has a double effect. Firstly, it assumes that victims must *want* to speak out, if only they could. Secondly, this prescriptive understanding of traumatised subjects places the psychoanalyst in a privileged social position vis-à-vis traumatised subjects, insofar as the psychoanalyst acts as the self-appointed key that unlocks the door to assimilated trauma. Once again, this view obscures the cultural and historical contexts in which victims may choose to speak out to claim victimhood, and places excessive emphasis on psychological factors without due attention to sociological factors. Indeed, in the context of the Aum Affair, it is evident that the causes of victims' silence are not solely attributable to psychological trauma. Amidst widespread reports of Aum as a 'death cult', and their history of attacking their critics including Nagaoka, many victims feared reprisals from the group by speaking publicly or suing Aum for damages. As a result, even survivors and bereaved families who publicly spoke about their experiences usually only did so on conditions of anonymity (Chikatetsu Sarin Jiken Higaisha no Kai 1998). Moreover, as clinical psychiatrist Stevan Weine points out, testimony might not be a priority for many survivors of violent events: 'there is a lot more to being a survivor … than trauma and torture … Only a small minority will accept psychotherapy, treatment, or testimony' (Weine 2006: 20). One cannot assume, therefore, that unwillingness to speak out stems from unassimilated trauma alone. Instead, one must look to the social context for a better understanding of when and why silences occur. In short, trauma theory provides an inadequate foundation for understanding why victims choose to narrate their experiences or not.

Towards a performative understanding of victimhood

As an alternative to the psychoanalytic model, this chapter proposes a performative framework for understanding different modalities, strategies, and goals pursued by actors who take up the role of 'victim' through social activism. This approach can be summed up as 'victimhood is as victimhood does.' Victimhood is a symbolic identity which is created and enacted through 'social performance': the public display and articulation of cultural norms and values through embodied action (Alexander 2009; 2016). While victimhood is grounded in existing cultural norms, the specific meanings attached to victimhood remain unarticulated and undetermined until they are mobilised through social action, such as making public claims to victimhood, providing testimony, accusing perpetrators, and participating in commemorative events.

Performance of victimhood is performative in two senses. In the first, more straightforward sense, victims perform victimhood by making public appearances 'on stage' to claim victimhood by narrating their experiences as 'protagonists' in a social drama, and to draw upon underlying cultural codes and rhetorical skill to convince their audience of the moral weight and authenticity of their experiences. In the second, philosophical sense, victims *create* the very meaning of victimhood through performative utterances. The philosopher J.L. Austin (1962) distinguished between constative utterances, which describe a situation or reality, and performative utterances, which create and change social reality. Performative utterances might range from validating a marriage or naming a pet dog to making promises or asking someone to close the window. Beyond the surface-level meaning of sentences, performative utterances are 'illocutionary', in that they express the speaker's intent, and also 'perlocutionary', in that they seek to affect the attitudes of others. In short, performative utterances create, reproduce, and change representations of social reality through language.

This perspective emphasises that victimhood is not an ontological category that exists in a social vacuum, but an identity that must be constructed through performative utterances by competing actors in a messy social arena where different actors have the potential to *become* victims due to their prior experience or perception of harm. In this sense, individuals who have received harm, or who perceive that they have received harm can be considered 'proto-victims' until they have made those experiences public, or have been identified as victims by third parties.

This may also mean, for instance, that individuals that previously claimed victimhood may relinquish their claims to victimhood in light of new information and contexts. This is exactly what happened to Nagaoka. After the Tokyo sarin attack, Nagaoka and other parents of Aum believers partially withdrew their public claims as victims, when their familial association with the perpetrators potentially compromised their social performance as victims, as compared with other potential victims and survivors of Aum's murders and terrorist attacks. Importantly, this suggests that an individual's performance and embodiment of victimhood is flexible and changeable with each iterative performance. Just like a theatrical performance, victimhood can be adjusted, reiterated, and revised over time according to the context and the performative strategies that one adopts.

Victimhood is polysemic – as it is open to multiple meanings as interpreted by different actors – but it is not an 'empty signifier' that can be filled with *any* meaning. Insofar as victimhood is predicated upon the performance of it, victimhood relies on the articulation of positive civil values, such as freedom, democracy, truth, and justice. In this sense, there is a presumption of 'innocence' and 'purity' expected of victims. This explains why Aum's dissident members who were killed by Aum or are survivors of abuse have rarely been acknowledged in commemorative discourse, and, by extension, why families of those victims have not spoken out in subsequent commemorative processes as victims. In addition, performance of victimhood is constrained by time: every public articulation of victimhood is unique and provisional. Each performance can succeed or fail (Alexander 2009). At the same time, repeated performances of victimhood can make the image of a victim fixed, enduring, and path dependent. While repeated, well-rehearsed performances can ensure the stability of a particular social reality created through performative utterances, the more this position becomes established, the harder it becomes the actor to dramatically change their views later on. One cannot enact a different notion of victimhood every time one makes a public intervention without risking damage to one's authenticity, sincerity, and credibility (Baert 2012).

By looking at variations in how different individuals enact and articulate these positive cultural values, it is possible to trace patterns indicating how victims value certain forms of justice over others, and how certain iterations of victimhood stand in conflict with others. To return to the idea of polyphony, there are situations in which multiple, irreconcilable interpretations of victimhood collide. For example, some victims may call for retributive justice by supporting harsh punishment for offenders such as the death sentence, while other may choose to engage in restorative justice measures by engaging in dialogue with offenders through policies such as Truth and Reconciliation Commissions.

In understanding the polyphonic models of victimhood in the aftermath of the Aum Affair, the two-by-two matrix depicted in Table 7.1 helps to delineate the different types of social performances by the three prominent victims according to two relational conditions: the actor's relationship with other victims, and the actor's relationship to offenders. As shown in Table 7.1, the actor's relationship with other victims can be divided into expressions of difference or solidarity. Expressions of difference accentuate the uniqueness of one's own experiences as being qualitatively different and incomparable to those of other victims. By contrast, expressions of solidarity seek to find common ground between victims by making demands at a collective level. The actor's relationship with perpetrators can be distinguished by whether they are antagonistic or reconciliatory. At the antagonistic end of the spectrum, victims are hostile to perpetrators, often calling for retributive justice or ostracism. At the reconciliatory end, victims seek to heal the divisions between themselves and the perpetrators through dialogue – for instance, by accepting public apologies, engaging in shared commemoration, or participating in restorative justice programmes.

Nagaoka fits the 'difference-antagonistic' model of victimhood. Despite being a survivor of a murder attempt himself, as the father of an ex-believer, he has emphasised the differences between himself and other survivors and bereaved families. At the same time, he has maintained an antagonistic attitude towards the remaining Aum/Aleph members by supporting the 'mind control' thesis. Takahashi has enacted a 'solidarity-antagonistic' model of victimhood. As the face of the public campaign demanding state restitution for victims of the subway sarin attack, she has consistently emphasised the shared trauma of sarin victims through numerous public interventions and commemorative actions. At the same time, she has personally maintained an antagonistic stance towards Aum, its successor organisations, and ex-members by denouncing Aum as a destructive cult, and has defended forms of retributive justice, including the death penalty, as necessary. Lastly, Kōno has espoused a radically different vision of victimhood that places reconciliation at the heart of his actions. In this 'solidarity-reconciliatory' version of victimhood, speaking out alongside other victims for state restitution goes hand-in-hand with engaging in reconciliatory dialogue with offenders. In addition to engaging in dialogue with members and ex-members of Aum as well as Aleph and Hikari no Wa, Aum's two successor organisations, Kōno has also openly criticised the death penalty in principle as unjust, in contrast to Nagaoka and Takahashi who have given qualified support for it.

		Actor's relationship with offenders	
		Antagonistic	**Reconciliatory**
Actor's relationship with other victims	**Difference**	*'difference-antagonistic'* Nagaoka Hiroyuki	*'difference-reconciliatory'*
	Solidarity	*'solidarity-antagonistic'* Takahashi Shizue, Kariya Minoru, Asakawa Kazuo, etc.	*'solidarity-reconciliatory'* Kōno Yoshiyuki

Table 7.1 Performative models of victimhood.

Of course, it is important to note that the matrix does not fully capture the complexity of the different modes of victimhood that have been discussed since the Aum Affair, or indeed across other historical cases of mass violence where victimhood has been articulated. As elaborated below, there are subtle differences in attitudes towards the death penalty as shown by Nagaoka and Takahashi – for example, as Nagaoka had campaigned for a reduced sentence for the twelve convicts sentenced to death (not including Asahara). Nevertheless, this matrix offers a useful heuristic to understand the polyphonic, and ultimately irreconcilable, meanings actors attribute to victimhood through political activism and commemoration.

Nagaoka Hiroyuki: The 'difference-antagonistic' model

Nagaoka Hiroyuki's encounters with religion, let alone new religions, was relatively limited. Born in 1938 to a relatively well-to-do family and educated at Waseda University, a prestigious private university in Tokyo, Nagaoka had had a successful career working in sales for a manufacturing firm. As part of the core post-war workforce that led Japan's economic recovery in the latter half of the 20th century, Nagaoka was hardly unique in his situation. For much of his working career, Nagaoka was the model 'salaryman' (*sararīman*) – a salaried employee – who poured his heart and soul into his work. He had no time for, or interest in, religious or spiritual matters. However, his son Tatsuya was different; as he had experienced some health problems as a child and teenager, he began to take an interest in religion. In 1987, Tatsuya, who was 19 years old at the time and studying at a Buddhist university, began to take an interest in Aum Shinrikyō. It was also around this time that Asahara had renamed his organisation Aum Shinrikyō from Aum Shinsen no Kai, effectively restructuring it from a yoga class to a religion that placed him as the omniscient and omnipotent guru. Nagaoka still recalls with shock when Tatsuya announced his intention to become a full-time renunciant (*samana*) in 1989, at the same time as asking his father for a cash donation to be made to Aum.[2] After Tatsuya left to become a *samana*, he cut off contact with his family, following Aum's teachings to minimise one's attachment to family and friends.

Nagaoka soon discovered other parents of Aum believers had experienced similar issues. Initially, parents' grievances mainly related to monetary issues and family breakdown. They were concerned that the prices for Aum's various 'initiation rituals' were extortionate, and that their children were being brainwashed in isolated environments with no family contact. The parents frequently protested

[2] Author's interview with Nagaoka Hiroyuki, 27 March 2015, Tokyo.

outside Aum's communes and shared accommodation to persuade their children to leave Aum, and sometimes took believers by force to 'deprogramme' them in physical isolation – a strategy which followed the examples of the contemporaneous 'anti-cult' movements in the US. This further deepened the gulf between Aum and the parents. In mid-1989, in response to Aum's request to be recognised as a religious corporation by the Tokyo Metropolitan Government, parents orchestrated a public petition demanding Aum's request to be turned down. Aum responded by organising a sit-in protest outside the Metropolitan Government building.[3] While the governor withheld a decision for some time, Aum was eventually granted religious corporation status in the summer of that year.

In October 1989, with the assistant of his wife Eiko and others, Nagaoka formed the Aum Shinrikyō Victims' Society (*Aum Shinrikyō Higaisha no Kai*), the first organised attempt to publicly express collective grievances against Aum. The Society was represented by the lawyer Sakamoto Tsutsumi, who had experience with dealing with the 'spiritual sales' of expensive products by new religious movements. The Society was formed out of a public media campaign against Aum Shinrikyō in the weekly contemporary affairs magazine *Sunday Mainichi*. Starting in October 1989, the magazine ran a seven-week series titled 'The Madness of Aum Shinrikyō' (*Oumu Shinrikyō no Kyōki*), accusing Aum of brainwashing believers and of generating income through unethical pseudo-scientific initiation rituals, as evidenced by the controversial 'initiation by blood', in which believers purchased phials of Asahara's bloody to be drunk by the initiand, supposedly to replicate Asahara's DNA inside their bodies. The series brought together parents sharing the same concerns, leading to the formation of an anti-Aum pressure group. The magazine was also the first major outlet to place Aum under public scrutiny.

The second development was the murder of Sakamoto Tsutsumi, and his wife and child, just two weeks after the Society's inception. After Sakamoto's discussions with Aum to resolve the situation fell through, Asahara ordered his disciples to kill Sakamoto by *poa*. Although Nagaoka persistently urged the police to investigate Aum as potential suspects, the case remained unsolved, and their bodies were not recovered until after the arrests of the main culprits in 1995.

The antagonism between Aum and the Victims' Society continued throughout the early 1990s, as Nagaoka continued to engage in protests and awareness-raising campaigns such as distributing leaflets requesting an investigation into the Sakamoto family's disappearance. His son Tatsuya quit Aum in 1990 following Aum's disastrous election campaign, and subsequently joined Nagaoka's Victims' Society as one of its core members to encourage other believers to quit the movement. Tatsuya later co-founded the Canary Society, a mutual support group for ex-members. Despite this success, Nagaoka's activism came at a personal cost.

[3] Ibid.

He was forced to quit his job after Aum continually harassed him by repeatedly making aggressive phone calls to his workplace.[4]

Unbeknownst to Nagaoka, Aum had also begun developing chemical weapons for *poa* on a massive scale. Starting in 1994, Aum began to attack its perceived enemies using sarin, VX, and phosgene, as well as attacking the lawyer Takimoto Tarō, who had taken over from Sakamoto in representing Nagaoka's group, and Egawa Shōko, a frequent media critic of Aum. Under Asahara's orders to kill either Nagaoka or his son, on 4 January 1995, assailants led by Niimi Tomomitsu sprayed VX solution on Nagaoka's neck as he was walking outside, which escaped his notice as it was raining. As he returned home, he collapsed and was hospitalised (Nagaoka 2009). Initially, the police failed to take the case seriously, instead informally feeding information to the press that Nagaoka had attempted suicide by drinking pesticide.[5] Nagaoka survived, but with severe physical impairment. Fearing further attacks by Aum, he did not dare stay in hospital for long, but left after two weeks. For the next two months, to protect himself from further attacks, he moved between various hotels near Tokyo, where he witnessed the horrors of the Tokyo sarin attack unfold. On the morning that the sarin attack occurred, he recalled that he could immediately tell that Aum was behind it.[6]

The Tokyo attack posed a new challenge for Nagaoka: it had created a new group of 'victims' distinct from the believers' parents whom he had represented. Although Nagaoka was undoubtedly a victim himself, and many parents believed themselves to be victims of family breakdown and financial loss, their claim to victimhood was becoming increasingly untenable. As 'parents of terrorists', the assumed moral purity as an innocent party had been compromised. Japan's specific cultural context, in which dishonour extends beyond individuals to families, complicated this ambiguous symbolic boundary between victim and perpetrator. It is common, for instance, for relatives of individuals arrested for serious crimes to make public apologies on behalf of the suspect.

Responding to these new developments, the Aum Shinrikyō Victims' Society renamed itself the Aum Shinrikyō Families' Society (*Oumu Shinrikyō Kazoku no Kai*) in June 1995 to better reflect the group's relational position vis-à-vis Aum Shinrikyō. Accentuating the difference between parents of believers and the victims of the sarin attacks, Nagaoka devised a new category of 'pure victims' (*junsui higaisha*) to describe victims of Aum's murders and terror attacks. This category indicated the symbolic 'purity' of victims of Aum's violence, without entirely abandoning parents' claims to victimhood. The Families' Society has made apologies on behalf of Aum's members and ex-members. On their official website, the Society makes a public apology to members of the public that their

[4] Ibid.
[5] Ibid.
[6] Ibid.

family members were involved in Aum's crimes, and that their efforts were not sufficient to prevent Aum's anti-social activities.[7]

In this readjusted performance, Nagaoka situates the experiences of believers' parents, including himself, as being separate and not directly comparable to victims of the sarin attacks. In this renegotiated symbolic space, believers' parents occupy an intermediary position between 'pure victims' and perpetrators. Stressing this difference, Nagaoka's public interventions have entailed a partial suppression of his own traumatic experiences as a survivor of a murder attempt, as exemplified in a press conference that he attended in January 2015 with reference to the trial of Takahashi Katsuya. A getaway driver in the Tokyo attack and an accomplice in the murder attempt against Nagaoka, Takahashi had evaded the police for 17 years under a false identity and was arrested in 2012 following a national manhunt. At the joint press conference held by Nagaoka and other victims of Takahashi's crimes, Nagaoka used the occasion to issue an apology to Takahashi Shizue and other 'pure victims' on behalf of other believers' parents for being unable to stop Aum's militarisation process earlier.[8] Nagaoka recalled that he felt conflicted to be sitting beside other victims such as Takahashi and Asakawa Kazuo, whose sister had been paralysed by the attack.[9]

In a talk given in 2009, Nagaoka's wife Eiko also re-emphasised this schism between believers' parents and other victims.

> We are not direct victims, and although we are victims of the VX gas, we also carry the burden of being families of perpetrators, so we are somewhat different from pure victims … I think we are not victims in the real sense. My son quit in January 1990, and my husband is a victim but can more or less live a normal life. That's different to victims who can't get back what they have lost. I think for [pure] victims, there is something greater than I can imagine. (Nagaoka 2009)

While the Tokyo attack prompted Nagaoka to adjust his position vis-à-vis other victims, he has maintained an antagonistic stance towards Aum and its successor organisations, Aleph and Hikari no Wa. Despite Hikari no Wa's public claims that they no longer worship Asahara as a spiritual leader, Nagaoka recognises the organisations as essentially the same, and views Jōyū as a cunning and untrustworthy figure.[10] Alongside many prominent anti-cult activists and intellectuals, Nagaoka has consistently supported the mind control thesis. In his words, the believers had lost the ability 'to think with their own heads'.[11] At the same time, Nagaoka acknowledges other social factors that prompted young people to join

[7] Oumu Shinrikyō Kazoku no Kai (n.d.), 'Ippan no minasama e' <http://aum-kazoku.boy.jp/?page_id=16> Accessed September 2021.

[8] Interview with Nagaoka.

[9] Ibid.

[10] Ibid.

[11] Ibid.

Aum, including parental neglect, miscommunication, and the excessive focus on school grades and rote learning. It is also on this principle of righting his (and other parents') past wrongs, that Nagaoka justifies the continuation of the Families' Society. For him, Aum was a problem that the 'adults' of contemporary society – himself included – created, and which they have a responsibility to address and resolve by working towards the group's dissolution.[12] Nagaoka also apportions blame to the state for failing to prevent the development of Aum's criminal activities. He has sharply criticised the Tokyo Metropolitan Government for granting religious corporation to Aum in 1989 and has been critical of the police's mishandling of criminal cases prior to the Tokyo attack, including both Sakamoto's case and the murder attempt on himself.[13]

While the Families' Society has fully endorsed retributive justice for Aum's offenders, its pursuit of justice has been slightly different to that of other Aum victims or public opinion at large. From the end of the criminal trial proceedings to the executions of the 13 convicts sentenced to death in 2018, the Families' Society had gathered and submitted multiple public petitions to the government for the death sentences of 12 convicts, excluding Asahara, to be commuted to life sentences. In their view, the core culprits, many of whom had renounced their faith after their arrests, were mind controlled and had limited agency at the time of committing the violent crimes.[14] Until the executions were carried out, Nagaoka had regularly met with convicts awaiting execution to offer them guidance and emotional support. Following the executions, Nagaoka expressed deep anger and disappointment that his pleas had not been heard and stated that he felt ashamed as a Japanese citizen that so many people had been executed at once.[15]

Takahashi Shizue: The 'solidarity-antagonistic' model

As a central figure who has built networks of solidarity among victims of the sarin attacks, Takahashi Shizue is one of the most recognisable victims of the Aum Affair. Before the attack, Takahashi worked part-time at a bank in Tokyo, while her husband Kazumasa worked at Kasumigaseki Metro Station as deputy station master. They had three children together. Kazumasa was one of two metro employees killed at the station; he was killed while cleaning up the spilled sarin solution. In the summer of 1995, Takahashi joined a class action lawsuit against

[12] Ibid.
[13] Ibid.
[14] Oumu Shinrikyō Kazoku no Kai (n.d.), 'Shomei katsudō ni tsuite' <http://aum-kazoku.boy.jp/?page_id=12> Accessed May 2022.
[15] *Tokyo Shimbun* (2018), '"Higai tsuzuite iru" Oumu zen shikeishū kei shikkō "tekisetsu" "shikkō wa gimon" yureru izoku, higaisha ra', 26 July 2018, p. 7.

Aum. Takahashi and her three children put their names down as plaintiffs in the first round of lawsuits. However, as many victims feared reprisal attacks, only 40 out of over 6,000 survivors and bereaved relatives initially agreed to be named as plaintiffs.[16]

The following year, the group filing the lawsuit officially formed the Subway Sarin Incident Victims' Society (*Chikatesu Sarin Jiken Higaisha no Kai*) with Takahashi as the 'representative-caretaker' (*daihyō sewanin*). This was the first civil group to claim to represent Aum's victims after the Families' Society partially relinquished its claim to victimhood. Takahashi took on the leadership role after lawyers representing them suggested she should publicise victims' demands to rally public support (Takahashi 2008). The Victims' Society has had four 'pillars' of activity. Firstly, a key aim was to recover losses through legal and financial means by suing for damages. Secondly, the group appealed for the need for a comprehensive health survey of survivors. Thirdly, it campaigned for a permanent and continuous treatment system for survivors through regular health checks. These have been provided through the efforts of local councils and charities. Fourthly, the group appealed for continued surveillance of Aum and its successor group, demanding that they be disbanded (Chikatetsu Sarin Jiken Higaisha no Kai 2015).[17]

Takahashi's performative logic entails both a deconstruction and a reconstruction of the Aum Affair as a national trauma. Her social performance is deconstructive because it challenges widespread representations of the Aum Affair that situated victimhood at the level of the nation. In contrast to mainstream media discourses that positioned victimhood at the national level, Takahashi locates victimhood at a strictly individual level: only individuals died, experienced the loss of a loved one, or suffered the physical and psychological trauma of sarin poisoning. In her view, if anything, state authorities had failed actual victims by letting Aum arm itself completely without being detected. Many victims echoed this sentiment, as evidenced by the collection of writings published by the Victims' Society, which expressed frustration with the media's insensitive and incessant harassment of victims in a bid to collect comments from them (Chikatetsu Sarin Jiken Higaisha no Kai 1998). These testimonies narrated victims' experiences in highly individual terms that defied attempts to appropriate and collect these experiences into a singular, overarching 'trauma narrative' for the Japanese nation.

This articulation of victimhood based on individual trauma is also reconstructive, because it ties directly into their collective demands for financial restitution. Takahashi argued that the scale of the Aum Affair warranted financial

[16] Author's interview with Takahashi Shizue, 6 April 2015, Tokyo.

[17] Ibid. Takahashi's vision for restorative justice here is therefore selective. Although she has campaigned for greater support for victims of crime, she has also distanced herself from efforts to achieve reconciliation through victim-offender talks, which is a key component of many restorative justice processes.

support from the government because anyone, at any time, could fall victim to terrorism. In opposition to the government's original position that compensation should be sought from perpetrators in a civil court, Takahashi argued that the victims acted as 'sacrifices' (*migawari*) for the state institutions Aum sought to destroy; the state therefore had a responsibility to make amends (Takahashi 2008: 91).

The Victims' Society's efforts to recover compensation encountered multiple obstacles. Plaintiffs of class action lawsuits had won multiple cases against Aum in the late 1990s, but this did not immediately result in the successful recovery of financial loss. Firstly, under existing laws, other debtors such as the state, local governments, and corporations were legally entitled to receive their share of compensation before individual debtors. In response, the government passed a law in 1998 to subordinate their compensation claims against Aum, thereby allowing victims to receive compensation first. This still left the issue of Aum's insolvency. Aum's total debt amounted to approximately ¥5.4 billion (around US$54 million), which led to its bankruptcy in 1996. Thus, victims could only expect to receive up to 10 per cent of the sum originally awarded to them in court.[18] The focus of the Victims' Society subsequently shifted towards establishing a state-funded compensation scheme to Aum's victims. After many years of campaigning alongside NGOs such as the Sarin Incidents Mutual Help Fund (*Sarin Jiken Tō Kyōjo Kikin*), Takahashi's lobbying eventually gathered cross-party support for a series of legal reforms aimed at providing relief to victims of crime. The landmark Victims Relief Act of 2008 established a system of state compensation in the form of 'relief payments' (*mimaikin*) to victims of the Aum Affair.

Takahashi's attempts to extend solidarity across victims of terrorism have had an international reach as she travelled to the United States to receive training related to victim care and to establish links with victim support charities. After the September 11 attacks, she was impressed by the level of care provided to victims of terrorism.[19] Later, she developed a long-standing friendship with Lee Ielpi, a retired firefighter and president of the September 11 Families Association who lost his son, also a firefighter, in the World Trade Center. In 2005, Takahashi invited Ielpi to speak at a symposium on the sarin attack, in which he strongly urged state support for terror victims (Takahashi 2008). Takahashi's international activities, as Mark Pendleton (2009) has argued, are indicative of transnational or even global modes of remembrance and mourning in response to terrorist attacks that have a moral impact beyond national borders.

Beyond her public role as the leader of the Victims' Society, Takahashi has occasionally expressed her personal support for capital punishment as necessary to reflect

[18] Ibid.
[19] Ibid.

the wishes of bereaved families (Takahashi 2008: 170–71). She expressed ambivalence towards perpetrators of the Aum attacks. In the trial of Hayashi Ikuo, who was responsible for her husband's death but who seemed to display genuine remorse during the trials, she declined to take the stand as a witness and did not explicitly demand the death sentence for Hayashi (ibid.: 100–11). At the same time, Takahashi has supported the death sentences for other Aum culprits (Pendleton 2015). Commenting in 2011 on the death sentence of Tsuchiya Masami, a key figure behind the sarin production, Takahashi stated that it was a relief that the rightful outcome had been reached.[20] Nonetheless, her feelings towards the death penalty do not seem to be fixed. Following the first round of mass executions, Takahashi stated that, while the justification for Asahara's execution was 'beyond question' (*tōzen*), she wished the six others could have spoken out more in the interests of counterterrorism.[21]

Like Nagaoka, Takahashi has maintained an antagonistic stance towards Aum, and views its successor organisations as anti-social cults. She has consistently called for Aum's successor organisations to be disbanded and has supported security agencies' continued surveillance of Aleph and Hikari no Wa.[22] She mistrusts the public apologies by both organisations as disingenuous media stunts. In her view, such apologies and reports of payments can be addressed directly to the Victims' Society without making a public show of remorse.[23] In my interview with her, when asked about Hikari no Wa leader Jōyū Fumihiro's claim that maintaining the organisation is necessary to continue paying out reparations, she responded: 'To be told that they can't disband because of compensation is outrageous. You can continue to pay compensation in different ways, as individuals, and there are people that do it like that. So we want them to make that kind of effort; and also, for them to be in a group, that's scary for everyone.'[24]

Takahashi's enactment of victimhood primarily through the pursuit of financial restitution raised the public profile of victims at a time when much of the media attention was focused on the perpetrators. Until Takahashi spoke out, victims were a marginal presence in media debates (ibid.: 96–7). This necessitated an expression of victimhood that differed from simplistic expectations of a 'victim' who feels anger towards the perpetrators and always agrees with prosecutors (ibid.: 96). Against this 'fabricated' (*tsukurareta*) image of a victim (ibid.: 96), she has represented victims as plural figures who are distanced from – and sometimes critical of – state institutions, and capable of making demands in their own terms. Reflecting on her activism over the past two decades, Takahashi speculates that a

[20] *Yomiuri Shimbun* (2011), 'Oumu Tsuchiya hikoku shikei kakutei e', 16 February, p. 36.

[21] NHK (2018), 'Oumu Shinrikyō Shikei Shikkō', <www3.nhk.or.jp/news/special/aum_shinrikyo/index.html?utm_int=news_contents_news-closeup_003> Accessed May 2022.

[22] Interview with Takahashi.

[23] Ibid.

[24] Ibid.

sea change has occurred in public understandings of victimhood as a direct result of the Victims' Society's actions. Before the Tokyo attack, victims of crime had to endure loss and hardship with no hope of publicly funded assistance. The fact that there has been no public criticism of the Victims Relief Act, in her opinion, reflects the widespread recognition of the fact that anyone at any time can become a victim of crime, terrorism, or natural disaster.[25]

For all its achievements, the Victims' Society nevertheless experienced tensions within the organisation. As Takahashi recalls in her memoir, the organisation's representation of both survivors and bereaved families elided some subtle subjective differences and priorities between the two groups on occasion. On the one hand, many survivors, who suffered from physical and psychological trauma, were interested in immediate financial restitution to recover their normal lives. Bereft families, on the other hand, were still grieving the loss of their loved ones, and were more interested in lobbying and staging commemorative activities (ibid.: 168–9; 178–9). There were also individuals who – for whatever reason – did not choose to join the Victim's Society. Her feelings towards the perpetrators have also differed from those of other victims and survivors; she recalls that others supported the death penalty for Hayashi (ibid.: 108–9), and that support for her group has sometimes been equivocal. Attendance was also quite poor at times. She recalls an instance in which she organised a survey via a newsletter and did not receive a single response, suggesting that internal support for her leadership has been mixed at times (ibid.: 160–61).

Despite these internal divisions and frictions, Takahashi has continued to host regular meetings among long-term members of the society, although these are relatively small in scale, numbering about a dozen people per event as of 2015.[26] Furthermore, as a memory agent, Takahashi has hosted various commemorative events on the Aum Affair, ranging from her annual visit to Kasumigaseki Station, holding press conferences and hosting symposia, to recording video interviews with people affected by the Tokyo attack. Takahashi has repeatedly warned that the memory of the Tokyo attack has been gradually 'weathering' (*fūka*). To address this, the group's more recent activities have included raising awareness of the long-term effects of sarin poisoning. In 2015, in collaboration with researchers at Tsukuba University, the Victims' Society published a study which found that over half the respondents experienced possible after-effects of sarin poisoning, such as headaches, tired eyes, loss of vision, and insomnia (Utsunomiya et al. 2015).

Takahashi's public interventions have some similarities to Nagaoka's, including their critical attitude towards failures of the security agencies and their antagonistic relations with Aleph and Hikari no Wa. However, Takahashi's interventions differ decisively from Nagaoka's in her emphasis on the necessity of the death

[25] Author's email correspondence with Takahashi Shizue, December 2015.
[26] Interview with Takahashi.

penalty as a requisite system for reflecting victims' retributive wishes. Takahashi's qualified support of capital punishment also differs substantially from victimhood as enacted by Kōno Yoshiyuki, a survivor and widower of the Matsumoto sarin incident.

Kōno Yoshiyuki: The 'solidarity-reconciliatory' model

As discussed in previous chapters, Kōno Yoshiyuki's experiences stand apart from other victims of Aum's violent crimes, as he was also a victim of false accusation by the police and media after being poisoned by the attack and eventually losing his wife to the effects of sarin poisoning. Kōno was hospitalised for a month after the attack, while his wife Sumiko, who suffered brain damage from the poisoning, fell into a coma until her eventual passing in 2008. Understandably, his public articulation of victimhood has been coloured by his traumatic experiences as a survivor and widower, which is compounded by his experiences as a suspect and a victim of a 'trial by media'. Following his total vindication over the course of the police investigation in 1995, Kōno began a prolific career as a writer and public speaker alongside his job as an office worker. To date, he has published a number of memoirs detailing his life experiences; his first book was based on a diary he kept while he was bedridden in hospital. In the memoir, he reconstructs the aggressive and malicious reporting by the news media, with examples of headlines and articles which were later retracted. The memoir vividly reconstructs the extent to which the police treated him as a suspect. For example, while he was in hospital, the police lied to his teenage son in informal interviews that Kōno had admitted responsibility for the attack to gain information (Kōno 2001).

However, his public interventions have rarely centred on his trauma testimony as such. He has written and spoken not only about his experiences as a sarin attack survivor and a suspect, but also about caring for his unconscious wife, his hobbies, and how he could enjoy life without being preoccupied with the past (Kōno 2008; 2012). By his own calculation, Kōno has spoken at over 2,000 events at institutional settings, ranging from journalism symposia and police functions to hospitals, nursing schools, and secondary schools.[27] Throughout these public interventions, he has consistently emphasised that the guilt of the suspect must be judged in a court of law, not the court of public opinion. He has also criticised the collusive relationship between the police and journalists. For example, journalists might gain unofficial, unverified information from anonymous police sources; investigators then use these published news reports as 'evidence' of guilt to gain information from potential suspects in highly pressurised police interviews (Kōno

[27] Author's interview with Kōno Yoshiyuki, 10 April 2015, Kagoshima.

2001). The false reports on the Matsumoto sarin incident occurred, Kōno believes, because intense competition over television ratings and newspaper readership led the media to 'stand side by side' (*yokonarabi*) to cover the same stories from the same angle with no variation (Kōno 2008: 138–41).[28]

Like Takahashi, Kōno has expressed solidarity with other victims by demanding greater institutional support for terror victims. He locates the 2003 Victims Relief Act as a milestone in providing a legal framework to support victims of crime. He has also suggested that beyond the Victims Relief Act, which was specifically established for Aum's victims, there should be a greater expansion of victims' rights by creating a comprehensive, public fund for crime victims.[29] In addition, he has served as a consultant to, and deputy director of, the Recovery Support Center (RSC), a charity set up in the aftermath of the Tokyo attack to provide care for victims of terrorism and natural disasters. Reflecting Kōno's opinion that victims require continued medical support and counselling, the RSC has conducted free regular health checks for victims of the Aum Affair, as well as victims of natural disasters.

Kōno's embodiment of victimhood is most distinctive in his stance towards the perpetrators. Unlike Nagaoka and Takahashi, who have been continuously critical of Aum and its successor organisations, he has interacted with Aleph and Hikari no Wa members on a regular basis (though this is not in itself an expression of 'forgiveness' as such). As Kōno explained in an autobiographical memoir, 'to hate or to hold a grudge against someone makes your life boring. Also, that kind of activity requires a tremendous amount of energy. If I am to use that energy, I'd rather spend that energy on something more worthwhile, including looking after Sumiko. That's my honest feeling' (Kōno 2008: 20). Prior to Sumiko's passing, Kōno had accepted visits to his wife by Aleph members, and had met with them on multiple occasions, such as at his talks.[30] In Kōno's view, ex-Aum members have been convicted and punished for their crimes, not their religious beliefs, so they should not be discriminated against for what they believe in. In the mid-2000s, Kōno put this principle into practice by befriending an ex-believer who had served a sentence for constructing the custom-made truck used to spray sarin in Matsumoto. When the man visited Kōno to apologise, he accepted the apology and the two forged a friendship (ibid.).[31] His friendship with an ex-believer was grounded in his belief to never turn down those who come to see him, and not to discriminate against ex-convicts: 'once you've come out of jail, and you've served your full time, you are an ordinary person, and you shouldn't need, in principle,

[28] Ibid.
[29] Ibid.
[30] Ibid.
[31] Ibid.

a title of "ex-so-and-so".'[32] Thus, Kōno has interacted with the ex-member 'as a human being', without judging him for his past beliefs and actions.[33] Following this principle, he had also met and conversed with some of Aum's death-row convicts, upon their request.[34]

His view that Aum members should be punished for their crimes, not their beliefs, is also reflected in his reconciliatory attitudes towards Aum's successor organisations. He has criticised civil rights violations against the remaining Aum believers, which included the refusal of municipal governments to accept resident records, and school boards' denial of compulsory education for children of Aum believers (including Asahara's children) (ibid.).[35] Arguing against the predominant depiction of Aum and its successor organisations as cults, Kōno recognises Aleph and Hikari no Wa as religions whose constitutional right of freedom of belief must be respected and safeguarded. This stance differs substantially from that of both Nagaoka and Takahashi, who have iterated wishes for both organisations to be disbanded. From 2011, Kōno served as the chairman of the External Audit Commission for Hikari no Wa, a third-party body set up to report on any criminal activity in the organisation. The commission comprised several experts such as criminologists and psychologists, some of whom served anonymously. Kōno explained the reasons for his appointment in my interview with him: 'Well, there are people who, at the first mention of Aum or Hikari no Wa, say that they are scared, even though they have no idea of what goes on inside. So then, you can tell them "What are you scared of? If you want to look inside we can show you everything," so I thought I could act as a kind of bridge to remove those anxieties, and that's why I accepted [the role].'[36]

His self-positioning as a bridge between Hikari no Wa and the local community to reduce social tension differs decisively from Nagaoka and Takahashi's models of victimhood, which stress an inherent opposition between victims and perpetrators. Moreover, his distinctive moral status as a terror victim arguably insulates him from criticisms that he was acting as a 'collaborator' with former terrorists and that the External Audit Commission is a disingenuous media stunt. In 2014, following the Public Security Intelligence Agency's (PSIA) successful application to extend the surveillance of Hikari no Wa under the Organisations Regulation Act, the External Audit Commission published an independent report detailing the nature of Hikari no Wa's religious activities, challenging the PSIA's decision. The report contradicted PSIA's claims that Asahara's teachings composed the core of the movement, and that the group could yet turn to criminal activity

[32] Ibid.
[33] Ibid.
[34] Ibid.
[35] Ibid.
[36] Ibid.

(Hikari no Wa Gaibu Kansa Iinkai 2014). After the publication of the report in 2014, Kōno left this role, citing family reasons. Hikari no Wa has continued to fight the extension of the ORA in court.

Kōno also stands apart from Nagaoka and Takahashi in his negative appraisal of capital punishment as a form of retributive justice. While Nagaoka appealed for clemency to avert the execution of the culprits (excluding Asahara), and Takahashi had expressed qualified support for the death penalty, Kōno has opposed the death penalty in principle, as his personal experience is testament to the potential risks of miscarriage of justice (Kōno 2008: 26; Pendleton 2015). Moreover, Kōno was critical of Asahara's death sentence as well as the court's decision that Asahara was 'faking illness' to avoid taking responsibility (ibid.: 20). In his view, Asahara was clearly suffering from mental illness and should have received medical treatment. In a press conference hosted by a group critical of Asahara's execution after the final round of executions, Kōno reiterated his opposition to the death penalty, and expressed sadness that culprits whom he felt had shown genuine remorse were executed.[37]

It is worth noting that Kōno's 'solidarity-reconciliatory' model of victimhood has arguably been made possible because he has acted largely as an individual. Unlike Nagaoka or Takahashi, who have acted as representatives of advocacy groups and have therefore had to consider and reflect the opinions of other constituent members, Kōno has served public positions as an individual. This may have afforded him more opportunities to speak out as an individual compared to the two other figures. Conversely, this has also meant Kōno's actions have arguably lacked the wide-reaching public impact that Nagaoka and Takahashi have had through their public campaigns, such as raising awareness about Aum's controversial activities, or pushing for legal reform. Nevertheless, Kōno's enactment of the victim as a defender of constitutional rights and due process suggests the potential of victims to contribute to an informal reconciliation process within a cultural climate which has occasionally permitted and justified the exclusion of Aum believers at the expense of the rule of law. Moreover, his social performance as a victim illustrates the polyphonic, open-ended, and clashing iterations of victimhood which cannot be reduced to simply 'narrating trauma'.

[37] *Asahi Shimbun* (2018), '"Oumu owaranai" Chikatetsu sarin, shinshin fuchō imamo; Shikei shikkō', 27 July, p. 33; see also *Kyodo News* (2018), '"Matsumoto sarin higai no Kōno-san kaiken "Shūkyō ga ōku no hito fukō ni"' 26 July, YouTube, <www.youtube.com/watch?v=Z6NtNQeVrfU> Accessed May 2022.

Conclusions

The very concept of the victim is a product of social and political mediation, created through the victims' relational positions vis-à-vis other victims on the one hand, and offenders on the other. Only by recognising this can one fully appreciate the diversity of interpretations that actors have produced as victims in the pursuit of their own definitions of justice. As this chapter has discussed, each actor has enacted and realised Wiesel's model of the victim as a witness and a bridge between the past and the future in contrasting ways. For Nagaoka, the subway attack necessitated a renegotiation of the symbolic position of believers' parents, leading to a partial relinquishing of victimhood as well as a suppression of his own experiences as a survivor of a horrific murder attempt. For Takahashi and the Subway Sarin Victims' Society, the articulation of victimhood in highly personal terms entailed reclaiming victimhood at a time when much of the media attention was focused on the biographies of the perpetrators and when there was little public support available for victims of crime. For Kōno, his experiences as a 'triple victim' – as a sarin attack survivor, widower, and a subject of false accusation – have shaped his activism for greater support for victims of crimes and has led him to champion the rule of law. While Nagaoka and Takahashi have continued to identify Aum's successor organisations as anti-social 'cults', Kōno has defended their constitutional rights to freedom of religion and has explored possible pathways to relieve social tension between Hikari no Wa and the local community. In contrast to the heavy media presence of the three figures, however, some other potential 'victims', such as families of members who died during Aum's training and families of dissident believers killed on Asahara's orders, have been entirely absent in commemorative discourses about victimhood.

While this chapter has largely discussed the differences between these three actors, it is important to not lose sight of what the three figures have held in common. At a fundamental level, all three agreed that Aum's crimes were abhorrent and that the instigators, including Asahara, should be held responsible for their actions. They have been united in their criticisms of state institutions in the handling of Aum Shinrikyō both in the period leading up to the terrorist attacks and in its aftermath regarding support for victims and the surveillance of Aum's successor groups. They also concurred that the Aum Affair deserves to be commemorated for future generations, although they did not necessarily agree on *how* it should be remembered. Importantly, it appears that, despite their significantly different positions, these differences never developed into an open dispute. With the exception of Nagaoka's reference to Takahashi's activism, there were few instances whereby the victims explicitly referred to activities by other actors; by and large, they tended to talk about their own activism, and not others'. This kind of 'respectful silence' in which differences of opinion are kept implicit rather than explicit, has possibly enabled these contrasting positions to coexist in relative harmony without developing into a competition for resources or an open disagreement.

As the next chapter explores, polyphony characterises not only the victims' experiences, but also the experiences of former Aum members. Just as victims of the Aum Affair have reached different viewpoints about justice, there is a remarkable diversity in how ex-members of different ranks have reflected upon their motives for joining the movement, their assessment of Asahara as a leader and guru, and the extent to which they have retained aspects of Aum's teachings in their post-Aum lives. These differences have resulted in acrimonious disputes among Asahara's children as well as within and between Aum's successor organisations.

8

The Trauma of Perpetrators

On New Year's Eve, 2011, around half an hour before midnight, a lone, tall figure emerged from the dark and approached the headquarters building of the Metropolitan Police Department in Kasumigaseki, a short walk from the epicentre of the sarin attack. Dressed in a black down jacket, jeans, and sneakers, he hardly struck a distinctive figure. Arriving at the entrance gate, he identified himself as Hirata Makoto, a fugitive wanted in relation to Aum's crimes including the kidnapping and death of Kariya Kiyoshi in early 1995. As Hirata later confessed, he decided to give himself up after the devastation of the '3.11' Tōhoku earthquake – the largest earthquake ever recorded in Japan and the fourth largest in the world since records began, which resulted in over 20,000 deaths and missing persons and the Fukushima Dai-ichi nuclear power plant disaster – compelled him to draw a line under his own past actions.[1] In a strange twist, handing himself in proved to be harder than he expected. The on-duty officers, having compared the photograph from the wanted poster to the man in front of them, decided that it was a hoax, and instructed Hirata to go to a different police station. It was only after Hirata identified himself again at Marunouchi police station, about 600 metres away, that he was questioned more thoroughly and placed under arrest several hours later. Hirata was sentenced to nine years in prison, a verdict which was upheld by the Supreme Court in 2016.[2]

The dramatic circumstances surrounding Hirata's arrest – from the police's blunder in turning him away from the police headquarters to the completely unexpected consequences of the 3.11 Tōhoku disaster – reinvigorated fresh public discourse about Aum. Hirata's arrest also marked the beginning of a new chapter in the Aum Affair, as the police launched a large-scale manhunt for the

[1] *Mainichi Shimbun* (2012), 'Oumu Jiken: Hirata yōgisha, taiho', 3 January, p. 1. The reasons for his surrender are disputed. Although he cited personal reasons for turning himself in, at a practical level, the arrest and subsequent trials reopened investigations and delayed the executions of Asahara and others on death row.

[2] *Mainichi Shimbun* (2016), 'Oumu saiban: Hirata hikoku, chōeki 9-nen kakutei e', 15 January, p. 27.

two remaining Aum suspects on the run: Kikuchi Naoko and Takahashi Katsuya. Kikuchi, a relatively low-ranking *samana*, was wanted in connection with sarin production and a letter bomb sent to the Tokyo Metropolitan Government. Takahashi was a getaway driver in the Tokyo attack and an accomplice in the murder of a member of the public using the nerve agent VX. As the public was once again captivated by the allure of a real-life crime drama, in February, the police doubled the bounty for information leading to the suspects' arrest.[3] Aum was back in the newspaper headlines and was the subject of the lead stories of news programmes.

Kikuchi was arrested in early June 2012, after a tip-off of a sighting. Takahashi, who had previously lived with Kikuchi but had since lived on his own, fled his home soon after Kikuchi's arrest. Over the next two weeks, the police expanded the manhunt to a national level and issued a bounty for information leading to his arrest. Re-enacting the media spectacle surrounding Asahara's arrest, the mass media once again took the lead in dominating the airwaves with live, rolling coverage of the manhunt, as reporters and commentators speculated about Takahashi's possible hiding places and his current appearance. Nearly two weeks after Kikuchi's arrest, Takahashi was arrested in Tokyo on 15 June in a 'manga café' – a popular haunt for those who need affordable overnight accommodation – after an employee raised the alarm. If the police's initial blunder in turning away a highly wanted suspect at the front gate of the Metropolitan Police Department was reflective of the nation's fading interest and attention in the Aum Affair, the subsequent media spectacle around the arrests of the two fugitives provided an opportune moment for tabloid and mass media to revive the trope of the 'destructive cult' in public discourse once again.

The following trials sustained public interest in the Aum Affair for several years. In a surprise verdict, Kikuchi was acquitted of all charges relating to her alleged role in terrorism-related activities in 2015. Takahashi was found guilty and was given an indefinite sentence in 2015. Takahashi appealed against the sentence, but the verdict was upheld in the High Court. Beyond bringing closure to the 'Aum trials', the arrests of the remaining fugitives also paved the way for the eventual executions of Asahara and 12 others sentenced to death; one of the most formidable roadblocks in preventing the government carrying out the executions had been that the testimonies of those on death row could be necessary for the trials of the fugitives.

[3] *Asahi Shimbun* (2012), 'Kenshōkin baizō 1-senmanen; Oumu Takahashi, Kikuchi ryō yōgisha', 2 February, p. 2 (Eve. Ed.)

The heavily mediatised manhunts and the ensuing trials raised once again pertinent questions about Aum's methods of organisational control, psychological manipulation, and the adherents' personal motivations for engaging in religious terrorism. The intense public interest in the arrests of Aum's last fugitives was demonstrative of an enduring public fascination with Aum members, past and present. Although Hirata, Kikuchi, or Takahashi have not publicly expressed their experiences in writing beyond public records of the trial proceedings, there has been a plethora of published biographical and autobiographical accounts by ex-members. These narratives have typically discussed a range of issues, such as their motivations for joining, their daily routines and training regimen, personal impressions of Asahara, personal guilt relating to Aum's crimes, and reasons and strategies for disaffiliation. Representations of their experiences have ranged from the sensational and melodramatic – a common feature of television documentaries and documentary dramas – to the more subdued and analytical interpretations by some religious scholars and public intellectuals. Most recently, the executions of the top disciples sentenced to death has resulted in posthumous publications of autobiographies and memoirs of Asahara's former disciples such as Inoue Yoshihiro (Kadota 2018) and Hirose Ken'ichi (2019) as per their last wishes.

This abundance of narratives as told from the position of the 'perpetrator' makes the discourses about the Aum Affair relatively unique from other cases of religious terrorism and of cultural traumas more generally. There are, of course, numerous accounts by former members of violent 'cults', including survivors of the Branch Davidians' siege in Waco, Texas (Wessinger 2009) as well as survivors of the Jonestown massacre.[4] What makes the Aum case unique, however, is that whereas many ex-cult members' accounts take the position of the 'victim' or 'survivor', many of these accounts are told from the perspective of the 'perpetrator'. In this sense, the narratives of these ex-members are comparable to German 'de-Nazification' narratives (Giesen 2004) and public apologies by formerly segregationist political leaders (Fine 2013) in which the narrator details their personal journeys towards forgiveness and moral redemption from the perspective of the offender. Such apologies have often been accompanied by various modes of redress, including the payment of financial reparations to victims, and the public recantation of their previous beliefs.

Ex-members' memoirs and autobiographies have played a significant part in the discursive struggles surrounding the scientific validity of brainwashing and mind control theories. While disillusioned members who underwent

[4] Accounts of survivors of Jonestown can be accessed on the Alternative Considerations of Jonestown & Peoples Temple <https://jonestown.sdsu.edu/?page_id=31383> Accessed May 2022.

disaffiliation procedures such as deprogramming and exit counselling have tended to become vocal proponents of the mind control narrative, there is also remarkable diversity in how ex-members have publicly articulated issues of personal guilt, trauma, and responsibility. In short, there is no single way of 'leaving Aum'. Although some ex-members support the claim that Asahara mind controlled his followers to become obedient puppets, other ex-members have also highlighted other social and cultural factors for joining and, perhaps more importantly, staying in Aum even after Aum's culpability in organised crime and terrorism became undeniable.

This chapter explores these contrasting examples through a comparative analysis of former members' autobiographical accounts, ranging from rank-and-file members to those who served Asahara as his closest aides, some of whom were and are leaders of Aum's successor organisations. It highlights how different individuals who self-identify and have been identified as 'perpetrators' have addressed this difficult identity with reference to concepts such as blind faith, guilt, and individual as well as collective responsibility. On the one hand, some ordinary renunciants (*shukkesha/samana*) who supported the brainwashing/mind control paradigm explained their past behaviours as the result of psychological manipulation. On the other hand, senior disciples in managerial positions, many of whom played instrumental roles in Aum's criminal activities, have been sceptical of claims of mind control. Instead, they have tended to characterise their actions as voluntary and borne out of choice, driven by strong, but ultimately misguided, faith.

Just as victimhood is a culturally mediated category that relies on the successful performance of a victim through the harnessing of underlying sociocultural norms and contexts, this chapter argues that the status of the 'perpetrator' is a socially mediated identity which arises out of the 'enactment' of a social identity associated with guilt, shame, and responsibility, rather than a self-explanatory transparent 'fact' of having harmed another, or having committed morally reprehensible acts. The status of the perpetrator as being separate from the commission of immoral acts is most evident in the discrimination that Asahara's children have faced in the aftermath of the Tokyo attack. In what follows, this chapter discusses how two of Asahara's children have negotiated the moral and social burdens of intergenerational guilt through contrasting approaches. While Asahara's third daughter Matsumoto Rika has detailed her experiences of discrimination and has challenged legal proceedings surrounding Asahara's trial, imprisonment, and execution as a breach of human rights, Asahara's fourth daughter, who uses the alias Matsumoto Satoka, has rejected her father's disreputable legacy by severing family ties, supporting his execution, and making clear her wishes for Aum's successor organisations to disband.

Recognising guilt – the view from 'below'

Viewing the archival television footage of initial days and weeks after the Tokyo attack, it is difficult not to form an impression of Aum believers as 'fanatics'. From the police's first raid into Aum's main facilities in Kamikuishiki and Tokyo, many Aum believers fiercely resisted the investigation, claiming religious persecution. Images and sounds of believers dressed in their signature all-white kurtas, screaming, tussling, and sometimes being dragged away by the police were reproduced widely across television and newspaper reports. These impassioned protests were likely the product of a combination of orders from above and natural reactions by ordinary members. Although rank-and-file members subscribed to Aum's millenarian eschatology that the end was nigh, most of them were ignorant of the true extent of the militarisation programme and therefore were more likely to believe that they were genuinely being persecuted by the state.

In spite of this stereotype of the typical Aum member as crazed and irrational, there was in fact a mass exodus of members in the first months after the Tokyo attack. For many of them, leaving Aum was a natural and foregone conclusion after witnessing what the '*Vajrayāna* plan' as a form of armed struggled meant in practice. Aum's membership declined rapidly after the police investigation began. At Kamikuishiki's main commune, which had housed up to a thousand *samana* until the police raid in March, the population had dwindled to around two hundred by October 1995.[5] Many had moved to smaller shared accommodation in other parts of the country or had left the movement altogether.

The Canary Society

It is not uncommon that ex-members of 'cults' become some of the most outspoken critics of the groups they once belonged to (Barker 2007; Bromley 2008). Among the hundreds of believers that quit Aum in the months after the Tokyo attack, some formed a mutual support network called the 'Canary Society' (*Kanariya no Kai*). Since its inception, the group has been represented by the lawyer and anti-cult activist Takimoto Tarō (see Chapter 6), who also represents the Aum Shinrikyō Families' Society (see Chapter 7). To date, the group has hosted meetings, offered exit counselling sessions to believers, and has published newsletters, which are archived and can be viewed online. The Canary Society has addressed issues of guilt and responsibility by closely

[5] *Asahi Shimbun* (1995), 'Kyūshinryoku ushinau Oumu Shinrikyō Jōkyū kanbu wa jisshitsu fuzai ni', 7 October, p. 34; *Mainichi Shimbun* (1995), 'Kyōsei sōsa kara hantoshi, Kamikuishikimura rupo; Oumu Shinrikyō, kanzen tettai no medo naku', 21 September, p. 27.

adhering to mind control theory and emphasising the need to remove nefarious psychological influences through 'de-mind control' (*datsu-maindo kontorōru*) and exit counselling.

The 1995 book *Escaping Mind Control* (*Maindo Kontorōru kara Nogarete*) by Takimoto and Nagaoka (1995), published several months after the Tokyo attack, exemplifies the Canary Society's position. Nagaoka Tatsuya is the son of Nagaoka Hiroyuki (see Chapter 7), the leader of the Aum Shinrikyō Families' Society. Nagaoka quit Aum in 1990 and became an anti-cult activist himself. In the book, former adherents detail and criticise Aum's use of alleged mind control techniques, such as limiting access to external information, punishing transgressions through corporal punishment, sleep deprivation, malnutrition, and physically taxing training regimes, all of which eventually moulded believers to be obedient puppets (ibid.: 59). Nagaoka repeatedly emphasises the difficulty of removing mind control; according to him, it takes time, effort, and a sympathetic voice provided by exit counselling (ibid.: 42–54). The testimonies of other ex-believers contained in the volume corroborate this view. They attest to the sense of losing agency, and the process of slowly recovering the ability to think for themselves through exit counselling. These ex-members also urged existing members to reach out for support (ibid.: 115–16). The testimonies, however, do not address issues of guilt or responsibility for having been an Aum believer. Rather, the narratives are records of their personal struggles to recover from what they considered to be damaging effects of mind control that also serve as warnings to others about the dangers of so-called 'cults'.

Another book by the Canary Society, published five years later, addresses collective guilt more explicitly. *We Who Quit Aum* (*Oumu o Yameta Watashitachi*) begins with a collective apology to victims of Aum's crimes (Kanariya no Kai 2000: vii). The book again positions Aum as a destructive cult that uses mind control (ibid.: 259–60). It describes examples of mind control techniques such as electro-shock, locking dissidents in metal containers (ibid.: 82–3), and administering hallucinogenic drugs in initiation rituals without the participants' knowledge and consent (ibid.: 102–4). Discussions of regret and remorse are more prominent compared to the group's previous publication. Some ex-believers recall their experience of apologising to Takahashi Shizue of the Victims' Society in person (ibid.: 138–40), while others express remorse for having supported Aum's violent doctrines, even if indirectly. They note that the Society collectively raised funds to give to Aum's victims (ibid.: 141–3). By completely rejecting Aum's doctrines as false and evil, this collective apology recognises their moral responsibility as former members, whilst reaffirming the collective values of Japanese civil society that they had initially opposed.

Separate from the question of the scientific validity of mind control, which has been discussed elsewhere in this book and in the wider literature on controversial religions, the vocabulary and choreography of exit counselling have a clear ritual function, similar to the stages of initiation rituals originally identified by Arnold van Gennep (1960) and Victor Turner (1967). Consequently, it may be more appropriate to consider exit counselling as a form of social ritual than as a legitimate form of psychotherapy backed by scientific evidence. The structure of exit counselling is usually as follows. In the first instance, the ex-believer is removed from the physical location which defines their former identity (e.g., the religious commune) and taken to a third (sometimes remote) location, such as a hotel or a safe house. There, the 'initiand' enters a liminal state where membership is fluid and indeterminate. In this liminal stage, initiands cannot contact the outside world and all aspects of their life are strictly controlled and monitored. During this stage, the exit counsellor – who may be a psychologist, therapist, or (in Japan) clergy of a traditional religion – strictly controls the ceremony to mark the initiand's transition from 'believer' (symbolically polluted, outsider to mainstream society) to 'ex-believer' (symbolically purified, rehabilitated member of mainstream society). This may include, for instance, exposing the initiand to 'negative literature', making insulting remarks about the leader, and making them explicitly denounce their leader in heated, emotional exchanges.

Once the ritual is complete, the initiand steps back into the social world and makes an announcement, usually to their parents, that they are no longer under the influence of mind control and that they positively affirm the norms and values of mainstream society. By completing this ritual, the subject 'regains' autonomy, simultaneously removing the stigma attached to the Aum believer and opening the possibility of social reintegration (Reader 2000a: 226–7). There is also a strong intergenerational dynamic to exit counselling, insofar as the ritual is premised upon parents 'bringing back' children (of legal adult age) into their care. If conventional initiation rites confer adulthood to initiands, deprogramming and exit counselling do the reverse, by returning ex-believers back into the role of the dependent child in the socially sanctioned structure of the nuclear family.

Whether the ritual of disavowal through 'de-mind control' has been totally successful in removing the stigma of Aum membership is questionable. To an extent, the mind control paradigm that situated Aum as a destructive cult has been the victim of its own success. In group discussions contained in the Canary Society's 2000 volume, several ex-members recounted the continuing social stigma attached to the status of 'ex-believers'. They have stated that the status of the 'ex-believer' carries connotations similar to 'ex-convicts', and they encounter comparable levels of social discrimination (Kanariya no Kai 2000: 205–6, 213). According to Noda Naruhito, who was nominally the leader of Aleph, informal discrimination against former members is common. Employers have terminated employment of ex-believers upon discovering their past, although the reason for dismissal is not usually attributed to their personal history. Moreover, contractual clauses that bar business transactions with 'anti-social forces' (*han-shakai seiryoku*) have prevented ex-members from opening bank accounts or applying for credit.[6]

Kaori's story

Despite the popularity of the mind control narrative in public discourse, many ex-believers deny that they had been under the influence of mind control. In the summer of 2016, I met one such ex-member who explicitly denied the efficacy of mind control in recounting the motivations for her joining, staying in, and eventually leaving Aum. Kaori (pseudonym) was in her late forties when we met – a relatively common age group for former Aum members. A polite and soft-spoken person, Kaori considered each of my questions carefully before reaching a thoughtful and nuanced answer. Her story of joining Aum shares similarities with the experiences of many former adherents, although it is by no means typical or generalisable.

Kaori became interested in Aum as a high-school student after her elder sister invited her to attend a local Aum *dōjō* in Tokyo. Her interest in religion was also shaped by her experience of losing her mother to an illness when she was younger. She did not find Asahara's personal charisma nor his promise to guide followers to enlightenment to be appealing. Rather, she was struck by the frankness and honesty with which Aum members seemed to interact with each other, qualities she felt were absent among her secondary school peers. After graduating from secondary school, she got a job near the *dōjō*, which allowed her to train daily as a part-time (*zaike*) worshipper after work, before joining full-time in 1993. She recalls that becoming a *shukkesha/samana* was not an easy choice, and her decision caused an intense argument between her and her family. She reflects that it was their vehement opposition to her and her sister's membership in Aum that effectively forced her to leave home abruptly and permanently. 'Perhaps I might not have become a *samana* if they hadn't been so obstinate', she says.[7]

During her time as a *samana*, Kaori lived in Kamikuishiki, where she worked in different sections, including as a cook and as a 'receptionist' handling incoming calls. Although sleep deprivation is often cited as a mind control technique by Aum's critics, she states that getting sleep was not difficult as she often dozed while meditating, as did many others. She remembers her section as being quite friendly and that they often chatted together despite official proscriptions against chitchat.

[6] Personal email correspondence with Noda, December 2015.

[7] Author's interview, anonymous, July 2016, location withheld.

When she heard the first reports of the Tokyo attack, she did not initially believe that Aum conducted the attack. However, as she started to gather information surreptitiously through the Internet, she gradually became convinced that Aum was responsible.

However, knowing about Aum's culpability did not lead to her renouncing her faith immediately. Kaori's disaffiliation narrative contrasts with those who underwent exit counselling, some of whom were forcibly taken by family members into physical isolation. Her disaffiliation in the late 2000s came not so much as a result of losing faith in the guru, but as a result of interpersonal difficulties with other members of the organisation. She found some part-time outside work while still a *samana*, allowing her to gradually regain financial independence. Around the same time, Aleph was undergoing a split with Hikari no Wa in a dispute over the organisation's future direction and the position of Asahara as a religious leader. However, she did not feel as though she identified with either camp and left the group instead. After leaving, she joined the charity sector, having been struck by stories of children growing up in poverty and struggling to eat regular meals. Although she worked for some time as a volunteer for a 'free school' programme – providing free meals and lessons to children after school – she became a *persona non grata* and was asked to stop attending after other staff members discovered her past membership in Aum. Despite these challenges, she has continued to work in the charity sector. As Erica Baffelli (2012: 32) has discussed, there are concrete and practical 'exit costs' that ex-members must be able to overcome, including income, food, housing, and social connections. Although Kaori's employment gave her financial independence not afforded to other *samana*, she struggled to be accepted back into mainstream society.

When I asked her if she felt guilt or remorse for Aum's crimes, she responded that she felt sorry for Aum's victims at an abstract level, but found it difficult to reconcile her own personal experiences as a *samana* with the organisational crimes that the leadership had committed. As she elaborated, her daily life as a training believer had little to do with Aum's 'secret work', therefore it was hard for her to feel a sense of responsibility even after knowing that Aum was behind the violent crimes. As a relatively low-ranking *samana*, she had little personal contact with Asahara beyond short conversations in seminars. However, when I asked if she still liked him even after leaving, after some hesitation, she stated that she may still have some 'emotional attachment' (*aichaku*) to him. Unlike those who cut off ties completely with Aum/Aleph, she has continued to have a relationship with some remaining members, including her older sister.

Reflecting on her experience as a *samana*, Kaori is adamant that she was not mind controlled or brainwashed. In her view, she and others chose to worship Asahara because they wanted to (*suki de yatta*). To this end, she discussed mind control in a critical manner as an 'easy way out' of denying individual agency.

She also stated that among her social circle of ex-members there are few, if any, who support the mind control paradigm.[8]

Kaori's story is but one of possibly thousands of disaffiliation narratives by ex-Aum members, but it is demonstrative of the breadth of autobiographical narratives that ex-Aum members have formed to make sense of their past membership that lie beyond the prescriptive format provided by proponents of mind control. Unlike others, she has chosen not to relate her experiences through a written medium. Although published testimonies of ex-believers explicitly critical of Aum tend to support mind control, other narratives, such as Murakami's (2003) and Aoki's (2010) collections of interviews, suggest that ex-members that support the mind control thesis may be relatively few in number.

Confessing guilt: Aum's killers

For many *samana* who quit the movement, moral questions that they confronted were 'associational': they had been members or, and had contributed to, what became a terrorist organisation. Their disavowal narratives are often framed in terms of the values that they once supported (absolute faith in a leader, hostility towards non-believers) rather than reflecting upon specific morally transgressive acts they may have committed. For Asahara's closest aides, however, they confronted moral questions of a different order: how to explain and come to terms with the violent criminal acts that they committed, including abduction, torture, murder, and the disposal of bodies. Notably, Niimi Tomomitsu and Yokoyama Masato never renounced their faith or expressed remorse for their actions. Others, however, have detailed their motivations for why they joined, and why they have lost faith in Asahara. Examining published accounts of two senior disciples – Hayashi Ikuo and Hayakawa Kiyohide – both of whom were responsible for Aum's most violent crimes, it becomes clear that they distance themselves from claims of mind control, and that they narrate their actions in terms of 'blind faith', as well as risks to personal safety if they disobeyed.

Hayashi Ikuo

Hayashi Ikuo was one of the most senior disciples in the organisation, selected to be one of the five men to board the trains in the Tokyo attack. Born in 1947, Hayashi was one of the few high disciples older than Asahara and had enjoyed a relatively long professional career before joining Aum. The son of a wealthy doctor, he followed in his father's footsteps, pursuing medicine and eventually

[8] Interview, anonymous.

becoming a heart surgeon. Despite his illustrious, international career, he became increasingly frustrated with what he saw the limits of modern medicine, which could treat illnesses or prolong life, but could not address fundamental questions about death and human suffering (Hayashi 2001: 30–31). He became interested in religion and joined the new religious movement Agonshū (of which Asahara was also briefly a member), which proclaimed to have rediscovered ancient esoteric Buddhism through the Agon sutra. Although he was a member of Agonshū for a decade, he became dissatisfied with the group and instead joined Aum as a *zaike* member, until becoming a *samana* with his wife and two children in 1990. Hayashi quickly rose through the ranks, was given the 'holy name' Krishnananda, and became a head of the medical section, which later came to be known as the Ministry of Treatment (ibid.: 138–51). Despite this senior position, in his memoir, Hayashi is keen to point out that Asahara viewed him as an annoyance (*kemutai sonzai*), since Hayashi had the expertise to challenge and contradict Asahara's medical guidance to adherents (ibid.: 152–4).

As the head of Aum's hospital unit, he devised training techniques such as taking scalding hot baths as a cleansing ritual – a practice which resulted in multiple accidental deaths.[9] He was also involved in several cases of kidnapping dissidents. Though Hayashi was not directly involved with the militarisation process, he was responsible for other aspects of Aum's organised violence; he devised a coercive interrogation method known as 'Narco' (*naruko*), in which subjects were interrogated after being injected with sodium thiopental, a barbiturate Aum considered to be a truth serum (ibid.: 311–13). Later, he also devised 'New Narco' (*nyū naruko*), a torturous procedure in which he administered high-voltage electric shocks to the head to erase memories of believers suspected to be spies (ibid.: 334–9). In February 1995, Hayashi placed Kariya Kiyoshi – a public notary who had been abducted by Aum – under 'Narco' for interrogation. Later, Kariya unexpectedly died while Hayashi had left his position to take a break – an action which he regrets as neglectful (ibid.: 412–33).

Although Hayashi was not involved in the militarisation programme, two days before the Tokyo attack, Asahara selected Hayashi to participate as part of the strike team. Hayashi recounts the moral conflict he felt immediately upon hearing the order from the chief scientist, Murai Hideo, in terms of familial dishonour. He states, 'I thought of my wife and children. They will carry a family line of a murderer. My heart wrenched. I would tarnish and cause great trouble to my family line. The feeling of "No, I don't want to do it" was overwhelming' (ibid.: 454). At the same time, he emphasises repeatedly that insubordination was not a choice.

[9] Scalding hot baths became compulsory after initiations in which drugs were used ('*kirisuto no inishiēshon*' and '*rudorachakurin no inishiēshon*'), intended to sweat out the drugs from the body.

Disobeying the order to engage in *poa* meant the ultimate betrayal of the guru, which would lead to eternal condemnation in hell (*mugen jigoku*), and possibly becoming a target of *poa* himself (ibid.: 456). In his narrative, Hayashi repeatedly expresses concerns for his family's safety: Hayashi saw his wife and children as Asahara's 'hostages' to ensure his lasting loyalty (ibid.: 202, 444, 457, 469, 471).

Despite his reservations, he justified the terrorist attack as a necessary realisation of *poa* and the *Vajrayāna* principles (ibid.: 461). Hayashi recalls that on the day of the attack, as he waited to board the designated train, he realised he was murdering not just state officials but innocent women and children too. 'In front of me, there were girls lined up with rucksacks, waiting for the train. There were also women. Until then, I had never thought about girls or women' (ibid.: 501). Nonetheless, he convinced himself that *poa* was necessary: 'This is a battle. Therefore, it is inevitable. Asahara has said "the battle has already begun." It's a battle, and it cannot be helped that people die. If I don't do it, Aum will be crushed … If I don't defend Aum, Truth will die out. I must do it. Even then, I don't want to kill women and children' (ibid.: 502).

Despite his hesitations, he pierced one of the bags of sarin solution as he disembarked. His part in the attack killed two station employees at Kasumigaseki Station and injured hundreds more. After returning to the Kamikuishiki headquarters, Hayashi went into hiding on Asahara's orders, but was arrested in April. During detention, he broke down and confessed to his crimes, detailing the extent of Aum's *Vajrayāna* plans and his own role in the Tokyo attack. Throughout his confession, Hayashi reiterates his feelings of guilt and remorse and repudiates his prior belief in *poa*. Notably, he characterises his actions as the outcome of faith, rather than external psychological manipulation. He states, 'What I did out of faith was a grave and irreparable error. I was ashamed of myself, ashamed that I was alive' (ibid.: 566). In the memoir, Hayashi offers an apology to the victims of the Aum Affair in the knowledge that his actions are 'unforgivable' (ibid.: 572–5). He was eventually sentenced to life in prison; he was the only one out of the five assailants that boarded the trains to avoid the death penalty.

Although Hayashi admits personal guilt and responsibility for his crimes in the autobiography, he simultaneously positions himself away from the 'core' group of perpetrators such as Asahara and Murai. Hayashi explains that he became involved in the Tokyo attack not because of his loyalty and devotion, but because Asahara fundamentally distrusted him. Hayashi recalls that on multiple occasions Asahara claimed that he could not read Hayashi's heart (ibid.: 400–04). Hayashi speculates that because he had witnessed Aum's illegal schemes, Asahara sought to silence him by making him complicit in murder. Hayashi also conjectures that Asahara felt threatened by Hayashi's age, medical career, and longer membership at Agonshū (ibid.: 152).

Throughout the memoir, Hayashi presents himself as a pawn who acted under duress, rather than a willing participant of Aum's *Vajrayāna* plan. However, his claim about his relative marginality must be considered in light of his active involvement in several prominent criminal cases such as the abduction and drugging of dissident believers and his involvement in the death of Kariya Kiyoshi. As a relatively senior *samana*, he was also privy to different areas of 'secret work' that low-ranking *samana* were not. Moreover, as the Minister of Treatment, he was responsible for introducing different training regimes that became standard across the organisation. Given these contextual factors, Hayashi arguably understates the power that he held within Aum's hierarchy and the level of zealous devotion he may have displayed in earning Asahara's trust. Nevertheless, his rationalisation of his actions as an act of faith rather than a consequence of psychological manipulation provides a significant point of contrast to the mind control narratives of the Canary Society.

Hayakawa Kiyohide

Hayakawa Kiyohide's published confession and autobiography follows a similar structure to Hayashi's by acknowledging the religious character of the violence Aum committed, expressing regret for his actions, and distancing himself from the 'core group' of perpetrators – namely, Asahara and Murai. Like Hayashi, Hayakawa was older than Asahara and had joined with an extensive professional career. Born in 1948, he worked as a landscaper for a large construction company. As he became increasingly interested in yoga and spiritualism, he briefly became a member of Agonshū like Asahara and Hayashi, although he did not know them personally. Like Hayashi, Hayakawa became dissatisfied with Agonshū's activities and joined the Aum Society of Sages in 1986. At the time, he did not consider it a religious conversion. For him, it was closer to joining a yoga society (Hayakawa and Kawamura 2005: 32–3). After Asahara changed the name of the group to Aum Shinrikyō in 1987, he became a full-time devotee along with his wife, donating all his assets as per Aum's regulation (ibid.: 59).

Under the 'holy name' Tirōpa, Hayakawa worked most closely with Asahara from the late 1980s to the early 1990s. He was one of five who killed the dissident believer Taguchi Shūji in 1989, the first case in which Asahara used *poa* as a justification for murder. Taguchi had witnessed the death of his friend, Majima Teruyuki, earlier in 1988, which had been covered up by Hayakawa and others. Fearing that Taguchi's disaffiliation would expose Majima's death to the public, Asahara ordered his murder. Hayakawa states that he tried to persuade Taguchi to change his mind, but when Taguchi refused, Hayakawa and four other accomplices killed him, incinerated his remains in an industrial microwave, and disposed of the ashes in a nearby lake (ibid.: 135–6). Hayakawa explains that he 'didn't want to murder anyone, even if it was *poa*' (ibid.: 138), but the group dynamic and his obedience to authority made it possible to kill without too much hesitation (ibid.: 138–9). Asahara picked Hayakawa to be one of the six assailants to murder Sakamoto's family in late 1989. Hayakawa claims he had hoped to find any reason to avoid murdering the Sakamoto family; but when Asahara gave the go-ahead, he obeyed the order. Like Hayashi, Hayakawa states he had doubts about the legitimacy of *poa*. Yet, he brushed these doubts aside as a sign of insufficient devotion to the guru (ibid.: 153). Afterwards, he fled briefly to Bonn, Germany, where he burned off his fingerprints on a hot frying pan in anticipation of a police investigation.

Hayakawa began to have doubts in Asahara after the disastrous election defeat in 1990, when Asahara gave the go-ahead for 'mass indiscriminate *poa*' using biological weapons (ibid.: 121; 165–6). As part of the *Vajrayāna* plan, Hayakawa played a key role in establishing connections in Russia. He was responsible for importing an AK-74 assault rife, military-grade equipment, and a military helicopter. He also smuggled ingredients for LSD to be used in initiation rituals (ibid.: 180–81). As Hayakawa was not part of the science and technology team, he was not selected as part of the gassing squad in Matsumoto or Tokyo. Using this as evidence for his marginal role in later *Vajrayāna* plans, Hayakawa positions himself away from the circle of perpetrators as he speculates that Asahara and Murai, the two core co-conspirators, considered him to be too passive in the *poa* schemes (ibid.: 195). Like Hayashi, Hayakawa arguably underplays his level of involvement in the militarisation programme, as he portrays himself as a reluctant figure who acted out of 'obedience to authority'. This has resulted in conspicuous moments of omission and compression surrounding his role in the programme. He quickly skims over his activities between 1990 and 1995 – the period of intense militarisation – reducing these to just over 30 pages, while devoting a similar amount of space for the period from 1988 to 1990.

Hayakawa renounced his faith in Asahara after his arrest, as did many of Asahara's followers. He explains his actions as acts of *religious* violence borne out of zealotry, not a result of mind control. In his view, the crimes he committed were the consequence of 'absolute devotion' (*zettaiteki kie*), which placed Asahara as an 'absolute authority' (*zettaiteki ken'i*) in a collective delusion that the masses needed to be saved through murder (ibid.: 205). He is adamant that the crimes 'no matter how crazed, occurred out of the guru's religious motives' (ibid.: 216). Although he notes elements of coercion existed – insofar as *poa* included the possibility of harm to him and his family if he ever decided to quit or disobey – he admits having played an active part in Aum's *Vajrayāna* process (ibid.: 122, 205). Hayakawa concludes the confession with an apology to Aum's victims, stating that he is prepared to pay for the crimes with his life should he be sentenced to death (ibid.: 214–16). Hayakawa was sentenced to death in 2000, a verdict which he appealed. The sentence was upheld by the Supreme Court in 2009.[10]

Former leaders of Aum and Aleph: Combining apology and redress

Besides Asahara, there have been several individuals who have represented Aum and Aleph. Many of them have since left Aleph, publicly renouncing their faith in Asahara and offering public apologies. However, the strategies for accounting for personal responsibility and offering apologies have varied considerably. Below we look at two figures who have had an active media presence following their departure from Aleph.

Jōyū Fumihiro: Continuing a (non)religious group

Jōyū Fumihiro has had a turbulent religious career, first as one of Aum's highest disciples, then as leader of Aleph, and finally as the founder of the splinter group Hikari no Wa (Circle of Rainbow Light) since 2007. Jōyū completed his undergraduate and master's degrees at Waseda University, specialising in communications followed by aeronautical engineering. As a university student, he also joined the debating society, where he honed his oratory and sophistic skills, for which he became notorious. As one of Aum's earliest members, he joined Aum in 1986 when he was a postgraduate student. Like other members with backgrounds in science, he found greater appeal in the world of religion than in scientific research. After becoming a renunciant the following year, he became one of Asahara's most valued protégés, completing enough training to be given the holy name Maitrēya and awarded the title of *Seitaishi*. Only four others – including Asahara's wife and third daughter Rika – have equalled him in rank. As a skilled orator, Jōyū served as Aum's spokesperson. In the early 1990s, Jōyū was involved in several *Vajrayāna* schemes, including several botched terrorist attempts. He briefly headed plans to construct the sarin plant at *Satyam* No. 7, after which Asahara sent him to work in Russia (Jōyū 2012: 102–3). As a result, Jōyū was not directly involved in Aum's various murders and terrorist attacks. Jōyū speculates that Asahara sent him to Russia either to preserve Aum's teachings after the impending Armageddon, or to remove him from a position of power, as Jōyū was known to occasionally contradict Asahara (ibid.: 104–5).

Following the Tokyo sarin attack, Jōyū was summoned back from Russia to handle Aum's media strategy. He appeared alongside other senior leaders on the

[10] *Yomiuri Shimbun* (2009), 'Oumu moto kanbu Hayakawa hikoku, Shikei kakutei e', 18 July, p. 38.

media circuit daily to deny responsibility and to accuse the state and media of religious persecution. His pugnacious performance and sophistic flair earned him the nickname *'Ā ieba Jōyū'* ('You say one thing, Jōyū says another'), a play on the idiom used to describe an argumentative personality *'Ā ieba sō yū'* ('You say one thing, they say another'). After Murai Hideo was stabbed to death and Asahara and other senior members were arrested *en masse*, Jōyū effectively became Aum's interim leader through a process of elimination, until he was also arrested in December 1995 for perjury in a case relating to a bogus donation of land in 1989. Jōyū served four years in jail, and upon his release he once again became the de facto leader, co-running the group with long-time member Muraoka Tatsuko before officially taking up the position in 2002.

Under Jōyū's leadership, Aum changed its name to Aleph in early 2000 and made its first official apology for the series of crimes the group committed. As Jōyū admits, this apology was part of a plan to appease public opinion towards Aum, which had hardened after the enactment of the Organisations Regulation Act. However, at the same time as admitting responsibility and promising to pay reparations to Aum's various victims, the group continued to worship Asahara (ibid.: 176–8). As Aleph's leader, Jōyū also began to de-emphasise Asahara as the primary object of worship; his publications in the early 2000s contain almost no references to Asahara as the guru, and instead emphasise Jōyū's charismatic authority as a religious leader (Jōyū 2002a; 2002b; 2003). According to him, this is a period in which he began to 'relativise' Asahara's abilities as a guru, while still worshipping him (Jōyū 2012: 202–3).

Jōyū's plan to dilute Asahara's importance in the group's beliefs and practices encountered strong opposition, especially from Asahara's wife, Matsumoto Tomoko, who had an indirect but powerful influence on the group (ibid.: 203–7). Jōyū was placed under 'intensive training' in 2003, which prevented him from communicating with ordinary members as a leader. Following a year of physical isolation, he gradually gained the support of some Aleph members who agreed with Jōyū's direction. By 2005, around 200 followers had identified themselves as the 'Jōyū-faction' or the 'representative faction' (*daihyō-ha*), distinct from the much bigger 'mainstream faction' (*shuryū-ha*), and began to organise their own events and use separate facilities. In 2007, Jōyū reached a legal agreement with Aleph to separate and form a new group called Hikari no Wa (Circle of Rainbow Light) along with around 160 supporters (Public Security Intelligence Agency 2008).[11] The group's name lends itself to a quasi-religious experience that Jōyū had at a pilgrimage site, when he saw a rainbow ring around the sun (Jōyū 2012: 237–8).

[11] This figure was corroborated through my interview with Hirosue Akitoshi, Hikari no Wa's spokesperson in 2016. However, the actual number of full-time members living in Hikari no Wa's shared accommodation is much smaller than this figure.

Although Jōyū has continued to act as Hikari no Wa's leader and representative, the group holds that it does not have particular objects of worship, and its followers are described as 'members' (*kaiin*), not 'believers' (*shinja*). Today, there are around 20 full-time members who live on site, while others pay a monthly membership fee and attend regular talks and events.

Jōyū and Hikari no Wa have had an active online presence since its inception, proactively using social networking sites and blogs to promote their activities (Baffelli 2018). On the front page of the group's website, the caption below the banner image reads, '"Hikari no Wa" is not a religion. It is a class for learning the wisdom, thought, and philosophy of happiness of East and West, including Buddhist thought, meditative methods and contemporary psychology without faith in particular founders, gods, or sects. You can study without joining. Please feel free to get in touch.'[12]

In my interview with Jōyū in July 2016, he maintained that, to his knowledge, there is no one in the group who continues to worship Asahara, and that those who still worshipped him would not be attracted to Hikari no Wa.[13] As a group, it offers a monistic view of the universe as a unified entity, with no clear separation of humans with each other, or of humans from nature (Jōyū 2012: 231–4). Hikari no Wa conducts regular tours across Japan's religious sites to encourage an appreciation of Japan's religious history as well as an appreciation of nature. The money raised from these tours contributes towards the payment of reparations. More recently, the group has conducted ascetic training under the supervision of *yamabushi*, practitioners of the religion Shugendō. Shugendō is a syncretic religion that combines Japanese esoteric Buddhism (Shingon Sect) with other traditions such as Shinto and Taoism.

According to Hikari no Wa's spokesperson Hirosue Akitoshi, the practice of *naikan* (introspection) is a core activity in Hikari no Wa that is not present in Aleph. *Naikan* refers to the practice of intensely reflecting on one's past experiences in a near-meditative state over several days, supervised by an expert. Reflecting on their past experiences, Hirosue says, allows one to realise one's indebtedness to the people around them. Consequently, it becomes impossible to sustain the good–evil and insider–outsider divisions that Aum and Aleph steadfastly kept.[14] Emphasising these connections with the secular world, Jōyū has proactively debated with writers and public figures in print (Jōyū 2012; Jōyū and Tahara 2013; Jōyū et al. 2013).

In my interview with Jōyū, he explicitly rejected the view that Aum used brainwashing or mind control extensively. With the possible exception of using

[12] Hikari no Wa (n.d.), 'Hikari no Wa' <www.joyu.jp/hikarinowa/> Accessed May 2022. Translation by author.

[13] Author's interview with Jōyū Fumihiro, 24 July 2016, Tokyo.

[14] Author's interview with Hirosue Akitoshi, 29 July 2016, Tokyo.

drugs in initial rituals without the participants' knowledge or consent, which could be a form of mind control, his view is that followers, including himself, idolised Asahara because they wanted to, not because they had been controlled to do so.[15] To him, Aum's failure was the result of uncritical 'blind faith' (*mōshin*) that refused to find or acknowledge flaws in the leader. Although he rejects mind control as a valid explanation of Aum's group dynamics, Jōyū differs from those academic critiques that deny there is a substantive difference between religions and cults. In Jōyū's opinion, the distinction of cult from religion is separate from the question of whether a group uses mind control. A cult can be identified by its anti-social, destructive character and the use of violence, whether or not it uses mind control techniques.[16] Perhaps unsurprisingly, Hikari no Wa has criticised Aleph and its leadership as an anti-social cult that has refused to learn lessons from the past.

Jōyū has also justified the continued presence of the group on the basis that they have a responsibility to continue to pay financial reparations to the victims. He has defended the de facto continuation of a communal lifestyle on the basis that individuals would likely struggle to pay reparations, and that there are elderly members to support. According to the spokesperson, Hirosue, the money raised through pilgrimage tours and public talks also contributes towards the payment of reparations.[17]

Not all critics accept Jōyū's narrative of moral reform and repudiation of Asahara as an object of worship. As Nagaoka Hiroyuki stated in my interview with him, he continues to consider Hikari no Wa and Aleph as one and the same.[18] Takahashi Shizue has also criticised the use of reparations as a justification of the group's continued existence as 'outrageous', arguing that dissolving the organisation altogether was the only acceptable solution for victims.[19] Local residents near Hikari no Wa's facilities have continued to organise regular rallies calling for the group's disbandment. Following the executions of the core culprits, a weekly tabloid magazine reported that Jōyū had been witness to a murder of a female adherent in 1991, thereby adding to concerns about his status as an unreliable narrator. The case was never brought to trial as Niimi Tomomitsu, one of the culprits according to the report, never made a formal confession before he was executed. Jōyū has defended his silence on this issue, stating that he could not speak out of fear of

[15] Interview with Jōyū. It is worth noting, however, that in his autobiography Jōyū refers to Aum's practices as 'brainwashing'. In an online blog post, Hikari no Wa also accuses Aleph of using 'brainwashing-like conversion' methods. See Hikari no Wa (2012), 'Arefu no sennō teki kyōka no higai ni awareta kata e', 9 September, <http://hikarinowa.net/public-info/departure/assistance/> Accessed December 2016.

[16] Interview with Jōyū.

[17] Interview with Hirosue.

[18] Interview with Nagaoka.

[19] Interview with Takahashi.

retaliation from Aleph.[20] However, this revelation has fuelled public criticisms that Jōyū may not have been entirely transparent and forthcoming about his activities during his tenure as Aum's spokesperson.

Despite Hikari no Wa's claim that it is entirely different from Aleph, the state has continued to treat it as a security threat. The Public Security Intelligence Agency successfully applied for the extension of surveillance of Hikari no Wa under the Organisation Regulation Act (ORA). In 2017, Hikari no Wa won a court decision in the Tokyo District Court that nullified the extension of the ORA in 2015.[21] However, the state appealed the decision and the Tokyo High Court reversed its decision in 2019, and this was upheld by the Supreme Court in 2020.[22] As the ORA has been extended for another three-years in 2021, Hikari no Wa will be under state surveillance until at least the end of 2024, barring future court rulings in their favour.

Noda Naruhito: Entrepreneurial reparations

If Jōyū has relied on apology and redress to defend his continuing his 'non-religious' pursuits as a group, former Aleph leader Noda Naruhito has addressed guilt and responsibility through entrepreneurship and the payment of financial redress as an individual. He is distinctive as a former senior member in embracing mind control and brainwashing. A contemporary of Jōyū, Noda abandoned his undergraduate degree in physics at the prestigious Tokyo University to become a renunciant with Aum. During the militarisation phase, Noda was tasked with developing a rail gun, a weapon designed to propel projectiles using electro-magnetism. This project was ultimately unsuccessful, and as a result he was not arrested or charged.

Known inside the organisation as Vajratikshnā, Noda was promoted to the rank of *Seigoshi* days before the Tokyo attack along with many of the other culprits, directly below Jōyū's *Seitaishi* title. During Jōyū's incarceration, Noda managed Aleph alongside other members with the *Seigoshi* title. After Jōyū's release from prison in late 1999, Noda had a relatively marginal role in the organisation until the conflict between Jōyū and Asahara's family escalated. Noda corroborates Jōyū's account that that Asahara's family forced Jōyū under 'intensive training' in 2003 (Noda 2010: 69–76). During Jōyū's solitary confinement, Noda was arrested and

[20] *Daily Shinchō* (2019), '"Jōyū Fumihiro" ga hita kakushi! Keisatsu mo shiranai "Asahara Shōkō" no josei shinja satsugai', 19 July <www.dailyshincho.jp/article/2018/07190557/> Accessed May 2022.

[21] *Mainichi Shimbun* (2017), 'Kansatsu shobun ihō Hikari no Wa "Arefu to betsu dantai"', 25 September.

[22] *Asahi Shimbun* (2019), 'Hikari no Wa, nishin de gyakuten haiso kansatsu shobun wa "tekihō" Tokyo Kōsai', 1 March, p. 38; *Jiji Tsūshin* (2020), '" Hikari no Wa" gyakuten haiso kakutei. Oumu kōkei bunha no kansatsu shobun – Saikōsai', <www.jiji.com/jc/article?k=2020031101099&g=soc> Accessed June 2020.

found guilty of selling unlicensed medical goods. He spent a year in custody and eventually received a suspended sentence. After being released from custody, Noda decided against leaving Aleph with Jōyū. He argues that this was because he felt it necessary to communicate what was happening inside Aleph to the outside world and also because he felt he needed to look after more junior members (ibid.: 102, 117–18). After Jōyū's departure, Noda claimed to have been elected by other *Seigoshi* members to serve as the new leader. However, middle-management members refused to recognise him as their leader and removed him from his key responsibilities (Public Security Intelligence Agency 2008). He was expelled from Aleph in 2009 after stating in his blog that Asahara's execution was necessary to free Aleph believers from the effects of brainwashing (Noda 2010: 105).

Since leaving Aleph, Noda has addressed his past by paying reparations as an individual and starting a business that provides housing to people on state benefits. Whilst making a public apology for his role as the former 'leader' of Aleph (although the extent to which he exercised authority as a leader is questionable), he has defended his business as a way of continually paying reparation to victims of the Aum Affair. In his view, his housing business is a rejection of both capitalism and Aum, both of which 'brainwashed' followers to submit uncritically to pernicious ideologies (Noda 2010; 2012). Although capitalism was anathema to Aum, Noda argues that both capitalism and Aum are examples of 'monotheism' (*isshinkyō*) grounded in moral absolutism and the demonisation of those who do not adopt their value system. Borrowing loosely from Weber's Protestant Ethic thesis, he draws an analogy between Aum and contemporary society; just as Asahara 'brainwashed' its believers into worshipping him as their saviour, capitalism has 'brainwashed' people into worshipping money as the only true god. Although Noda has unequivocally rejected Asahara as a guru, there is a strong millenarian dimension that underlines his motivations for running the social business. He argues in his self-published book (Noda 2012) that global capitalism is like the Tower of Babel, growing bigger and bigger to the point of collapse. He anticipates there will be an imminent collapse of capitalism to be replaced by an entirely new social system characterised by what he calls 'polytheism', which he defines as a proliferation of pre-modern forms of social life unregulated by a single value system.[23] Noda's social business, therefore, represents an antidote to monotheistic principles of contemporary capitalism, as well as an economic safeguard against impending catastrophe.

Beyond the religious interpretation Noda has attributed to his own current activities, the social enterprise has helped to finance compensation to Aum's victims. According to his website, as of March 2022, Noda had cumulatively

[23] Interview with Noda Naruhito, 30 March 2015, Saitama Prefecture.

donated ¥14.2 million through the profits made from his business.[24] Unlike Hikari no Wa, Noda has not faced large-scale criticism or social protests, although some have criticised his business model of profiting off those living on state benefits as an exploitative 'poverty business'.[25] Since starting the business, Noda states that he has encountered challenges as an ex-believer. According to him, one property deal fell through when the seller discovered Noda's past and withdrew the offer, and he has been denied bank loans as he is blacklisted as a member of an 'anti-social force' (*hanshakai seiryoku*).[26]

Although Jōyū and Noda have followed very different trajectories since leaving Aum/Aleph, there are some similarities between how they have sought reconciliation with victims and the public at large. For both, disaffiliation marks a fundamental break from their former biographical identities as a 'believer' (*shinja*), and they have both repeatedly renounced Asahara as an object of worship in their public interventions. In addition, they have both relied on the payment of reparations as a partial justification for their activities after Aum.

Nevertheless, there are also key differences between how Jōyū and Noda have chosen to express their identities as perpetrators. Jōyū has chosen to continue practices based on 'studying' religion alongside many former Aleph members, while Noda has chosen to run his business individually. In addition, whereas Jōyū denies the brainwashing/mind control narrative to describes his actions as outcomes of 'blind faith', Noda fully embraces the thesis to develop an abstract critique of contemporary society as being 'brainwashed' by capitalism. In either affirming or rejecting mind control, their contrasting responses resemble those of rank-and-file members like Kaori and members of the Canary Society who have had to construct biographical narratives of 'life after Aum'.

Intergenerational guilt and perpetrators' trauma

So far, this chapter has examined how ex-members have dealt with subjective dimensions of 'guilt' from the perspective of adult adherents. However, in more recent public debates surrounding Aum, there have also been concerted efforts by two of Asahara's daughters to influence public opinion. Understanding societal reactions to Asahara's children in the aftermath of the Aum Affair is not only crucial for understanding Japan's cultural attitudes towards familial, intergenerational guilt and shame, but also for understanding how individuals who bear the stigma

[24] Noda Naruhito (2022), 'Baishō kiroku' <http://alephnoda.blog85.fc2.com/blog-entry-1122.html> Accessed May 2022.

[25] *Mainichi Shimbun* (2015), 'Sutōrī: Chikatetsu sarin jiken 20 nen', 15 March.

[26] Personal email correspondence with Noda, December 2015.

of being 'children of perpetrators' have negotiated this difficult identity through divergent media strategies.

Matsumoto Rika

Questions of guilt and responsibility have haunted Asahara's children, some of whom spent their entire childhoods as pariahs in Japanese society, being subjected to intense discrimination and prejudice that is difficult to describe in words here. It is perhaps unsurprising that many of them have chosen to shun the media and to live privately away from prying eyes. Matsumoto Rika, the third eldest child in Asahara's household, has been exceptional in this regard for having had a public-facing life, especially since 2015.[27] The publication of Rika's autobiography *The Stopped Clock* (*Tomatta Tokei*) coincided with the 20th anniversary of the Tokyo attack (Matsumoto 2015). Explaining her motivation for writing the autobiography, she situates the book as a way of reflecting on the past to put it behind her, and to restart the figurative 'clock' which had stopped since childhood (ibid.: 13).

Rika's autobiography reconstructs the trauma of living as 'Asahara's third daughter' after the Tokyo attack and the arrest of both her parents. Born in 1983, Rika grew up in a position of privilege inside the organisation, even compared with Asahara's other children. Known inside the group by her holy name Ācharī, Rika held the prestigious rank of *Seitaishi* as a child without having much experience of training or meditation. She remembers Asahara as a distant figure with whom she had little personal contact after he declared himself an omniscient guru. Eleven years old at the time of the Tokyo attack, she was largely an object of worship and admiration by the followers.

Growing up was especially harsh for Asahara's children. Whereas many children of Aum members were taken into care or reunited with relatives following the police raids, this was not the case for Asahara's children. After the arrests of Asahara and his wife Tomoko, Rika was raised by her two older, adult sisters and personal attendants who had acted as her guardians. After moving away from the commune in Kamikuishiki, she grew up in several Aum facilities around the country, where she was met with virulent protestors. Responding to these protests, municipal state authorities reacted by initially refusing to accept resident records or admit her to middle school. Her younger siblings and half-siblings faced similar issues elsewhere in the country. Rika's difficult and peripatetic upbringing, together with a strained relationship with her mother after her release from prison, and worries about her father's trial proceedings, has had a massive psychological

[27] Asahara had six children with his wife Tomoko: the four oldest were girls, the two youngest were boys. He also fathered between six (Jōyū 2012: 118) and nine (Matsumoto 2010: 92) children with other female devotees.

effect; she has suffered from severe depression, which she has tried to address through self-harm and a suicide attempt.

Education posed a significant hurdle for her throughout her childhood and early adulthood. Having missed compulsory education while growing up in Kamikuishiki, Rika's educational abilities were several years behind her cohort. Her delay in starting education meant that she had to catch up with her education through independent study and a correspondence course. Furthermore, when applying for a correspondence course, she was refused admission on multiple occasions, even when she was qualified (ibid.: 181). She continued to face discrimination when applying to university, as several refused to accept her even when she met the entry requirements. She took legal action against Bunkyo University – a private university in Tokyo – and was re-offered a place after the court found the university's action to be unconstitutional (ibid.: 208–10). Rika describes her life as a university student as a daunting but enjoyable experience. She graduated with a bachelor's degree in psychology in 2008 and has expressed an interest in becoming a psychological counsellor.

She continued to have personal contact with Aum members and ex-members, although she firmly denies having ever had a leadership position and insists that she never became a member of Aleph when Jōyū changed the group's name (ibid.: 165). According to Rika, she only had a casual and intermittent relationship with Aleph (ibid.: 187–91), including with her mother and senior figures like Jōyū. Rika claims that her mother used Rika's religious authority without her knowledge to subvert Jōyū's leadership (ibid.: 202–3, 238–40). In 2014, Aleph formally 'expelled' Rika after opposing a policy her mother attempted to introduce, which would establish her youngest brother to be the group's new spiritual leader to replace Asahara (ibid.: 254–6).[28]

Throughout the autobiography, Rika argues that Asahara was mentally ill during and after the trials, although her pleas for treatment were ultimately unheeded. Regarding issues of responsibility and guilt, whilst admitting that Aum was collectively responsible for the crimes, Rika 'withheld' an explicit acknowledgement of Asahara's culpability until she could directly communicate with him (ibid.: 166). Rika suggests the possibility that the disciples could have committed the crimes using Asahara's religious authority to justify their actions without Asahara's consent (ibid.: 224, 276).

Since the book's publication, there have been multiple criticisms of Rika's account, especially regarding the extent of her personal involvement in Aum and Aleph. Although she argues she only had a nominal role within Aleph, both Jōyū and Noda's accounts place her as a key decision-maker in the group's shift away

[28] This also raises the question of why Rika had to be 'expelled' if she never had joined Aleph in the first place.

from apology and reconciliation and towards continued worship of Asahara (Jōyū 2012: 203–7; Noda 2010: 69–85). To this end, Hikari no Wa has published extensive blog articles contradicting Rika's version of events.[29] The anti-cult lawyer Takimoto Tarō has also criticised Rika's account for omitting details of her influential position as an authority figure within Aum/Aleph, and for continuing to receive material support from ex-believers.[30] However, perhaps the most notable and the most vocal critic, who appeared in 2015, was Rika's younger sister, Satoka.

Matsumoto Satoka

Satoka made multiple media appearances after 2015 following the publication of Rika's autobiography, during which she claimed that Rika's account was full of falsehoods and that it did not sufficiently address Asahara's status as a perpetrator.[31] Five years before Rika's memoir, she had also published an autobiographical account. Like Rika, Satoka experienced a traumatic childhood marked by discrimination and rejection from local communities and public institutions. However, in her autobiography *Why Was I Born as Asahara Shōkō's Daughter?* (Matsumoto 2010) and a published interview (Aoki 2010), Satoka has narrated her position as Asahara's daughter in a completely different way to Rika. Like many other autobiographies by former believers, Satoka uses her narrative not only as an outlet for her own traumatic experiences, but also as a public apology to Aum's victims (Matsumoto 2010: 8–9).

Born in 1989, Satoka experienced similar difficulties to Rika's as a child. Raised by attendant caretakers, she moved frequently across the country, and went to several schools, encountering rejection from a school board and experiencing bullying in those schools to which she was eventually admitted. She recounts her long-standing struggles with depression and self-harm, which had led to several suicide attempts. In one instance, perhaps illustrative of societal attitudes to Asahara's children, when her family raised the issue of her self-harm and bullying to the school, the head teacher replied, 'Satoka-san, you have one life. But your father killed a lot of people. It can't be helped [*shikata ga nai*)] even if you die' (Matsumoto 2010: 131).

As Satoka was not given access to outside media and information, Satoka recalls that she was not aware of the full extent of Aum's involvement in the

[29] Hikari no Wa (2015), 'Kanseiban. Asahara sanjo Matsumoto Rika shi "Tomatta tokei" (Kōdansha) no kyogi naiyō 1–6', 12 May. <www.joyu.jp/hikarinowa/news/00news/1464.html> Accessed November 2016.

[30] Takimoto Tarō (2015), 'Sanjo – Matsumoto Rika san', 20 March. *Ikiteiru fushigi, Shindeiku fushigi* <http://sky.ap.teacup.com/applet/takitaro/20150320/archive> Accessed May 2022.

[31] *Shūkan Asahi* (2015) '"Chichi wa hitori no ningen to shite aisarenakatta" kyōdan o hanareta Asahara yonjo ga kataru.' 27th March, p.25.

crimes until she was 15 (ibid.: 32). According to her, she fled home at 16 after becoming distressed that her family had refused to take responsibility for Aum's crimes. After leaving home, anti-Aum journalist Egawa Shōko (see Chapter 7) initially agreed to serve as Satoka's legal guardian, but Satoka left after several months, following disagreements over house rules and worries about her future (ibid.: 168–72). Egawa relinquished her guardianship after Satoka reunited with several ex-members, reportedly to start a new religious movement. Since then, she has lived an independent life without contact with any of her family members, having worked various jobs as a temporary contract worker whilst still struggling with mental health issues. She recounts an incident when the police and the intelligence agency made a visit to her employer, demanding them to make her redundant (ibid.: 179–80). She concludes her memoir with a reflection on her childhood: 'I put down this pen with the prayer that a day will come in Japan when children are not discriminated against for the parent's name or forced into a parent's beliefs' (ibid.: 241).

Unlike Rika, who has 'withheld' an acknowledgement of Asahara's culpability, Satoka holds her father ultimately responsible for Aum's violence. She considers it 'impossible' that someone like 'Murai would commit crimes without father's orders' (ibid.: 232). She has echoed popular representations of Aum as a brainwashing cult and has warned that hidden forms of Aum may yet threaten Japan's national security (ibid.: 56–60). Directly contradicting Rika's argument that Asahara was mentally ill, Satoka argued that he was faking illness, recalling that when she visited Asahara in 2007, he whispered her name under his breath (ibid.: 34–9). Before the execution, Satoka accepted Asahara's execution as necessary and inevitable and stated that 'Now that I have renounced my faith, my father to me is just one criminal who put Japan in turmoil. I believe my father's death penalty must be enforced.'[32] In late 2017, she announced that she had severed legal ties with her parents, ending any claims to inheritance. She is currently represented by the anti-cult lawyer Takimoto Taro.

Just as Satoka has criticised Rika's account, Rika has criticised Satoka for a partial representation of events. According to Rika, Satoka had gathered her followers after leaving home to become the leader of a new movement, then abandoned them abruptly to live with Egawa (Matsumoto 2015: 230–32). Jōyū's autobiography also states that Satoka had tried to start a new movement, which resulted in breaking a promise she had made with Egawa not to associate herself with Aleph members (Jōyū 2012: 217–18), a fact that Satoka alludes to but does not explicitly acknowledge or elaborate upon (Aoki 2010: 285). Given these conflicting

[32] *Shūkan Asahi* (2015), '"Chichi wa hitori no ningen to shite aisarenakatta" kyōdan o hanareta Asahara yonjo ga kataru', 27 March, p. 25.

interpretations of events, neither of their autobiographies provides an impartial or completely reliable account of their life events and their motivations.

The public fallout between Rika and Satoka since 2015 has left a rift between them that has only grown wider since Asahara's execution. After Asahara was executed, the government announced that his cremated remains would be handed over to Satoka according to Asahara's final wishes. Satoka issued a public statement via her lawyer Takimoto announcing that she intended to scatter Asahara's ashes over the Pacific Ocean to prevent any one place becoming a holy site for Aleph members. Asahara's wife and Rika contended that Asahara could not have made such decisions before his execution given his mental illness, and contested the custody of his remains in the Family Court. In 2020, the Tokyo Family Court ruled that there was insufficient evidence that Asahara had explicitly specified Satoka as the custodian of his remains and awarded custody to Rika and the second daughter.[33] The Supreme Court upheld this decision in 2021, awarding custody to Asahara's second daughter.[34]

Conclusions

Former believers have presented polyphonic and sometimes irreconcilably different interpretations of their motivations for joining, staying in, and leaving Aum. Contrary to popular claims that mind control turns adherents into obedient 'robots' or 'zombies', many of these accounts demonstrate that many of the individuals critically reflected upon the moral weight of the decisions they undertook, even when they were committing the most violent crimes. Nor did many of them require exit counselling to lose faith in Asahara – many left Aum following critical self-reflection and interaction with like-minded peers. Moreover, some, like Kaori, have kept ties with other ex-members without subscribing to the mind control paradigm.

As 'perpetrators' in the public eye, former members have also addressed emotions of guilt, shame, and responsibility through a variety of performative strategies. For low-ranking members of the Canary Society, this has meant attributing their past actions to mind control, thereby effectively conferring responsibility to a higher authority figure. As perpetrators of Aum's violent crimes, Hayashi and Hayakawa both admitted individual responsibility for their actions and used their publications to make public apologies. Importantly, their expressions of guilt and regret are not merely symbolic gestures but are connected to material interests;

[33] *Asahi Shimbun* (2020), 'Matsumoto moto shikeishū no ikotsu, jijo ni hikiwatashi Tokyo Kasai ga kettei', 17 September.

[34] NHK (2021), 'Oumu Shinrikyō Matsumoto Chizuo moto shikeishū ikotsu Jijo hikitori kakutei; Saikōsai', 5 July, <www3.nhk.or.jp/news/html/20210705/k10013120881000.html> Accessed May 2022.

both Jōyū and Noda have cited the payment of reparations as partial justifications for their respective post-Aum careers as the leader of a splinter group and founder of a social housing business.

From the media spectacle surrounding the manhunt for Aum's fugitives to the mediatised feud between Asahara's daughters, there has been a continuing public interest in the ex-members' experiences. The posthumous publications of Asahara's closest aides after the July 2018 executions serve to illustrate that there appears to be an enduring demand for the consumption of insider knowledge about Aum.

Whether the preponderance of ex-believers' accounts has resulted in more complex understandings of Aum Shinrikyō beyond straightforward narratives of believers as passive, mind-controlled subjects is an entirely separate question. On the one hand, the diversity of published accounts by former members and Asahara's family seems to have consolidated, not challenged, media characterisations of Aum as a destructive cult marked by a strict separation from the outside world, a justification for violence, blind obedience to Asahara, and intense internal factionalism, regardless of whether any alleged forms of mind control were effective in practice. On the one hand, Rika and Satoka's public interventions have shed light on how established narratives of Aum and its affiliated individuals as 'polluting' threats to civil society have resulted in patterns of harassment by resident groups and legal transgressions by public authorities such as municipal governments, school boards, and universities. Despite their contrasting responses to issues surrounding the intergenerational guilt and trauma of perpetrators, their lives have both been irreversibly shaped by experiences of social ostracism, rejection, and the breakdown of a 'normal' family life.

Finally, given the polyphony of interpretations put forward by a range of actors associated with Aum, it is important to consider the possibility of adjudicating between the veracity of claims. For instance, while Hayashi's and Hayakawa's accounts leave no doubts about Asahara's involvement in ordering murders and terrorist attacks, Rika subtly questions the extent of her father's involvement by suggesting the disciples possibly misused Asahara's authority to commit violent crimes. Asahara's silence on the matter – voluntary or not – has created large gaps which various ex-members have filled through trial testimonies, confessions, and memoirs, often by portraying themselves as passive and reluctant figures.

Dissonance has arguably been most acute regarding the inner workings of Aleph in the 2000s. Whilst Jōyū and Noda largely agree with each other's presentations of facts, Hikari no Wa has strongly disputed Rika's version of events and her self-positioning as a marginal figure in Aleph. Likewise, Satoka rejects Rika's claim that she no longer has associations with Aleph. At the same time, Jōyū has suggested Satoka's original intention to leave Aleph was to start her own religious group, a detail Satoka mostly omits from her autobiographical account.

The crossfire of narratives is reminiscent of Akutagawa Ryūnosuke's short story *In a Grove (Yabu no Naka)*, adapted as a film by Kurosawa Akira in the masterpiece *Rashōmon*. In the short story, the reader is presented with polyphonic, dissonant witness accounts of a case of murder-robbery. Likewise, these different autobiographical accounts by Aum's affiliates present the reader with varied, clashing narratives, each one portraying the narrator in a more positive light. Considering the narrator's unreliable position, the reader must be wary of considering one narrative as being truer than others. But perhaps, following Bakhtin's exhortations, we do not necessarily need to come to judgements of truth or falsehood. The sociological benefit of dialogue and polyphony lies an awareness that the analyst must treat the narrator as expressing a *legitimate* and *valid* representation of reality, even if not objectively *true*; recognising that there exist multiple subjective worlds that are beyond reconciliation does not mean we have to pick one 'correct' version of social reality. After all, the inclusion of multiple perspectives promises a richer and more complex understanding of social reality than simplifying (and simplistic) master concepts and narratives.

9

Conclusions

Even past meanings, that is, those born in the dialogue of past centuries, can never be stable (finalized, ended once and for all)—they will always change (be renewed) in the process of subsequent, future development of the dialogue.

Bakhtin 1986: 170

In the last quarter-century, the Aum Affair has resurfaced time and time again as a cultural *leitmotif* in public debates around cults, religious terrorism, and organised violence in Japan and elsewhere. Most recently, Aum Shinrikyō returned to newspaper headlines, television news, and trending words on social media when the executions of Asahara and six of his former associates – Endō Seiichi, Hayakawa Kiyohide, Inoue Yoshihiro, Nakagawa Tomomasa, Niimi Tomomitsu, and Tsuchiya Masami – were carried out on 6 July 2018. Less than three weeks later, on 26 July, a second round of executions ended the lives of six other convicts – Hashimoto Satoru, Hayashi (Koike) Yasuo, Hirose Ken'ichi, Okasaki (Miyamae) Kazuaki, Toyoda Tōru, and Yokoyama Masato – completing the executions of all 13 convicts sentenced to death in relation to Aum Shinrikyō's organised acts of criminal violence.

Following the conclusion of the Aum trials, the timing of the executions was meticulously calculated by key governmental decision-makers (RIRC 2018). Since Emperor Akihito's announcement in 2016 that he intended to abdicate – bringing an end to the imperial *Heisei* Era that began in 1989 – there had been widespread speculation that the executions would be carried out in the months before the abdication and the coronation of the new emperor in April 2019. Various observers had suggested that, as the Aum Affair was a defining event of the *Heisei* Era, the state would seek to bring closure to the Affair through the executions of the convicts before the coronation of the new emperor. The timing, however, was a delicate matter, as holding the executions too close to the coronation would tarnish the auspiciousness of the occasion. Anticipating that the executions might be carried out soon, in the spring of 2018, the filmmaker Mori Tatsuya and the sociologist Miyadai Shinji formed the Society for Pursuing the Truth of the Aum

Affair (*Oumu Jiken Shinsō Kyumei no Kai*), calling for a stay on Asahara's execution. They argued that medical evidence gathered by the defence team suggested that Asahara was too mentally ill to be executed, and that medical treatment was necessary to extract a full confession from him before he was to be executed.[1] Separately, the anti-cult activist Nagaoka Hiroyuki and the lawyer Takimoto Tarō had campaigned for the sentences of the 12 convicts excluding Asahara to be commuted to life sentences. Much to the dismay of both camps, their calls were not heeded by the government. The executions were condemned as failing to deliver justice by Amnesty International and by the Japan Federation of Bar Associations, a national body representing attorneys in Japan.[2] Beyond these protestations, the executions seem to have been welcomed, or at least taken as inevitable, by much of the Japanese population.

Neither the timing of the executions nor the high levels of interest that the executions generated were themselves surprising. Nonetheless, there were some unexpected social reactions to the mass executions. In a macabre spectacle, during the initial hours of reporting the first round of executions, the national television broadcaster Fuji Terebi ran a live news programme in which presenters held up boards showing portrait photographs of the convicts' faces, placing stickers labelled 'executed' on them as the news of their deaths rolled in. On the Internet, anonymous posters bombarded a blog run by Asahara's third daughter Matsumoto Rika, posting insulting comments that celebrated her father's death. While the executions may have brought a sense of closure to many of the victims affected by Aum's violence, they also laid bare the nation's deep-seated trauma of the Tokyo attack and the intense hatred that a proportion of the population held towards Asahara and Aum as quintessential signifiers of evil.

The Aum Affair may appear to much of the Japanese population as a thing of the past, but there are still unresolved legal and social issues. As Aum's successor organisations continue to be active, there remain social tensions between the groups and local residents. As annual reports by the Public Security Intelligence Agency (2017, 2018, 2019) have repeatedly emphasised that the remaining members pose a continued threat to public safety, the potential for remaining members – who remain under state surveillance – to engage in organised crimes or in future terrorist activities is likely overstated.

[1] The group argued for a stay on Asahara's execution until he had been treated. However, they did not call for his sentence to be commuted on medical grounds.

[2] Amnesty International (2018), 'Japan: Executions of Seven Aum Cult Members Fails to Deliver Justice', 6 July, <www.amnesty.org/en/latest/news/2018/07/japan-aum-cult-executions-fails-to-deliver-justice/> Accessed May 2022; Japan Federation of Bar Associations (2018), 'Statement Strongly Protesting Today's Executions and Calling for an Immediate Moratorium and the Abolition of the Death Penalty by 2020', 6 July, <www.nichibenren.or.jp/en/document/statements/180706.html> Accessed May 2022.

Indeed, the future direction of Aleph has become even more uncertain since the founder's demise. Asahara's family members, some of whom were instrumental in deciding Aleph's trajectory, are split more than ever, as demonstrated not only by the rift between Rika and Satoka, but also by the successful legal action brought by Asahara's elder son to stop Aleph from acclaiming him as its spiritual leader.[3] While Asahara's wife and second son are said to continue to be involved in the organisation, how the group will evolve in the future amidst an ageing membership remains opaque to external observers, if not to the members themselves (Baffelli 2020). As the core membership has now entered their fifties and sixties, there are questions over its durability over the coming years and decades. Nevertheless, as opportunities for gainful employment outside of the organisation become increasingly difficult as the members age, the practical 'exit costs' of disaffiliation may prove too high for many.

The Aum Affair in Japanese culture

In many ways, the Aum Affair was a product of the specific cultural, historical, and religious landscape of Japan in the 1980s and 1990s. From its inception, Aum benefited from a broader 'boom' of charismatic new religions, expanding youth subcultures, and a growing discontent among young people that conventional career paths were unappealing and undesirable. Beneath the glitzy surface of Japan's bubble economy in the 1980s, there flowed a consistent undercurrent of social frustration and dissatisfaction that material wealth could not provide satisfactory answers to questions about life, death, and one's purpose in the world: questions to which Aum and many other religious movements claimed to have found ultimate answers.

Whereas the factors that contributed to Aum's growth could be located in Japan's religious and cultural milieux of the time, the factors for Aum's turn to violence lie primarily in Aum's intra-group dynamics and its frictions with external stakeholders. Over the course of several years prior to the Tokyo attack, Asahara's increasing paranoia pushed Aum to pursue violence as a legitimate method for achieving religious ends. Asahara's closest aides were only too eager to carry out these orders. Given these unique characteristics that made Aum far more violent and dangerous than many other minority religions and controversial cults, it would be difficult if not contrived to reach general conclusions about religious terrorism or religious violence from this case alone. Nevertheless, by examining the social consequences of the Aum Affair, it is possible to suggest some general

[3] Nikkei (2020), 'Arefu ni sonshō no shiyō kinjiru Asahara motoshikeishū no chōnan', 25 March, <www.nikkei.com/article/DGXMZO57210180V20C20A3CR8000/> Accessed March 2020.

theoretical observations about the societal aftermaths of religious terrorism that have implications for fields including memory studies, the sociology of religion, and cultural sociology.

Firstly, violent events such as the Tokyo sarin attack become cultural traumas when stakeholders make concerted attempts to narrate the incident as a *collective* experience in relation to their shared identities and memories. As the initial aftermath of the Matsumoto attack showed, not all events that have the potential to become cultural traumas achieve this symbolic transformation. Whether this narration process occurs immediately, latently, or not at all, is contingent on a number of social factors, such as the availability of factual information relating to the nature of the attack, the skills of different 'carrier groups' (including but not limited to journalists, public intellectuals, artists, and academics) in being able to present morally compelling narratives, and the narrators' access to means of communication.

The Aum Affair demonstrated that an event becoming a cultural trauma does not mean that there is a singular narrative or meta-narrative of the event. Rather, cultural traumas are borne out of a competition between multiple narratives, some of which become more successful than others. In the quarter-century since the Tokyo attack, the Aum Affair has produced numerous conflicting interpretations, ranging from whether Aum was a 'religion' or a 'cult', whether followers were brainwashed, and whether remaining groups constituted continuing security threats. While the orthodox narrative of Aum as a brainwashing cult has been reproduced by the state and the mass media alike, other actors have posed counter-narratives to this hegemonic frame by offering alternative perspectives for understanding the causes and consequences of Aum's violence.

This book has stressed that the ability to narrate and to commemorate past events as cultural traumas is shaped by hierarchies of social power and resources within and across societies. The uneven distribution of material and symbolic resources that actors have access to in modern societies indirectly functions as a selection mechanism for who partakes in public struggles over meaning. The Aum Affair, above all, demonstrated the overwhelming power of the mass media – especially television – to mobilise national public opinion against the 'public enemy', the result of which was a moral battle against an 'enemy force' on a scale scarcely seen since the Second World War. By contrast, actors with fewer social resources had to turn to other methods to disseminate their narratives to the public, such as the Victims' Society self-publishing a collection of memoirs, or Mori Tatsuya self-financing an independent film after being turned down by multiple television production companies. The central role of television as the primary medium for news reports, which was the case in the latter half of the 20th century, seems to have declined in the age of social media. As social media companies like Twitter, Facebook, Instagram, and TikTok occupy a greater share of people's attention space, the ways people witness and respond to news events have changed dramatically since the immediate aftermath of the Aum Affair. While the rise of social media may have 'democratised' the playing field somewhat in terms of lowering the barriers to entry for ordinary people to engage in public discourse, however, the dominance of these companies in shaping public opinion have also arguably fuelled social division with the global rise of populism and 'fake news'. Nevertheless, it would be a mistake to reduce cultural patterns to economic or political power; cultural discourse is and always will be a matter of struggle, even if some actors are more powerful than others.

These are all, of course, general theoretical arguments about the nature of collective memory and the politics of commemoration. But what can a study of the Aum Affair reveal about Japanese culture more specifically? The book has argued the following points.

Above all, the aftermath of the Tokyo attack revealed and strengthened a national aversion to 'religion' (*shūkyō*), as a phenomenon to be approached cautiously and at arm's length. Unlike other cultural contexts in which religions or religious symbols can provide solace and moral guidance in the face of collective adversity, Japan does not consider religion to be part of the civil sphere. Even when religion serves a cultural function – such as visiting temples and shrines, local festivals, Imperial rituals, and visiting family graves – these practices are often framed in the language of 'culture', 'tradition', and 'family traditions', rather than as explicit expressions of faith and religious affiliation. While the transition of Japan to an increasingly 'non-religious' (*mushūkyō*) society did not begin with the Aum Affair, it certainly intensified people's aversion to organised religion as a potential danger to society.

Moreover, the Aum Affair brought to the surface Japan's cultural tendency to employ social ostracism as a primary response mechanism against potentially threatening people and objects. Like many other societies, Japan has historically responded to the cultural 'Other' through social ostracism and the imposition of a physical and social barrier between the majority population and minority groups. Historically, a practice known as '*mura hachibu*' has been a major mechanism for punishing normative transgressions in village communities in which the transgressors are shunned and excluded from communal activities. *Mura hachibu* is a practice that continues in some rural communities today. Similarly, social ostracism has been a major component of racialised discrimination against *burakumin*, an underclass of people who historically engaged in occupations associated with ritual pollution, including executions, undertaking, butchery, leather tanning, and leather crafts. *Burakumin* historically lived in segregated areas, known as 'discriminated settlements' (*hisabetsu buraku*), and in spite of decades of assimilation policies and public works (*dōwa seisaku*) in the 20th century, socio-economic disparity between *buraku* and non-*buraku* communities has remained and discrimination against *burakumin* has persisted in various areas of social life, including hiring and marriage.

To be sure, the point here is not to suggest that Aum members are in any way related or similar to *burakumin* nor that they deserve any sympathy as victims of discrimination. Rather, the point is that many actors' responses to Aum in the aftermath of the Tokyo attack are illustrative of wider patterns of societal reactions to perceived threats and sources of symbolic pollution. In the years following the Aum Affair, many local authorities and resident groups near Aum/Aleph's communes instituted a modern-day *mura hachibu*. For the first several years after the passing of the Organisations Regulation Act in 1999, authorities illegally refused to process resident records submitted by Aleph members, while residents often enforced 'shunning' by refusing to engage in conversations with Aleph members beyond what was absolutely necessary. Aum and Aleph, whose teachings already prohibited contact with outsiders, continued to minimise contact and maintain its 'world-rejecting' stance, contributing to their own isolation in the neighbourhoods they inhabited.

Finally, the Aum Affair has shown that restorative justice remains inchoate and underdeveloped in a cultural context which sees capital punishment as both desirable and necessary. The enduring public support for the death penalty in public opinion has rested on two assumptions: first, that the state is responsible for avenging victims and their families, and second, that offenders who commit serious crimes are beyond moral redemption and must pay for their crimes with their lives. Following the terrorist attacks and during the trials, many bereaved families and survivors expressed their wish that the culprits be put to death. The death sentences for Asahara and the twelve aides were seen as inevitable, if not desirable. Although organisations including the Japanese Federation of Bar Associations and Amnesty International have repeatedly called for an end to the practice, it continues to be defended as a necessary mechanism for delivering retributive justice. Furthermore, because of this strong moral impetus to 'punish' transgressors, there are few institutional opportunities whereby victims and perpetrators can reach any reconciliation. Despite the best efforts of figures such as Kōno Yoshiyuki, who has been a steadfast advocate for greater dialogue and reconciliation between perpetrators and victims, these actions do not seem to have been considered in any serious way by many other victims, public intellectuals, the mass media, and, most importantly, the state. In a cultural climate in which the death penalty is justified for murderers and terrorists, and in which any negotiation or compromise is seen as a breach of the norm of social ostracism, reconciliation remains a distant, if not unachievable, possibility.

Final remarks

Collective memory necessarily evolves as societies encounter new challenges and past events regain a new significance in the light of emerging events. Since the Tokyo sarin attack, Japan has encountered multiple events which have become cultural traumas on a scale perhaps even greater than the Aum Affair, including the 2009 global financial crisis and recession, the 2011 East Japan earthquake and the subsequent tsunami and nuclear disaster, and the COVID-19 pandemic. Each of these momentous events has had a fundamental impact on how Japan sees itself and how Japan relates to the world. Just as the Aum Affair raised questions about structural faults and dysfunctions in society, these cultural traumas have prompted fundamental questions about what constitutes a 'normal' and 'healthy' society, from the reliance on nuclear energy to the risks that the most vulnerable people face from unemployment, natural disasters, and pandemics. As the perceived social significance of the Aum Affair relative to these more recent cultural traumas gradually declines, and as the core stakeholders such as victims and ex-members age, it appears inevitable that the frequency and intensity of commemorative speech acts surrounding the Aum Affair will only reduce with the passage of time.

The rise of new cultural traumas does not mean, however, that old traumas disappear. Even in the present day, older historical traumas of the atomic bombings, the remembrance of the war dead, and Japan's colonial and wartime actions continue to stir intense domestic and international debates. As those with first-hand experiences of the Second World War inevitably pass away, these issues have become, first and foremost, about intergenerational memory and 'post-memory'. Progressive and conservative memory narratives by children, grandchildren, and great-grandchildren of those with first-hand experience of Japanese colonialism and the Second World War are constantly emerging and re-emerging (Ushiyama 2021). Likewise, just as the past several years have seen the interventions of Asahara's daughters, discourses of the Aum Affair are increasingly contested as 'post-memory', as children of victims and perpetrators inherit the trauma of their parents, producing new interpretations in new contexts. In this sense, the Aum Affair has not truly ended. Even as collective memory has a structural and long-term effect on how a society views itself, it is always open to revision and challenge.

Appendix: Glossary of Terms

Glossary of Aum terminology

Aleph	Aum Shinrikyō's biggest successor organisation, renamed in 1999. The spelling of Aleph has changed over the years (first, from *Ārefu*, then to *Arefu*); currently it is written as 'Aleph' in Roman characters. Jōyū Fumihiro and his followers split from Aleph in 2007 to form the schismatic group Hikari no Wa in 2007. Another smaller group known by security authorities as the 'Yamada et al. group' (*Yamada-ra no shūdan*) broke off from Aleph in 2015.
Aum Shinrikyō	Originally founded as Oumu no Kai (Aum Society, later the Aum Society of Sages) by Asahara Shōkō in 1984. Was renamed in 1987 as Aum Shinrikyō and was awarded religious corporation status in 1989 by the Tokyo Metropolitan Government. Aum lost its religious corporation in June 1995 but continued as a voluntary association (*nin'i dantai*) without recognition as a legal person.
Gotai tōchi	A form of prostration in which participants 'throw' their limbs and head onto the ground repeatedly to express devotion for the guru and the god Shiva.
Hikari no Wa	Splinter organisation of Aum Shinrikyō, which separated from Aleph in 2007 over disagreements over teachings and Asahara's position. Led by Aum's former spokesperson Jōyū Fumihiro.
Hinayāna	Translated as 'small vehicle', it is one of the 'vehicles' to enlightenment. *Hinayāna* emphasises individual self-enlightenment through yogic practice and meditation.
Holy name	Name entrusted by Asahara to those who completed the *Raja* Yoga stage and were qualified to be 'leader' (*shi*). Once given, the holy names were used exclusively. Names were taken from Buddhist scriptures.
Initiation	Aum used a wide range of 'initiation rituals' to deepen faith in Asahara. In the late 1980s, 'initiation by blood' (*chi no inishiēshon*) involved drinking a phial of Asahara's blood,

	supposedly to replicate Asahara's DNA in the initiand's body. Later, initiations used hallucinogenic drugs to simulate mystical experiences, which were forcibly given without the initiand's knowledge or consent. This included 'Christ's initiation' (*kirisuto no inishiēshon*) using LSD, and 'Rudorachakurin's initiation' (*rudochakurin no inishiēshon*) using LSD and methamphetamines.
Karuma otoshi	Literally translated to 'dropping karma', or 'cleansing karma'. Aum believed that 'bad karma' from a person's past lives were cleansed by experiencing pain and suffering in the present. Practices such as corporal punishment and self-flagellation with bamboo swords (*shinai*) were justified on this ground. Physical injury, illnesses, and harm towards others was also justified and celebrated as signs of *karuma otoshi*.
Mahāmudrā	A difficult challenge or task set by Asahara or a superior *samana* as a test of faith. Many members willingly committed crimes believing that their absolute obedience to Asahara (and to their superiors) was being tested.
Mahayāna	Translates to 'big vehicle', it is one of the 'vehicles' to enlightenment. In Aum's doctrinal hierarchy, *Mahayāna* emphasises the salvation of others through proselytising work.
Ministerial system *(shōchōsei)*	In 1994, Aum introduced various ministries, with senior members taking the title of 'Minister'. For instance, Murai Hideo was Minister of Science and Technology, Inoue Yoshihiro was Minister of Intelligence, and Hayashi Ikuo was Minister of Treatment.
Perfect Salvation Initiation (PSI)	An initiation ritual in which the user wore a headgear device which passed a weak electrical current to the head. Shaped like a helmet and lined with electrodes touching the scalp, the PSI claimed to synchronise Asahara's brainwaves with the initiand's.
Poa	Derived from '*phōwa*', a ritual of soul transference practiced in Tibetan Buddhism. *Poa* came to mean murdering Aum's 'enemies'. It became a thinly veiled euphemism to kill off Aum's enemies, used as a verb 'to poa' (*poa suru*).
Samana	Aum's term for a believer living full-time in Aum's facility or commune. Also known interchangeably as *shissha*, *shukke shinja* (renunciant believer), or *shukkesha*.
Satyam (Satian)	Name for a building block located in Aum's headquarters in Kamikuishiki. Satyam No. 7 was intended to become a sarin factory, but the construction work was never completed.

Seigoshi — The rank awarded to senior followers, ranking directly below *Seitaishi* and above '*shi*'. Many of the culprits of the Tokyo attack were promoted to the rank of *Seigoshi* days before the attack. *Seigoshi* wore purple kurtas.

Seitaishi — The highest rank that disciples could attain, directly beneath Asahara. The only *samana* that held the title were Ishii Hisako, Jōyū Fumihiro, and Murai Hideo. The other *Seitaishi* were Asahara's wife Tomoko and third daughter Rika (holy name: Ācharī). *Seitaishi* wore light green kurtas.

Secret work — Term used to describe 'work' conducted in secrecy, which often involved illegal or criminal activities. Believers engaged in secret work were prohibited from talking about it to other members.

Shaktīpat — An initiation ritual in which the spiritual leader 'injects' energy into the initiand's forehead, resulting in a mystical experience. This was administered by Asahara and other senior members.

Shi — Literally translated to 'master', *shi* were middle-management followers who were given 'holy names' chosen by Asahara. Originally known as *swami*.

Shukkesha — See *samana*.

Spy check (supai chekku) — As Asahara constantly feared that Aum was being infiltrated by state agents, suspected spies and saboteurs were often tortured and interrogated for hours on end in a process known as a 'spy check'. Methods of interrogation included 'narco' (*naruko*), in which the suspected spy was injected with sodium thiopental, a barbiturate, and 'new narco' (*nyū naruko*), in which they were given high-voltage electric shocks to the head to erase their memories. A *samana*, Tomida Toshio, was killed by 'spy check' after he was accused of poisoning the well water.

Tantra Vajirayāna — Translates to the 'diamond vehicle' towards enlightenment. It is the highest form of teaching in Aum's doctrinal hierarchy, above *Hinayāna* and *Mahayāna* vehicles. The *Vajrayāna* doctrine justified the enlightened guru to commit violence if the overall outcome was seen to be more beneficial for the person and the world. For example, it would be justified to kill someone whom the guru knew was going to commit murder in the future, as it would save the life of the future murder victim and guarantee a better reincarnation for the would-be murderer.

Work (wāku) Daily duties conducted for the running of the organisation, separate from their training regimen. This included, for example, preparing meals, cleaning, media work, and construction.

Zaike shinja Part-time members who did not live in shared accommodation or commune. They comprised the vast majority of Aum's 'membership'.

Glossary of names: individuals associated with the Aum Affair

Aoyama Yoshinobu (1960–) Holy name: Apājaha. A *samana* and Aum's attendant lawyer. At the time, he was the youngest person in the country to pass the bar at 21 years old.
He was jailed for falsifying documents relating to a land deal in 1989 but was not involved in Aum's violent crimes.

Asahara Shōkō (1955–2018) Born in Yatsushiro, Kumamoto as Matsumoto Chizuo, he founded Aum in 1984. Claiming that he had achieved enlightenment in the Himalayas in 1986, he invented the title *Sonshi* (supreme leader) to be worshipped as a guru. Asahara gave direct orders for Aum's *poa* schemes, including murders, attempted murders, and terrorist attacks. Executed in 2018.

Egawa Shōko (1958–) Originally a journalist for the regional newspaper *Kanagawa Shimbun*, she subsequently became a freelance journalist. She took an interest in Aum beginning in the late 1980s and wrote about Aum's various controversies before the Tokyo attack. She was attacked but survived an assassination attempt by Aum using phosgene gas. She received the Kikuchi Kan Award in 1995 for contributions to culture. She temporarily acted as the legal guardian of Asahara's fourth daughter.

Endō Seiichi (1960–2018) Holy name: Jīvaka. One of the core scientists behind Aum's militarisation programme. He synthesised sarin and other chemicals used in Aum's criminal schemes. A culprit in the Matsumoto sarin attack. Executed in 2018.

Hayakawa Kiyohide (1949–2018) Holy name: Tirōpa. Originally a landscaper, he was involved in many construction projects. As a de facto diplomat for Aum, he was later instrumental in smuggling weapons and military equipment from Russia. One of the culprits of the Sakamoto murders. Executed in 2018.

Hayashi Ikuo (1947–) Holy name: Krishnananda. A heart surgeon by training, he became the head of Aum's medical section. Introduced the method of drugging suspected spies (*naruko*) and administering electric shocks to erase memories (*new naruko*). One of the culprits of the Tokyo sarin attack. Sentenced to life in prison.

Hayashi Yasuo (1957–2018) Holy name: Vajrachitta Ishidinna. One of the culprits in the Tokyo attack. An electrical engineer by training, Hayashi was also a member of the Science and Technology team. He was a fugitive until he was arrested in 1998. Married while in prison and changed his surname to Koike. Executed in 2018.

Hirata Makoto (1965-) Holy name: Pōsha. One of the culprits of the kidnapping of Kariya Kiyoshi, he went into hiding until he handed himself in on New Year's Eve, 2011. He was sentenced to nine years in prison.

Inoue Yoshihiro (1969–2018) Holy name: Ānanda. One of Asahara's youngest aides, he was responsible for intelligence gathering and was involved in kidnapping and assassination cases. He coordinated the ground-level operation during the Tokyo attack. Executed in 2018.

Ishii Hisako Holy name: Mahā Keima. One of the oldest and most devoted adherents, Ishii had an early leadership role in the late 1980s alongside Jōyū as a model adherent and held the highest title of *Seitaishi*. Asahara's lover, she gave birth to two of his children, and she had a much less prominent role within Aum during the 1990s due to her child-rearing responsibilities.

Jōyū Fumihiro (1962–) Holy name: Maitrēya. He was one of the earliest adherents to join Aum and served as Aum's spokesperson. He was stationed in Russia at the time of the terror attacks. Jailed for perjury and falsification of documents in a 1989 land deal. He was the de facto leader of Aleph after 2000 but was put into physical isolation in 2003 following disagreements with Asahara's family. Left Aleph in 2007 to start Hikari no Wa with around 160 followers.

Kōno Yoshiyuki (1950–) A survivor of the Matsumoto Sarin Incident. He was initially falsely accused as a suspect in the Matsumoto attack. He became a prolific public speaker and an advocate for victims' rights. As an opponent of the death penalty, he criticised the executions of the culprits in 2018.

Matsumoto Rika (1983–) Holy name: Ācharī. Asahara's third daughter, Rika was raised by various *samana* attendants following the arrests

	of her parents. Held the title *Seitaishi*. She contended that Asahara was mentally ill prior to his execution.
Matsumoto Satoka (alias) (1989–)	Asahara's fourth daughter, Satoka has taken a fiercely critical view of Aum as a 'brainwashing cult' and has severed legal ties with her family. The government initially announced that Asahara had specified her to be custodian of his remains, but this was overturned in court after a legal challenge by Rika and other family members.
Matsumoto Tomoko (1958–)	Asahara's wife. Holy name: Mahāmāya, later Yasōdharā. Tomoko held the title *Seitashi*. Tomoko has played a leading role in running Aleph following Asahara's arrest.
Mori Tatsuya (1956–)	Documentary filmmaker and writer. Creator of independent films *A* (1998) and *A2* (2001). In the nonfiction book *A3* (2012), he argued that Asahara was mentally ill. He opposed the executions of Asahara and his accomplices in 2018.
Murai Hideo (1958–1995)	Holy name: Manjushrī. As the head of the Science and Technology team, Murai directed many parts of Aum's militarisation programme. He was one of the culprits in the Sakamoto murders and the Matsumoto attack in addition to planning and overseeing the Tokyo attack. He was murdered outside Aum's Tokyo office in April 1995.
Murakami Haruki (1949-)	Novelist and writer. Published the *Underground* series, a collection of interviews with victims (volume 1) and members/ex-members (volume 2). His 2009 novel *1Q84* was partly inspired by the Aum Affair.
Nagaoka Hiroyuki (1938–)	Father of a former Aum member and a representative of the Aum Shinrikyō Victims' Society, which was renamed Aum Shinrikyō Families' Society in 1995. Survived an assassination attempt using the nerve agent VX in 1995.
Noda Naruhito (1966–)	Holy name: Vajratikshnā. Originally a physics student at Tokyo University, he was head of the transport section. He briefly acted as the representative of Aleph but was expelled from Aleph in 2010.
Okasaki Kazuaki (1960–2018)	Holy name: Angulimāla. One of the culprits in the murders of Taguchi Shūji and the Sakamoto family. He fled Aum in 1990 with large amounts of the group's cash and negotiated his safety with Asahara for a one-off payment. Okasaki changed his surname to Miyamae after being adopted by a supporter. Executed in 2018.
Takahashi Katsuya	Holy name: Sumangala. One of the getaway drivers in the Tokyo sarin attack. He fled soon after the attack and lived in

(1958–)	hiding until he was arrested in 2012 following a nation-wide manhunt. Was sentenced to a life term.
Takahashi Shizue (1947–)	Leader of the Subway Sarin Incident Victims' Society. A widow of the Tokyo attack, she campaigned for state compensation for Aum's victims, and has engaged in various commemorative activities including self-publishing testimonies and hosting annual symposia.
Takimoto Tarō (1957–)	Lawyer. Became the lawyer for the Aum Shinrikyō Victims' Society (later the Aum Shinrikyō Families' Society) following Sakamoto Tsusumi's disappearance. Also the leader of the ex-member group Kanariya no Kai (Canary Society) and formerly a director of Japan De-Cult Council (renamed Japan Society for Cult Prevention and Recovery).
Tsuchiya Masami (1965–2018)	Holy name: Ksitigarbha. A chemist by training, he played a central role in Aum's militarisation scheme. One of the culprits of the Tokyo attack. Executed in 2018.

Bibliography

Notes on Methodology

For qualitative media content analysis, I consulted two Japanese broadsheet national newspapers *Yomiuri Shimbun* and *Asahi Shimbun* as my main primary sources for newspaper reports. There were several advantages in the selection of these two papers. Firstly, the *Yomiuri* and the *Asahi* are the best-selling (7.4 million copies per day in 2021) and second-best selling (4.9 million per day in 2021) newspapers in the country respectively (*Yomiuri Shimbun* 2021). They are therefore indicative of the general tone and direction of national media discourse. Secondly, the *Yomiuri* is a leading conservative paper, while the *Asahi* is known for its progressive agenda: comparing the two enabled me to see how different political leanings shaped reactions to the Aum Affair as expressed through their editorials and news reports. Thirdly, on a more practical note, both papers were accessible through online digital archives, making archival work in the UK considerably easier than it would have been otherwise.

As additional sources, I have included articles from the national newspapers *Mainichi Shimbun* and *Sankei Shimbun*, and some contemporary affairs magazines such as *AERA* and *Bungei Shunjū,* limiting the analysis to editorials in the first month after the Tokyo attack (March to April 1995). Both *Mainichi* and *Sankei* are widely read national newspapers: *Mainichi* has a daily circulation of 2.1 million copies, while *Sankei* has 1.2 million daily readers as of 2021 (*Yomiuri Shimbun* 2021). They have contrasting political stances, with the *Mainichi* widely regarded as a centrist and liberal newspaper, while the *Sankei* is the most right-wing of major national papers. Due to time constraints during my fieldwork, these newspapers comprise a small sample of the overall data, but nonetheless provide useful comparisons to the *Yomiuri* and the *Asahi.*

For each newspaper, I searched for articles containing key words in Japanese such as 'Aum Shinrikyō', 'Sarin', 'Matsumoto Sarin Incident' and 'Subway Sarin Incident'. Given the massive number of media reports on the Aum Affair, I narrowed down the date range of search for each topic to recover the most relevant articles.

For initial reports on the Matsumoto Sarin Incident (which occurred on 27 June 1994) and Subway Sarin Incident (which occurred on 20 March 1995), I covered the period between June 1994 and December 1995. I then looked at commemorative media coverage of the Matsumoto Sarin Incident in June between 1996 and 2015, and in March between 1996 and 2015 for the Tokyo Subway Sarin Incident. This enabled an extensive but still manageable collection of articles. Many of the articles that I included were general news reports from the 'society' (*shakai*) section, editorials and opinion columns, letters to the editor, and special reports. All the articles were written in Japanese, and all translations are my own.

A unique aspect of Japanese newspapers is that different regional offices have a degree of editorial independence. This means that there is some variation in how regional editions print stories. For instance, cover stories may have different lengths depending on the relevance to the region and may have different layouts. There are also stories printed only in regional editions. In principle, I have privileged articles printed in 'national' editions. However, where there have been detailed reports on Aum in region-only editions, I have chosen to include them to demonstrate possible regional variations in media coverage of the Aum Affair.

One of the drawbacks of relying on online archives was the removal of visual data in the archival format. Visual information – such as photographs, cartoons, tables and figures, and diagrams – is a key component of print media, and especially so for newspapers, which rely on eye-catching headlines and photographs as part of their storytelling. Due to the storage format of archived articles as well as copyright issues, visual data presented in newspapers had to be omitted from the analysis, and where possible, I have considered other forms of visual media, such as magazines, television, and film.

Primary Sources

Interviews

Date	Name (surname/first name)	Title/Occupation
18 March 2015	Shimada Hiromi	Independent scholar, Religious Studies
25 March 2015	Inoue Nobutaka	Academic, Religious Studies
27 March 2015	Nagaoka Hiroyuki	Anti-Aum activist, survivor of an assassination attempt by Aum

Date	Name (surname/first name)	Title/Occupation
30 March 2015	Noda Naruhito	Former leader of Aleph
31 March 2015	Ōta Toshihiro	Academic, Religious Studies
6 April 2015	Takahashi Shizue	Spokesperson for Subway Sarin Incident Victims' Society
10 April 2015	Kōno Yoshiyuki	Survivor and widower of Matsumoto Sarin Incident
8 July 2016	Aoki Yumiko	Freelance book editor
20 July 2016	Mori Tatsuya	Film director; writer
24 July 2016	Jōyū Fumihiro	Leader, Hikari no Wa. Formerly leader of Aleph
29 July 2016	Anonymous	Former member of Aum/Aleph
29 July 2016	Hirosue Akitoshi	PR spokesperson for Hikari no Wa

Television programmes

Broadcaster	Title	Original Air Date
Fuji Terebi	Tsumayo! Matsumoto sarin jiken hannin to yobarete … Kazoku o mamorinuita 15 nen	26 June 2009
Fuji Terebi	Chikatetsu sarin jiken 15 nen me no tatakai	20 March 2010
Fuji Terebi	Gekido! Seiki no daijiken Oumu Shinrikyō to tatakatta 'kazoku no zenkiroku'	20 March 2015
NHK	Ningen Dokyumento. Tsuma Shizue san no haru: Chikatetsu sarin jiken izoku no hibi	15 April 2005
NHK	Mikaiketsu jiken File No.2 Oumu Shinrikyō Jiken	26, 27 May 2012
TV Tokyo	Hōdō sukūpu purojekuto Oumu wa imamo ikiteiru: sōryoku tsuiseki! Chikatetsu sarin jiken 20 nen	7 March 2015
Yomiuri Terebi	NNN Dokyumento Ashiato Matsumoto sarin jiken 20 nen	30 June 2014

Films

Kumai, K. (2000) *Nihon no Kuroi Natsu: Enzai*. Drama, Nikkatsu.
Mori, T. (1998) *A*. Documentary, "A" Production Committee.
Mori, T. (2001) *A2*. Documentary, "A" Production Committee.

Laws

1995. Sarin tō ni yoru jinshin higai no bōshi ni kansuru hōritsu. 21 April. Act No. 78.
1995. Shūkyō hōjinhō no ichibu o kaisei suru hōritsu. Act No.134.
1998. Oumu Shinrikyō ni kakawaru hasan tetsuzuki ni okeru kuni no saiken ni kansuru tokurei ni kansuru hōritsu. 24 April. Act No. 45.
1999. Musabetsu tairyō satsujin o okonatta dantai no kisei ni kansuru hōritsu. Act No. 147.
1999. Tokutei hasan hōjin no hasan zaidan ni zokusubeki zaisan no kaifuku ni kansuru tokubetsu sochihō. Act No. 148.
2004. Hanzai higaisha tō kihon hō. 8 December. Act No. 161.
2008. Oumu Shinrikyō hanzai higaisha tō o kyūsai suru tameno kyūfukin no shikyū ni kansuru hōritsu. 18 June. Act No. 80.

Publications by Aum Shinrikyō/Aleph

Asahara, S. 1986b. *Seishi O Koeru*. Tokyo: Oumu Shuppan.
Asahara, S. 1989a. *Metsubō Kara Kokū E: Zoku Metsubō no Hi*. Tokyo: Oumu Shuppan.
Asahara, S. 1989b. *Metsubō No Hi*. Tokyo: Oumu Shuppan.
Asahara, S. 1991[1986]. *Chōnōryoku Himitsu No Kaihatsuhō*. Tokyo: Yamato Shuppan.
Asahara, S. 1991b. *Asahara Shōkō No Sekai Part 2: Sonshi, Asahara Shōkō Ga Kiru!* Tokyo: Oumu Shuppan.
Asahara, S. 1991c. *Jinrui Metsubō No Shinjitsu*. Tokyo: Oumu Shuppan.
Asahara, S. 1995a. *Bōkoku Nihon No Kanashimi*. Tokyo: Oumu Shuppan.
Asahara S. 1995b. *Hi Izuru Kuni, Wazawai Chikashi*. Tokyo: Oumu Shuppan.
Jōyū, F. 2002a. *Jōyū Fumihiro ga kataru: Kunō kara no kaihō*. Tokyo: Higashiyama.
Jōyū, F. 2002b. *Kakusei Shinseiki*. Tokyo: Higashiyama.
Jōyū, F. 2003. *Jōyū Fumihiro ga kataru (2) Kokoro to shinpi no sekai*. Tokyo: Higashiyama.

Secondary sources

Alexander, Jeffrey C. 2004a. "On the Construction of Moral Universals: The 'Holocaust' from War Crime to Trauma Drama". Pp. 196–263 in *Cultural Trauma and Collective Identity*. Berkeley, CA: University of California Press.

Alexander, Jeffrey C. 2004b. "Towards a Theory of Cultural Trauma". Pp. 1–30 in *Cultural Trauma and Collective Identity*. Berkeley, CA: University of California Press.

Alexander, Jeffrey C. 2009. "Public Intellectuals and Civil Society". Pp. 19–28 in *Intellectuals and their publics: Perspectives from the Social Sciences*, edited by C. Fleck, A. Hess, and E. S. Lyon. Surrey: Ashgate.

Alexander, Jeffrey C. 2016. "Dramatic Intellectuals". *International Journal of Politics, Culture, and Society* 29(4):341–58.

Alexander, Jeffrey C., and Elizabeth Butler Breese. 2011. "Introduction: On Social Suffering and Its Cultural Construction". Pp. xi–xxxv in *Narrating Trauma: On the Impact of Collective Suffering*, edited by R. Eyerman, J.C. Alexander, and E.B. Breese. Boulder, CO: Paradigm.

Altglas, Véronique. 2010. "Laïcité Is What Laïcité Does: Rethinking the French Cult Controversy". *Current Sociology* 58(3):489–510.

Anthony, Dick, and Thomas Robbins. 2008. "Conversion and 'Brainwashing' in New Religious Movements". Pp. 243–97 in *The Oxford Handbook of New Religious Movements*, edited by J.R. Lewis. Oxford: Oxford University Press.

Aoki, Yumiko, ed. 2010. *Oumu o ikite: moto Shinja tachi no Chikatestu sarin jiken kara 15 nen*. Tokyo: Saizō.

Aonuma, Yōichirō. 2007. *Ōmu Saiban Bōshōki*. Shohan. Tokyo: Shōgakkan.

Asahara Kōsoshin Bengonin, ed. 2006. *Gokuchū de mita Asahara Shōkō*. Tokyo: Inpakuto Shuppan.

Austin, John L. 1962. *How to Do Things with Words*. Oxford: Clarendon.

Baert, Patrick. 2012. "Positioning Theory and Intellectual Interventions". *Journal for the Theory of Social Behaviour* 42(3):304–24.

Baert, Patrick. 2015. *The Existentialist Moment: The Rise of Sartre as a Public Intellectual*. Cambridge: Polity.

Baert, Patrick, and Alan Shipman. 2012. "Transforming the Intellectual". Pp. 179–204 in *The Politics of Knowledge*, edited by F.D. Rubio and P. Baert. London: Routledge.

Baffelli, Erica. 2012. "Hikari No Wa: A New Religion Recovering from Disaster". *Japanese Journal of Religious Studies* 39(1):29–49.

Baffelli, Erica. 2018. "Aum Shinrikyō". Pp. 193–210 in *Handbook of East Asian New Religious Movements*, edited by L. Pokorny and F. Winter. Leiden: Brill.

Baffelli, Erica. 2020. "Did Aum Shinrikyō Really End?" Pp. 49–66 in *The Demise of Religion: How Religions End, Die, or Dissipate*, edited by M. Stausberg, S.A. Wright, and C.M. Cusack. London: Bloomsbury Academic.

Baffelli, Erica, and Ian Reader. 2011. "Competing for the Apocalypse: Religious Rivalry and Millenial Transformations in a Japanese New Religion". *International Journal for the Study of New Religions* 2(1):5–28.

Baffelli, Erica, and Ian Reader. 2012. "Editors' Introduction. Impact and Ramifications: The Aftermath of the Aum Affair in the Japanese Religious Context". *Japanese Journal of Religious Studies* 39(1):1–28.

Bakhtin, Mikhail M. 1981. *The Dialogic Imagination: Four Essays*. edited by M. Holquist. Austin, TX: University of Texas Press.

Bakhtin, Mikhail M. 1984a. *Problems of Dostoevsky's Poetics*. edited by C. Emerson. Minneapolis: University of Minnesota Press.

Bakhtin, Mikhail M. 1984b. *Rabelais and His World*. Bloomington, IN: Indiana University Press.

Bakhtin, Mikhail M. 1986. *Speech Genres and Other Late Essays*. 1st ed., edited by M. Holquist and C. Emerson. Austin: University of Texas Press.

Bakhtin, Mikhail M., Pavel N. Medvedev, and V. N. Voloshinov. 1994. *The Bakhtin Reader*. edited by P. Morris. London: Edward Arnold.

Barker, Eileen. 1984. *The Making of a Moonie: Choice or Brainwashing?* Oxford: Basil Blackwell.

Barker, Eileen. 2007. "Charting the Information Field: Cult-Watching Groups and the Construction of Images of New Religious Movements". Pp. 309–30 in *Teaching New Religious Movements*, edited by D.G. Bromley. Oxford: Oxford University Press.

Bartmanski, Dominik, and Ron Eyerman. 2011. "The Worst Was the Silence: The Unfinished Drama of the Katyn Massacre". Pp. 237–66 in *Narrating Trauma: On the impact of Collective Suffering*, edited by R. Eyerman, J.C. Alexander, and E.B. Breese. Boulder, CO: Paradigm.

Benedict, Ruth. 1967. *The Chrysanthemum and the Sword: Patterns of Japanese Culture*. London: Routledge & Kegan Paul.

Billig, Michael. 1995. *Banal Nationalism*. London: SAGE.

Bromley, David G. 2008. "Leaving the Fold: Disaffiliating from New Religious Movements". Pp. 298–314 in *The Oxford Handbook of New Religious Movements*, edited by J.R. Lewis. Oxford: Oxford University Press.

Buruma, Ian. 2009. *The Wages of Guilt: Memories of War in Germany and Japan*. London: Atlantic.

Caruth, Cathy. 1996. *Unclaimed Experience: Trauma, Narrative, and History*. Baltimore, MD: Johns Hopkins University Press.

CCCS Popular Memory Group. 1982. "What Do We Mean by Popular Memory?" Centre for Contemporary Cultural Studies.

Chikatestu Sarin Jiken Higaisha no Kai. 1998. *Soredemo Ikite Iku – Chikatetsu sarin jiken higaisha shukishū*. Tokyo: Sanmāku.

Chikatestu Sarin Jiken Higaisha no Kai. 2007. *Watashi Ni Totte No Chikatetsu Sarin Jiken: Jiken Hassei 12 Nen o Mukaete*. Self-published.

Chikatestu Sarin Jiken Higaisha no Kai. 2015. "20 Nenkan No Dekigoto".

Cohen, Stanley. 1972. *Folk Devils and Moral Panics: The Creation of the Mods and Rockers*. London: MacGibbon and Kee.

Connerton, Paul. 1989. *How Societies Remember*. Cambridge: Cambridge University Press.

Conway, Brian. 2010a. *Commemoration and Bloody Sunday: Pathways of Memory*. Basingstoke: Palgrave Macmillan.

Conway, Brian. 2010b. "New Directions in the Sociology of Collective Memory and Commemoration". *Sociology Compass* 4(7):442–53.

Cowan, Douglas E. 2002. "Exits and Migrations: Foregrounding the Christian Counter-Cult". *Journal of Contemporary Religion* 17(3):339–54.

Dorman, Benjamin. 2001. "Aum Shinrikyo". *Religion in the News*. Retrieved 25 February 2017 (www.trincoll.edu/depts/csrpl/RINVol4No1/aum_shinrikyo.htm).

Dorman, Benjamin. 2012a. *Celebrity Gods: New Religions, Media, and Authority in Occupied Japan*. Honolulu: University of Hawai'i Press.

Dorman, Benjamin. 2012b. "Scholarly Reactions to the Aum and Waco Incidents". *Japanese Journal of Religious Studies* 39(1):153–77.

Dower, John W. 1999. *Embracing Defeat: Japan in the Aftermath of World War II*. London: Allen Lane.

Ducharme, Lori J., and Gary Alan Fine. 1995. "The Construction of Nonpersonhood and Demonization: Commemorating the Traitorous Reputation of Benedict Arnold". *Social Forces* 73(4):1309–31.

Durkheim, Émile. 2008. *The Elementary Forms of Religious Life*. Oxford: Oxford University Press.

Edelman, Bryan, and James T. Richardson. 2005. "Imposed Limitations on Freedom of Religion in China and the Margin of Appreciation Doctrine: A Legal Analysis of the Crackdown on the Falun Gong and Other 'Evil Cults.'" *Journal of Church and State* 47(2):243–67.

Egawa, Shōko. 1991. *Kyūseishu no yabō: Oumu Shinrikyō o otte*. Tokyo: Kyoīku shiryō shuppan-kai.

Egawa, Shōko. 1995. *Oumu Shinrikyō Tsuiseki 2200 Nichi*. Tokyo: Bungei Shunjū.

Erikson, Kai. 1976. *Everything in Its Path: Destruction of Community in the Buffalo Creek Flood*. New York: Simon and Schuster.

Erll, Astrid. 2011. *Memory in Culture*. Basingstoke: Palgrave Macmillan.

Eyerman, Ron. 2001. *Cultural Trauma: Slavery and the Formation of African American Identity*. Cambridge: Cambridge University Press.

Eyerman, Ron. 2004. "The Past in the Present: Culture and the Transmission of Memory". *Acta Sociologica* 47(2):159–69.

Eyerman, Ron. 2011. "Intellectuals and Cultural Trauma". *European Journal of Social Theory* 14(4):453–67.

Eyerman, Ron. 2015. *Is This America? Katrina as Cultural Trauma*. Austin: University of Texas Press.

Eyerman, Ron. 2019. *Memory, Trauma, and Identity*. Basingstoke: Palgrave Macmillan.

Fine, Gary Alan. 2013. "Apology and Redress: Escaping the Dustbin of History in Postsegregationist South". *Social Forces* 91(4):1319–42.

Freud, Sigmund. 1917. "Mourning and Melancholia". Pp. 243–58 in *The Standard Edition of the Complete Psychological Works of Sigmund Freud: "On the History of the Post Psychoanalytic Movement", "Papers on Metapsychology" and Other Works*. Vol. XIV. London: Hogarth.

Friedlander, Saul. 1992. "Trauma, Transference and 'Working through' in Writing the History of the 'Shoah.'" *History and Memory* 4(1):39–59.

Fromm, Erich. 2001. *Fear of Freedom*. London: Routledge.

Fujita, Shōichi. 2011. "Oumu Shinrikyō Jiken No Genryū: Shanbara Oukoku Gensou Kara Musabetu Gairyō Satsujin Eno Doutei". Pp. 19–56 in *Jōhō jidai no Oumu Shinrikyō*, edited by N. Inoue and Shūkyō Jōhō Risāchi Sentā. Tokyo: Shunjūsha.

Fujiwara, Shinya. 2006. *Yomi no Inu*. Tokyo: Bungei Shunjū.

Furihata, Ken'ichi. 2000. *Oumu Saiban to Nihonjin*. Tokyo: Heibonsha.

Gardner, Richard A. 1999. "Lost in the Cosmos and the Need to Know". *Monumenta Nipponica* 54(2):217–46.

Gardner, Richard A. 2002a. "'A' Revisited". *Monumenta Nipponica* 57(3):339–48.

Gardner, Richard A. 2002b. "'The Blessing of Living in a Country Where There Are Senryū!': Humor in the Response to Aum Shinrikyō". *Asian Folklore Studies* 61(1):35–75.

Gardner, Richard A. 2003. "Aum and Humor: More Blessings From the Land of Senryu". *Sophia International Review* 25:1–34.

Gardner, Richard A. 2008. "Aum Shinrikyō and a Panic about Manga and Anime". Pp. 200–218 in *Japanese Visual Culture: Explorations in the World of Manga and Anime*, edited by M. MacWilliams. New York: M.E. Sharpe.

Geilhorn, Barbara, and Kristina Iwata-Weickgenannt, eds. 2017. *Fukushima and the Arts: Negotiating Nuclear Disaster*. London; New York: Routledge.

Giesen, Bernhard. 2004. *Triumph and Trauma*. Boulder, CO: Paradigm.

Hacking, Ian. 2000. "What Did Aum Shinrikyo Have in Mind?" *London Review of Books*, 19 October, 3–8.

Halbwachs, Maurice. 1992. *On Collective Memory*. edited by L.A. Coser. Chicago, IL: University of Chicago Press.

Hardacre, Helen. 2007. "Aum Shinrikyô and the Japanese Media: The Pied Piper Meets the Lamb of God". *History of Religions* 47(2/3):171–204.

Hashimoto, Akiko. 2015. *The Long Defeat: Cultural Trauma, Memory, and Identity in Japan*. Oxford: Oxford University Press.

Hassan, Steven. 1993. *Maindo Kontorōru No Kyōfu*. Tokyo: Kōyū Shuppan.

Hayakawa, Kiyohide, and Kunimitsu Kawamura. 2005. *Watashi ni totte Oumu towa nandattanoka*. Tokyo: Popurasha.

Hayashi, Ikuo. 2001. *Oumu to watashi*. Tokyo: Bungei Shunjū.

Hikari no Wa Gaibu Kansa Iinkai. 2014. "Gaibu Kansa Kekka Hōkokusho (2014 Nen 11 Gatsu 27 Nichi)".

Hirano, Naoko, and Hotaka Tsukada. 2015. "Media Hōdō Eno Shūkyō Riterasī: 'Senmonka' Ga Katatta Koto o Tegakari Ni". Pp. 213–56 in *"Oumu Shinrikyō" o kenshō suru*, edited by N. Inoue and Shūkyō Jōhō Risāchi Sentā. Tokyo: Shunjūsha.

Hirose, Ken'ichi. 2019. *Kaigo: Oumu Shinrikyō moto shinto, Hirose Ken'ichi no shuki*. Tokyo: Asahi Shimbun Shuppan.

Hughes, Christopher W. 1998. "Japan's Aum Shinrikyo, the Changing Nature of Terrorism, and the Post-cold War Security Agenda". *Pacifica Review: Peace, Security & Global Change* 10(1):39–60.

Human Rights Without Frontiers. 2011. Japan: Abduction and Deprivation of Freedom for the Purpose of Religious De-conversion. Brussels: Human Rights Without Frontiers International.

Igarashi, Yoshikuni. 2007. "Dead Bodies and Living Guns: The United Red Army and Its Deadly Pursuit of Revolution, 1971–1972". *Japanese Studies* 27(2):119–37.

Inoue, Madoka. 2011. "Roshia Ni Okeru Oumu Shinrikyō No Katsudou". Pp. 385–405 in *Jōhō jidai no Oumu Shinrikyō*, edited by N. Inoue and Shūkyō Jōhō Risāchi Sentā. Tokyo: Shunjūsha.

Inoue, Nobutaka. 1999. *Wakamono to Gendai Shūkyō: Ushinawareta Zahyōjiku*. Tokyo: Chikuma Shobō.

Inoue, Nobutaka. 2011. "Shūkyō Hōjin Kaisan to Arefu/Hikari No Wa". Pp. 410–30 in *Jōhō jidai no Oumu Shinrikyo*, edited by N. Inoue and Shūkyō Jōhō Risāchi Sentā. Tokyo: Shunjūsha.

Inoue, Nobutaka, Michio Takeda, and Kiyoyasu Kitabatake. 1995. *Oumu Shinrikyō to Wa Nani Ka: Gendai Shakai Ni Toikakeru Mono*. Tokyo: Asahi Shimbunsha.

Irons, Edward A. 2018. "The List: The Evolution of China's List of Illegal and Evil Cults". *Journal of CESNUR* 2(1):33–57.

Ishii, Kenji. 2013. "The Stereotyping of Religion in Contemporary Japan". *Journal of Religion in Japan* 2(1):63–83.

Jōyū, Fumihiro. 2002a. *Jōyū Fumihiro Ga Kataru: Kunō Kara No Kaihō*. Tokyo: Higashiyama.

Jōyū, Fumihiro. 2002b. *Kakusei Shinseiki*. Tokyo: Higashiyama.

Jōyū, Fumihiro. 2003. *Jōyū Fumihiro Ga Kataru (2) Kokoro to Shinpi No Sekai*. Tokyo: Higashiyama.

Jōyū, Fumihiro. 2012. *Oumu Jiken 17-Nenme No Kokuhaku*. Shohan. Tokyo: Fusōsha.

Jōyū, Fumihiro, Kunio Suzuki, and Hiroyuki Jo. 2013. *Owaranai Oumu*. Tokyo: Rokusaisha.

Jōyū, Fumihiro, and Sōichirō Tahara. 2013. *Kiken na shūkyō no miwakekata*. Tokyo: Popurasha.

Kadota, Ryusho. 2018. *Oumu shikeishū tamashii no henreki: Inoue Yoshihiro subete no tsumi wa wagami ni ari*. Tokyo: PHP Kenkyūjo.

Kanariya no kai, ed. 2000. *Oumu o Yameta Watashi Tachi*. Tokyo: Iwanami Shoten.

Kavitha, Rao, and Mutsuko Murakami. 1997. "The Human Cost: The Aum Shinrikyo Victims Have Their Say". Asiaweek, 3 October.

Kim, Mikyoung, and Barry Schwartz, eds. 2010. *Northeast Asia's Difficult Past: Essays in Collective Memory*. Basingstoke: Palgrave Macmillan.

Kisala, Robert J. 2001. "Religious Responses to the 'Aum Affair.'" Pp. 107–32 in *Religion and social crisis in Japan: understanding Japanese society through the Aum affair*, edited by R. Kisala and M. Mullins. Basingstoke: Palgrave.

Klein, Axel. 2012. "Twice Bitten, Once Shy: Religious Organizations and Politics after the Aum Attack". *Japanese Journal of Religious Studies* 39(1):77–98.

Koike, Yasushi. 2011. "Mori Tatsuya Kantoku Eiga 'A' 'A2' o Megutte". Pp. 340–45 in *Jōhō jidai no Oumu Shinrikyō*, edited by N. Inoue and Shūkyō Jōhō Risāchi Sentā. Tokyo: Shunjūsha.

Komiya, Hiromi. 2011. "Oumu Shinrikyō Kara No Dakkaisha Tachi". Pp. 346–59 in *Jōhō jidai no Oumu Shinrikyō*, edited by N. Inoue and Shūkyō Jōhō Risāchi Sentā. Tokyo: Shunjūsha.

Kōno, Yoshiyuki. 2001. *"Giwaku" wa hareyoutomo: Matsumoto sarin jiken no hannin to sareta watashi*. Tokyo: Bungei Shunjū.

Kōno, Yoshiyuki. 2008. *Inochi Aru Kagiri: Matsumoto Sarin Jiken o Koete*. Tokyo: Daisan Bunmeisha.

Kōno, Yoshiyuki. 2012. *Ima o Ikiru Shiawase*. Tokyo: Hoshoin.

Kumai, Kei. 2000. *Nihon No Kuroi Natsu: Enzai*. Nikkatsu.

Kurasawa, Fuyuki. 2009. "A Message in a Bottle: Bearing Witness as a Mode of Transnational Practice". *Theory, Culture & Society* 26(1):92–111.

LaCapra, Dominick. 2001. *Writing History, Writing Trauma*. Baltimore, MD: Johns Hopkins University Press.

Lewis, James R., ed. 2011. *Violence and New Religious Movements*. Oxford: Oxford University Press.

Lewis, James R. 2016. "Brainwashing and 'Cultic Mind Control.'" Pp. 174–85 in *The Oxford Handbook of New Religious Movements: Volume II*, edited by J.R. Lewis and I. Tollefsen. Oxford: Oxford University Press.

Lifton, Robert Jay. 1999. *Destroying the World to Save It: Aum Shinrikyō, Apocalyptic Violence, and the New Global Terrorism*. New York: Henry Holt and Co.

Manne, Robert. 2009. "On the Political Corruptions of a Moral Universal". Pp. 135–45 in *Remembering the Holocaust: A Debate*. Oxford: Oxford University Press.

Matsubara, Hiroshi. 2002. "Aum Grows Again, Guru Still Revered". *The Japan Times Online*, 8 August.

Matsumoto, Rika. 2015. *Tomatta Tokei: Asahara Shōkō No Sanjo Ācharī No Shuki*. Tokyo: Kōdansha.

Matsumoto, Satoka. 2010. *Watashi Wa Naze Asahara Shōkō No Musume Ni Umareteshimatta Noka: Chikatetsu Sarin Jiken Kara 15 Nenme No Kokuhaku*. Tokyo: Tokuma.

McLaughlin, Levi. 2012. "Did Aum Change Everything? What Soka Gakkai Before, During, and After the Aum Shinrikyo Affair Tells Us About the Persistent 'Otherness' of New Religions in Japan". *Japanese Journal of Religious Studies* 39(1):51–75.

McLuhan, Marshall. 1964. *Understanding Media: The Extensions of Man*. London: Routledge & Kegan Paul.

Misztal, Barbara. 2003. *Theories of Social Remembering*. Maidenhead: Open University Press.

Miyadai, Shinji. 1995. *Owarinaki nichijō o ikiro: Oumu kanzen kokufuku manyuaru*. Tokyo: Chikuma Shobō.

Mori, Tatsuya. 1998. *A*. "A" Production Committee.

Mori, Tatsuya. 2002. *A: Masukomi Ga Hōdō Shinakatta Oumu No Sugata. A*. Tokyo: Kadogawa Bunko.

Mori, Tatsuya. 2012. *A3 (2 Volumes)*. Tokyo: Shūeisha.

Mori, Tatsuya, and Takaharu Yasuoka. 2001. *A2*. Tokyo: Gendai Shokan.

Mullins, Mark. 2016. "Neonationalism, Politcs, and Religion in Post-Disaster Japan". Pp. 107–31 in *Disasters and Social Crisis in Contemporary Japan: Political, Religious, and Sociocultural Responses*, edited by M. Mullins and K. Nakano. Basingstoke: Palgrave Macmillan.

Mullins, Mark, and Koichi Nakano. 2016. "Introduction". Pp. 1–20 in *Disasters and social crisis in contemporary Japan: political, religious, and sociocultural responses*. Basingstoke: Palgrave Macmillan.

Murakami, Haruki. 1997. *Underground*. Tokyo: Kōdansha.

Murakami, Haruki. 2001. *Underground 2 Yakusoku sareta basho de*. Tokyo: Bungei Shunjū.

Murakami, Haruki. 2003. *Underground: The Tokyo Gas Attack and the Japanese Psyche*. London: Vintage.

Nagaoka, Eiko. 2009. "Oumu Shinrikyō Ni Kakawatte". Retrieved 14 October 2020 (http://ww4.tiki.ne.jp/~enkoji/nagaoka.htm).

National Police Agency. 2010. *Oumu Shinrikyō Hanzai Higaisha Kyūsai Hō No Sekō Jōkyō Tō Ni Tsuite*. Tokyo: National Police Agency.

Nishi, Kumiko. 2009. "'Shūkyōteki Na Mono' Ni Hikareru Nihonjin". *Hōsō Kenkyū to Chōōsa* 59(5):66–81.

NHK Supesharu Shuzaihan. 2013. *Mikaiketsu Jiken, Ōmu Shinrikyō Hiroku*. Tōkyō: Bungei Shunjū.

Noda, Naruhito. 2010. *Kakumei ka sensō ka: Oumu wa gurōbaru shihon shugi eno keishō datta*. Tokyo: Saizō.

Noda, Naruhito. 2012. *Isshinkyō Shihai No Shūen*. Self-published.

Nora, Pierre. 1989. "Between Memory and History: Les Lieux de Mémoire". *Representations* (26):7–24.

Olick, Jeffrey K. 1999. "Collective Memory: The Two Cultures". *Sociological Theory* 17(3):333–48.

Olick, Jeffrey K. 2007. *The Politics of Regret: On Collective Memory and Historical Responsibility*. New York; Abingdon: Routledge.

Olick, Jeffrey K. 2016. *The Sins of the Fathers: Germany, Memory, Method*. Chicago, IL: The University of Chicago Press.

Olick, Jeffrey K., Vered Vinitzky-Seroussi, and Daniel Levy, eds. 2011. *The Collective Memory Reader*. New York: Oxford University Press.

Ōta, Toshihiro. 2011. *Oumu Shinrikyō No Seishinshi: Roman Shugi, Zentai Shugi, Genri Shugi*. Tokyo: Shunjūsha.

Palmer, Susan. 2011. *The New Heretics of France: Minority Religions, La Republique, and the Government-Sponsored "'War on Sects.'"* Oxford: Oxford University Press.

Pendleton, Mark. 2009. "Mourning as Global Politics: Embodied Grief and Activism in Post-Aum Tokyo". *Asian Studies Review* 33(3):333–47.

Pendleton, Mark. 2011. "Subway to Street: Spaces of Traumatic Memory, Counter-Memory and Recovery in Post-Aum Tokyo". *Japanese Studies* 31(3):359–71.

Pendleton, Mark. 2014. "Theme Parks and Station Plaques: Memory, Tourism, and Forgetting in Post-Aum Japan". Pp. 75–94 in *Death Tourism*, edited by B. Sion. London: Seagull Books.

Pendleton, Mark. 2015. "Memory, Justice, and Postterror Futures". Pp. 202–20 in *Historical Justice and Memory*, edited by K. Neumann and J. Thompson. Madison, WI: University of Wisconsin Press.

Public Security Intelligence Agency. 2008. "Naigai Jōsei No Kaiko to Tenbō".

Public Security Intelligence Agency. 2017. "Naigai Jōsei No Kaiko to Tenbō".

Public Security Intelligence Agency. 2018. "Naigai Jōsei No Kaiko to Tenbō".

Public Security Intelligence Agency. 2019. "Naigai Jōsei No Kaiko to Tenbō".

Qurashi, Fahid. (2018) "The Prevent Strategy and the UK 'War on Terror': Embedding Infrastructures of Surveillance in Muslim Communities". *Palgrave Communications* 4(1): 1–13.

Radstone, Susannah. 2007. "Trauma Theory: Contexts, Politics, Ethics". *Paragraph* 30(1):9–29.

Reader, Ian. 2000a. *Religious Violence in Contemporary Japan: The Case of Aum Shinrikyō*. Richmond: Curzon.

Reader, Ian. 2000b. "Scholarship, Aum Shinrikyo, and Academic Integrity". *Nova Religio* 3(2):368–82.

Reader, Ian. 2001. "Consensus Shattered: Japanese Paradigm Shift and Moral Panic in the Post-Aum Era". *Nova Religio* 4(2):225–34.

Reader, Ian. 2012. "Secularization, R.I.P? Nonsense! The 'Rush Hour Away from the Gods'and the Decline of Religion in Contemporary Japan". *Journal of Religion in Japan* 1(1):7–36.

Richardson, James T. 2011. "Deprogramming: From Private Self-Help to Governmental Organized Repression". *Crime, Law and Social Change* 55(4):321–36. doi: 10.1007/s10611-011-9286-5.

Richardson, James T., and Massimo Introvigne. 2007. "New Religious Movements, Countermovements, Moral Panics, and the Media". Pp. 91–112 in *Teaching New Religious Movements*, edited by D.G. Bromley. Oxford: Oxford University Press.

RIRC. 2018. "Oumu Shinrikyō No Shikei Shikkoku Ni Taisuru <kokunai> Media No Hannō". *RIRC Dayori*, 30 November, 41–45.

Rojas-Perez, Isaias. 2017. *Mourning Remains: State Atrocity, Exhumations, and Governing the Disappeared in Peru's Postwar Andes*. Stanford, CA: Stanford University Press.

Rothberg, Michael. 2009. *Multidirectional Memory: Remembering the Holocaust in the Age of Decolonization*. Stanford, CA: Stanford University Press.

Saaler, Sven. 2005. *Politics, Memory and Public Opinion: The History Textbook Controversy and Japanese Society*. München: Iudicium.

Said, Edward W. 1994. *Representations of the Intellectual: The 1993 Reith Lectures*. 1st American ed. New York: Pantheon Books.

Said, Edward W. 1995. *The Politics of Dispossession: The Struggle for Palestinian Self-Determination, 1969–1994*. London: Vintage.

Saito, Hiro. 2006. "Reiterated Commemoration: Hiroshima as National Trauma". *Sociological Theory* 24(4):353–76.

Saito, Hiro. 2017. *The History Problem*. Honolulu: University of Hawai'i Press.

Sakurai, Yoshihide. 2014. *Karuto Mondai to Kōkyōsei: Saiban, Media, Shūkyō Kenkyū Wa Dō Ronjita Ka*. Sapporo: Hokkaidō Daigaku Shuppankai.

Sanpo, Ketsun, and Shin'ichi Nakazawa. 1981. *Niji No Kaitei: Chibetto Mikkyō No Meisou Shugyō*. Tokyo: Hiraga.

Schwartz, Barry. 2012. "Rethinking Conflict and Memory: The Case of Nanjing". Pp. 529–63 in *The Oxford Handbook of Cultural Sociology*, edited by J.C. Alexander, R.N. Jacobs, and P. Smith. Oxford: Oxford University Press.

Schwartz, Barry, and Howard Schuman. 2005. "History, Commemoration, and Belief: Abraham Lincoln in American Memory, 1945–2001". *American Sociological Review* 70(2):183–203.

Searle, John R. 1995. *The Construction of Social Reality*. London: Penguin.

Seaton, Philip A. 2007. *Japan's Contested War Memories: The "Memory Rifts" in Historical Consciousness of World War II*. London; New York: Routledge.

Sennett, Richard. 2012. *Together: The Rituals, Pleasures and Politics of Co-Operation*. London: Allen Lane.

Seraphim, Franziska. 2006. *War Memory and Social Politics in Japan, 1945–2005*. Cambridge, MA: Harvard University Asia Center.

Shimada, Hiromi. 2012. *Oumu Shinrikyō Jiken (2 volumes)*. Tokyo: Toransubyū.

Shimazono, Susumu. 1995. "In the Wake of Aum: The Formation and Transformation of a Universe of Belief". *Japanese Journal of Religious Studies* 22(3/4):381–415.

Shimazono, Susumu. 1997. *Gendai shūkyō no kanōsei: Oumu Shinrikyō to bōryoku*. Tokyo: Iwanami Shoten.

Shimazono, Susumu. 2001. *Posuto Modan No Shinshūkyō: Gendai Nihon No Seishin Jōkyō No Teiryū*. Tokyo: Tōkyōdō shuppan.

Shupe, Anson, David Bromley, and Susan E. Darnell. 2008. "The North American Anti-Cult Movement: Vicissitudes of Success and Failure". Pp. 184–205 in *The Oxford Handbook of New Religious Movements*, edited by J.R. Lewis. Oxford: Oxford University Press.

Simko, Christine. 2012. "Rhetorics of Suffering: September 11 Commemorations as Theodicy". *American Sociological Review* 77(6):880–902.

Sims, Calvin. 2000. "Japan Software Suppliers Linked to Sect". The New York Times, 2 March.

Smelser, Neil J. 2004a. "Epilogue: September 11, 2001 as Cultural Trauma". Pp. 264–82 in *Cultural Trauma and Collective Identity*. Berkeley, CA: University of California Press.

Smelser, Neil J. 2004b. "Psychological Trauma and Cultural Trauma". Pp. 31–59 in *Cultural Trauma and Collective Identity*. Berkeley, CA: University of California Press.

Smith, Andrea L. 2004. "Heteroglossia, 'Commond Sense,' and Social Memory". *American Ethnologist* 1(2):251–69.

Takahashi, Hidetoshi. 2012. *Oumu Kara No Kikan*. Tokyo: Sōshisha.

Takahashi, Shizue. 2008. *Koko ni iru koto: Chikatetsu sarin jiken no izoku to shite*. Tokyo: Iwanami Shoten.

Takayama, Fumihiko. 2006. *Asahara Shōkō No Tanjō*. Tokyo: Bungei Shunjū.

Takimoto, Tarō, and Tatsuya Nagaoka. 1995. *Maindo Kontorōru Kara Nogarete: Oumu Shinrikyō Dakkaisha Tachi No Taiken*. Tokyo: Kōyū Shuppan.

Taylor, Diana. 2003. *The Archive and the Repertoire: Performing Cultural Memory in the Americas*. Durham, NC: Duke University Press.

Thomas, Jolyon Baraka. 2012. "Horrific 'Cults' and Comic Religion Manga after Aum". *Japanese Journal of Religious Studies* 39(1):127–51.

Tsukada, Hotaka. 2011. "Shinritō No Undō Tenkai to Katsudō Naiyō". Pp. 307–27 in *Jōhō jidai no Oumu Shinrikyō*, edited by N. Inoue and Shūkyō Jōhō Risāchi Sentā. Tokyo: Shunjūsha.

Turner, Victor W. 1967. *The Forest of Symbols; Aspects of Ndembu Ritual*. Ithaca, NY: Cornell University Press.

Turner, Victor W. 1982. *From Ritual to Theatre: The Human Seriousness of Play*. New York: Performing Arts Journal Publications.

Umehara, Takeshi, and Tetsuo Yamaori. 1995. *Shūkyō no jisatsu: Nihonjin no atarashii shinkō o motomete*. Tokyo: PHP Kenkyūjo.

Ushiyama, Rin. 2019a. "Discursive Opportunities and the Transnational Diffusion of Ideas: 'Brainwashing' and 'Mind Control' in Japan after the Aum Affair". *The British Journal of Sociology* 70(5):1730–53.

Ushiyama, Rin. 2019b. "Latency Through Uncertainty: The 1994 Matsumoto Sarin Incident as a Delayed Cultural Trauma". *International Journal of Politics, Culture, and Society* 32(1):21–41.

Ushiyama, Rin. 2021. "'Comfort Women Must Fall'? Japanese Governmental Responses to 'Comfort Women' Statues around the World." *Memory Studies* 14(6):1255–71.

Ushiyama, Rin, and Patrick Baert. 2016. "Cultural trauma, counter-narratives, and dialogical intellectuals: the works of Murakami Haruki and Mori Tatsuya in the context of the Aum affair". *Theory and Society* 45(6):471–99.

Utsunomiya Kenji, Nakamura Yūji, and Matsui Yutaka. 2015. "Chikatetsu Sarin Jiken Higaisha/Gokazoku Ankēto Chōsa Kekka Sokuhō".

Van Gennep, Arnold. 1960. *The Rites of Passage*. Chicago, IL: University of Chicago Press.

Vinitzky-Seroussi, Vered. 2002. "Commemorating a Difficult Past: Yitzhak Rabin's Memorials". *American Sociological Review* 67(1):30–51.

Voloshinov, Valentin N. 1986. *Marxism and the Philosophy of Language*. Cambridge, MA.: Harvard University Press.

Wagner-Pacifici, Robin. 1986. *The Moro Morality Play: Terrorism as Social Drama*. Chicago, IL: University of Chicago Press.

Wagner-Pacifici, Robin, and Barry Schwartz. 1991. "The Vietnam Veterans Memorial: Commemorating a Difficult Past". *American Journal of Sociology* 97(2):376–420.

Wallis, Roy. 1984. *The Elementary Forms of the New Religious Life*. London: Routledge & Kegan Paul.

Watanabe, Manabu. 1998. "Religion and Violence in Japan Today: A Chronological and Doctrinal Analysis of Aum Shinrikyo". *Terrorism and Political Violence* 10(4):80–100.

Watanabe, Manabu. 1999. "Karuto' Ron e No Ichi Shiten: Amerika No Maindo Kontorōru Ronsō". *Nanzan Shūkyō Bunka Kenkyū Jo Kenkyūshohō* 9:82–91.

Watanabe, Manabu. 2005. "Kyūsai to Bōryoku: Oumu Shinrikyō Moto Kanbu No Nyūshin to Dakkai No Ichi Jirei". *Journal of Religious Studies* 79(2):375–98.

Weine, Stevan. 2006. *Testimony after Catastrophe: Narrating the Traumas of Political Violence*. Evanston, IL: Northwestern University Press.

Wessinger, Catherine. 2009. "Deaths in the Fire at the Branch Davidians' Mount Carmel: Who Bears Responsibility?" *Nova Religio* 13(2):25–60.

Wessinger, Catherine. 2011. "Millennialism in Cross-Cultural Perspective". Pp. 3–24 in *The Oxford Handbook of Millennialism*, edited by C. Wessinger. Oxford: Oxford University Press.

Wiesel, Elie. 2006. *Night*. London: Penguin.

Winter, Franz. 2018. "Japanese New Religious Movements: An Introduction". Pp. 17–32 in *Handbook of East Asian New Religious Movements*, edited by L. Pokorny and F. Winter. Leiden; Boston: Brill.

Winter, Jay. 2010. "Sites of Memory". Pp. 312–24 in *Memory: Histories, Theories, Debates*, edited by S. Radstone and B. Schwarz. New York: Fordham University Press.

Winter, Jay. 2014. *Sites of Memory, Sites of Mourning: The Great War in European Cultural History*. Cambridge: Cambridge University Press.

Yamada, Marc. 2014. "Trauma and Historical Referentiality in Post-Aum Manga". *Japanese Studies* 34(2):153–68.

Yang, Fenggang. 2012. *Religion in China: survival and revival under Communist rule*. Oxford: Oxford University Press.

Yomiuri Shimbun. 2021. *Yomiuri Shimbun 2021–22 Media Guide*. Tokyo: Yomiuri Shimbun.

Yoneyama, Lisa. 1999. *Hiroshima Traces: Time, Space, and the Dialectics of Memory*. Berkeley: University of California Press.

Zerubavel, Eviatar. 2003. *Time Maps: Collective Memory and the Social Shape of the Past*. Chicago, IL; London: University of Chicago Press.

Index